Pillsbury

Christmas

2010

published by

Taste of Home Books
Reiman Media Group, Inc.
5400 S. 60th St., Greendale WI 53129

Taste of Home® is a registered trademark
of Reiman Media Group, Inc.

Bake-Off® is a registered trademark
of General Mills.

All recipes were previously published
in a slightly different form.

Front Cover Photograph:
Grasshopper Cupcakes p. 298,
Snowball Cupcakes p. 306,
Mini Cherry Cheesecakes p. 280.

Title Page Photograph:
Linzer Sandwich Cookies p. 247.

Back Cover Photographs:
Skillet Chicken Parmigiana p. 155,
Easy Pesto Pinwheels p. 22,
Crème de Menthe Truffles p. 215,
Tropical Waffle Bake p. 173,
Snow Fun Snowmen p. 234.

credits

GENERAL MILLS, INC.
EDITORIAL DIRECTOR: Jeff Nowak
PUBLISHING MANAGER: Christine Gray
COOKBOOK EDITOR: Grace Wells
EDITORIAL ASSISTANT: Lisa Olson
DIGITAL ASSETS MANAGER: Carrie Jacobson
PRODUCTION MANAGER: Michelle Tufts
RECIPE DEVELOPMENT AND TESTING: Pillsbury Test Kitchens
PHOTOGRAPHY: General Mills Photography Studio

REIMAN MEDIA GROUP, INC.
EDITOR IN CHIEF: Catherine Cassidy
VICE PRESIDENT, EXECUTIVE EDITOR/BOOKS: Heidi Reuter Lloyd
CREATIVE DIRECTOR: Howard Greenberg
SENIOR EDITOR/BOOKS: Mark Hagen
EDITOR: Krista Lanphier
ART DIRECTOR: Rudy Krochalk
CONTENT PRODUCTION SUPERVISOR: Julie Wagner
LAYOUT DESIGNERS: Kathy Crawford, Nancy Novak
PROOFREADER: Linne Bruskewitz
COVER PHOTOGRAPHY: Reiman Media Group Photo Studio
  PHOTOGRAPHER: Dan Roberts
  FOOD STYLIST: Sarah Thompson
  SET STYLIST: Jennifer Bradley Vent

NORTH AMERICAN CHIEF MARKETING OFFICER: Lisa Karpinski
VICE PRESIDENT, BOOK MARKETING: Dan Fink
CREATIVE DIRECTOR/CREATIVE MARKETING: Jim Palmen

READER'S DIGEST ASSOCIATION
PRESIDENT AND CHIEF EXECUTIVE OFFICER: Mary G. Berner
PRESIDENT, NORTH AMERICAN AFFINITIES: Suzanne M. Grimes

For additional holiday recipes and other delicious dishes, visit
Pillsbury.com.

International Standard Book Number (10): 0-89821-822-5
International Standard Book Number (13): 978-0-89821-822-0
International Standard Serial Number: 1930-1685
Printed in U.S.A.
Second Printing

contents

The Most Wonderful Time of the Year!

Holiday celebrations are easier than ever, because all the mouthwatering recipes you'll ever need are in this eye-catching *Pillsbury Christmas 2010* cookbook.

p. 237

p. 44

p. 213

p. 146

p. 94

p. 131

"Tis the season to celebrate the spirit of Christmas with those you love. The spirit of the season wouldn't be the same without elaborately adorned tables filled with your favorite holiday recipes and Yuletide dishes.

Whether you enjoy hosting formal dinners with elegant specialties, prefer intimate get-togethers that feature comforting dishes or having a casual cocktail party with tasty finger foods, you'll find hundreds of wonderful dishes in Pillsbury Christmas 2010.

For more than 100 years, family cooks have turned to Pillsbury to make mealtime special…and that's certainly true when holiday celebrations begin. With this beautiful collection right at your fingertips, it's never been easier to find amazing hors d'oeuvres everyone clamors for, hearty soups that warm the soul and memorable entrees destined to become family traditions.

This beautiful cookbook offers more than *300 recipes* with chapters such as "Yuletide Bites & Beverages" (p. 6), "Blissful Breads & Baked Goods" (p. 40) and "Seasonal Soups, Sides & Salads" (p. 58). There are also sections devoted entirely to main courses, edible gifts, breakfast, Christmas treats and lovely desserts.

Need a special present for a friend who has everything? Check out the chapter "Gifts from the Kitchen" (p. 196) that offers dozens of beautiful homemade goodies. You'll also find darling Christmas-themed treats in "Winter Wonderland Sweets" (p. 222), and dozens of decadent delights in "Joyous Cookies & Bars" (p. 244) and "Divine Desserts" (p. 278). You can also browse through the "Merry Christmas Morning" (p. 164) chapter for glorious breakfast recipes.

A sample of some of the yummy treats in the pages that follow are pictured at left, such as Whole Wheat Gingerbread Cutouts, Poinsettia Coffee Cake and Sugar and Spice Nuts. And you can't go wrong with robust, hearty main dishes such as Cabbage Rolls in Creamy Bacon Sauce and So-Simple Flank Steak (both pictured left) or French Onion-Beef-Noodle Bake (pictured above right). And, there are plenty of scrumptious desserts throughout the book, including Rich Espresso Bars with Buttercream Frosting (pictured lower right).

Take comfort in knowing that each recipe was tested in the Pillsbury Kitchen so it meets our standards of easy preparation, reliability and great taste. And for even more added assurance, we've included many of our Bake-Off® Contest winners…so you know you're preparing the best of the very best!

We've also included *cook's notes* with many of the recipes. These tidbits suggest ways to trim prep time, substitute ingredients and more. Similarly, *kitchen tips* offer sensible advice on tasks from streamlining cleanup to selecting the best produce. We even share a *special touch* for some recipes that offer advice on dressing up buffet tables or how to make menus unforgettable.

Filled with the irresistible flavors of the holiday season, this is one recipe collection you'll turn to time and again. We hope that Pillsbury Christmas 2010 will rekindle heartwarming memories of Christmas past…and spark plenty of new ones, too. *Merry Christmas!*

p. 249

Yuletide Bites
& Beverages

Share the spirit of Christmas with loved ones at

your next holiday party. Whether it's casual or fancy, these

festive appetizers and frosty sippers will delight everyone.

p. 19

p. 24

p. 26

p. 22

p. 13

pastry-wrapped cranberry brie p. 34

cook's notes

Take the stress out of last-minute party preparations by placing the chips on your serving tray and measuring out the other ingredients so they are ready to go. When it's time to serve, it will only take minutes to have these appetizers on the table.

veggie ranch scoops

READY IN: 35 Minutes ✳ **SERVINGS:** 10

1/3 cup ranch dressing

3 cups scoop-style tortilla chips (about 30 chips)

1 small carrot, shredded (about 1/3 cup)

2 tablespoons finely chopped red bell pepper

1 cup very small (1/2 inch) broccoli florets (about 30)

1 Spoon scant 1/2 teaspoon dressing in center of each chip. Top each with pinch of carrot, bell pepper and 1 broccoli floret. Place on serving plate or tray; serve immediately.

NUTRITION INFORMATION PER SERVING: Calories 80 • Total Fat 6g • Saturated Fat 1g • Cholesterol 0mg • Sodium 105mg • Total Carbohydrate 6g • Dietary Fiber 0g • Protein 0g. DIETARY EXCHANGES: 1/2 Starch • 1 Fat • 1-1/2 Carb Choices.

coconut shrimp with gingered cocktail sauce

PREP TIME: 15 Minutes ✳ **READY IN:** 30 Minutes ✳ **SERVINGS:** 16

Shrimp

- 1 cup shredded coconut
- 1/2 cup Progresso® plain bread crumbs
- 1/4 teaspoon salt
  Dash ground red pepper (cayenne)

- 1-1/2 lb. uncooked medium shrimp, peeled, deveined
- 1/4 cup honey

Sauce

- 1 jar (12 oz.) cocktail sauce
- 1/4 teaspoon ground ginger

1 Heat oven to 425°F. Line large cookie sheet with foil; lightly spray foil with cooking spray. In food processor, place coconut, bread crumbs, salt and ground red pepper; process 10 seconds to mix slightly. Place in pie pan or shallow dish.

2 Pat shrimp dry with paper towels; place in medium bowl. In 1-quart saucepan, heat honey over low heat just until melted. Pour over shrimp; toss to coat. Roll shrimp in coconut mixture to coat; place in single layer on cookie sheet.

3 Bake 9 to 12 minutes or until shrimp turn pink and coconut begins to brown. In small serving bowl, mix sauce ingredients. Arrange shrimp on serving platter; serve with sauce.

NUTRITION INFORMATION PER SERVING: Calories 110 • Total Fat 2.5g • Saturated Fat 2g • Cholesterol 40mg • Sodium 380mg • Total Carbohydrate 15g • Dietary Fiber 0g • Protein 5g. DIETARY EXCHANGES: 1 Other Carbohydrate • 1/2 Very Lean Meat • 1/2 Fat • 1 Carb Choice.

kitchen tip

To devein peeled shrimp, run a sharp knife down the back of the shrimp and lift the sandy-colored vein from the shrimp. Rinse to remove any excess vein.

onion and herb tart

PREP TIME: 20 Minutes ✱ **READY IN:** 30 Minutes ✱ **SERVINGS:** 18

- 1 can (8 oz.) Pillsbury® refrigerated crescent dinner rolls
- 1 large sweet onion (about 12 oz.)
- 2 teaspoons olive oil
- 2 teaspoons chopped fresh rosemary leaves or 1 teaspoon dried rosemary leaves, crushed
- 2 tablespoons packed brown sugar
- 4 oz. coarsely chopped Brie cheese

1 Heat oven to 375°F. Grease or spray large cookie sheet. Unroll dough into 1 large rectangle on cookie sheet; press into 13x9-inch rectangle, firmly pressing perforations to seal. Fold edges over 1/2 inch to form edges on crust. Bake 9 minutes.

2 Meanwhile, cut the root end off onion, creating flat surface. Place flat surface on cutting board; cut the onion in half vertically, and peel off the outer layer. Place the large flat side down; cut into 1/8-inch slices.

3 In 10-inch skillet, heat oil over medium heat. Add onion and rosemary; cook 8 to 10 minutes, stirring frequently, until onions are caramelized. Stir in brown sugar.

4 Arrange cheese evenly over partially baked crust; top with onions. Bake 4 to 6 minutes longer or until crust is golden brown. Cut into 6 rows by 3 rows. Serve warm.

NUTRITION INFORMATION PER SERVING: Calories 90 • Total Fat 5g • Saturated Fat 2g • Cholesterol 5mg • Sodium 140mg • Total Carbohydrate 8g • Dietary Fiber 0g • Protein 2g. DIETARY EXCHANGES: 1/2 Starch • 1 Fat • 1/2 Carb Choice.

crescent holiday appetizer tree

PREP TIME: 15 Minutes ✱ **READY IN:** 45 Minutes ✱ **SERVINGS:** 16

1 can (8 oz.) Pillsbury® refrigerated crescent dinner rolls or Pillsbury® Crescent Recipe Creations® refrigerated seamless dough sheet

1 container (8 oz.) chives-and-onion cream cheese spread

1 tablespoon milk

3/4 medium red bell pepper

1/4 medium yellow bell pepper

1/2 cup chopped fresh broccoli

2 tablespoons sliced ready-to-eat baby-cut carrots

1 tablespoon chopped cucumber

1 Heat oven to 375°F. Remove the dough from can in 1 long roll; do not unroll or separate. Cut the roll into 16 slices.

2 Place slices, cut side down, on ungreased cookie sheet. To form tree, start by placing 1 slice for top; arrange 2 slices just below, with sides touching. Continue arranging a row of 3 slices, then a row of 4 slices, ending with a row of 5 slices. Use remaining slice for tree trunk.

3 Bake 11 to 13 minutes or until golden brown. Cool 1 minute; carefully loosen from cookie sheet with spatula and slide onto wire rack. Cool completely, about 15 minutes.

4 Place tree on serving platter or tray. In small bowl, mix cream cheese spread and milk until smooth. Spread mixture over baked tree.

5 Cut strips from red bell pepper for garland; chop any remaining red pepper. With small star-shaped canapé cutter, cut star from yellow bell pepper; chop remaining yellow pepper. Decorate tree with bell peppers, broccoli, carrots and cucumber. Serve immediately, or cover loosely and refrigerate up to 24 hours before serving.

NUTRITION INFORMATION PER SERVING: Calories 100 • Total Fat 7g • Saturated Fat 3.5g • Cholesterol 15mg • Sodium 210mg • Total Carbohydrate 7g • Dietary Fiber 0g • Protein 2g. DIETARY EXCHANGES: 1/2 Starch • 1-1/2 Fat • 1/2 Carb Choice.

special touch

If desired, top the baked tree trunk with the cream cheese mixture and 1 tablespoon sliced almonds. Sprinkle tree with additional 1 tablespoon of almonds.

roasted bell pepper dip

roasted bell pepper dip

READY IN: 20 Minutes ✳ **SERVINGS:** 12

1   package (8 oz.) cream cheese, softened

1/4 cup sour cream

1/2 cup finely chopped roasted red bell peppers (from a jar)

3   tablespoons chopped fresh cilantro

1/4 teaspoon red pepper sauce

1   clove garlic, finely chopped

2   fresh cilantro sprigs

    Bite-size round tortilla chips or crackers

1 In medium bowl, mix all ingredients except cilantro sprigs and tortilla chips. Spoon into serving bowl. Garnish with cilantro sprigs.

2 Serve immediately with tortilla chips, or cover and refrigerate until serving time. If refrigerated, let stand 10 to 15 minutes before serving.

NUTRITION INFORMATION PER SERVING: Calories 160 • Total Fat 12g • Saturated Fat 5g • Cholesterol 25mg • Sodium 160mg • Total Carbohydrate 12g • Dietary Fiber 0g • Protein 3g. DIETARY EXCHANGES: 1 Starch • 2 Fat • 1 Carb Choice.

salmon canapes with dilled honey mustard

READY IN: 25 Minutes ✳ **SERVINGS:** 24

1   tablespoon finely chopped red onion

3   tablespoons Dijon mustard

1   tablespoon honey

2   teaspoons chopped fresh dill weed

12 slices cocktail pumpernickel or rye bread

2   to 3 tablespoons soft cream cheese

1/4 lb. smoked salmon (lox), broken into 24 pieces

24 sprigs fresh dill weed

1 In small bowl, combine onion, mustard, honey and chopped dill weed; mix well. Spread each bread slice with cream cheese; top with mustard mixture. Cut each bread slice in half diagonally. Top each bread triangle with salmon and dill sprig. Serve immediately.

NUTRITION INFORMATION PER SERVING: Calories 25 • Total Fat 1g • Saturated Fat 0g • Cholesterol 0mg • Sodium 110mg • Total Carbohydrate 3g • Dietary Fiber 0g • Protein 1g. DIETARY EXCHANGES: 1/2 Starch • 1/2 Other Carbohydrate.

spicy honey chicken drumettes

PREP TIME: 10 Minutes ✳ **READY IN:** 2 Hours 10 Minutes ✳ **SERVINGS:** 12

1/4 cup honey

1/4 cup soy sauce

1/4 cup chili sauce

1/2 teaspoon hot pepper sauce

1/4 teaspoon ginger

1/4 teaspoon dry mustard

12 chicken drumettes

1 In 12x8-inch (2-quart) baking dish, combine the honey, soy sauce, chili sauce, hot pepper sauce, ginger and dry mustard; mix well. Add the drumettes; turn to coat. Cover; refrigerate 1 hour to marinate.

2 Heat oven to 375°F. Uncover dish. Bake chicken in marinade at 375°F for 45 to 60 minutes or until chicken is tender and no longer pink next to bone, brushing with marinade occasionally.

NUTRITION INFORMATION PER SERVING: Calories 50 • Total Fat 3g • Saturated Fat 1g • Cholesterol 15mg • Sodium 120mg • Total Carbohydrate 2g • Dietary Fiber 0g • Protein 4g. DIETARY EXCHANGE: 1 Lean Meat.

cook's notes

For variety, add crisp bagel chips, whole wheat crackers and cocktail breads to the serving platter.

italian appetizer wedges

PREP TIME: 20 Minutes ✳ READY IN: 1 Hour 10 Minutes ✳ SERVINGS: 12

SHERRY D. JOHNSTON
Ft. Lauderdale, Florida
Bake-Off® Contest 40, 2002

APPETIZERS

- 1 Pillsbury® refrigerated pie crust, softened as directed on package
- 1/2 cup Progresso® Italian-style bread crumbs
- 1/3 cup chopped fresh basil
- 1/4 cup grated Romano cheese
- 1/4 teaspoon salt
- 1/4 teaspoon freshly ground black pepper
- 1 cup part-skim ricotta cheese
- 3 tablespoons extra-virgin olive oil or olive oil
- 3 Italian plum tomatoes, seeded, diced

GARNISH

- 1 Italian plum tomato, sliced, if desired
- 8 fresh basil leaves, if desired

Kitchen tip

To seed a tomato, cut in half horizontally and remove the stem. Holding a tomato half over a bowl or sink, scrape out seeds with a small spoon or squeeze the tomato to force out the seeds.

1 Heat oven to 400°F. Remove crust from pouch; unfold crust. Place on ungreased cookie sheet; press out fold lines. With rolling pin, roll to form 12-inch round.

2 In medium bowl, combine bread crumbs, chopped basil, Romano cheese, salt, pepper, ricotta cheese and oil; mix well. Stir in diced tomatoes. Spoon and spread over crust to within 3 inches of edge. Fold edge of crust 3 inches over filling; crimp crust slightly.

3 Bake at 400°F for 25 to 35 minutes or until golden brown. Cool 15 minutes. Cut into wedges. Garnish with tomato slices and basil leaves. Serve warm or cool.

NUTRITION INFORMATION PER SERVING: 1/12 of Recipe: Calories 160 • Total Fat 10g • Saturated Fat 4g • Cholesterol 10mg • Sodium 230mg • Total Carbohydrate 14g • Dietary Fiber 1g • Protein 4g. DIETARY EXCHANGES: 1 Starch • 1 Other Carbohydrate • 2 Fat.

golden glow punch

READY IN: 10 Minutes ✳ **SERVINGS:** 25

1 can (6 oz.) frozen lemonade concentrate, thawed

1 can (6 oz.) frozen orange juice concentrate, thawed

1 can (6 oz.) frozen tangerine juice concentrate, thawed

2 cups cold water

2 bottles (33 oz. each) ginger ale, chilled
Ice cubes or ice mold

1 In large nonmetal pitcher or punch bowl, combine juice concentrates and water; mix well. Just before serving, add ginger ale and ice; stir to blend. Garnish as desired.

NUTRITION INFORMATION PER SERVING: Calories 70 • Total Fat 0g • Saturated Fat 0g • Cholesterol 0mg • Sodium 10mg • Total Carbohydrate 17g • Dietary Fiber 0g • Protein 0g. DIETARY EXCHANGES: 1 Other Carbohydrate • 1 Carb Choice.

special touch

For a pretty presentation, float orange slices and edible flowers in the punch bowl.

pastry-wrapped jalapeño brie with fruit

pastry-wrapped jalapeño brie with fruit

PREP TIME: 15 Minutes ✳ READY IN: 1 Hour ✳ SERVINGS: 12

- 1 can (8 oz.) Pillsbury® refrigerated crescent dinner rolls
- 1 round (8 oz.) Brie cheese, about 4 inches in diameter
- 2 tablespoons green or red jalapeño jelly or hot pepper jelly
- 2 tablespoons chopped fresh cilantro

- 1 egg, beaten
- 8 small clusters seedless red or green grapes
- 1 kiwifruit, unpeeled, sliced
- 1/2 cup fresh strawberry halves
- 1/2 orange, cut into wedges

1 Heat oven to 350°F. Spray cookie sheet with cooking spray. Unroll dough onto cookie sheet; pat dough and firmly press perforations to seal.

2 Cut cheese horizontally into 2 equal layers. Place bottom half of cheese on center of dough on cookie sheet. Spread jelly over cheese. Sprinkle with chopped cilantro. Top with remaining cheese half.

3 Lift and gently press dough evenly around cheese. Gather dough together over top of cheese; twist to form bow. Brush dough with beaten egg.

4 Bake 20 to 25 minutes or until golden brown. Cool 15 minutes before serving. To serve, place warm pastry-wrapped Brie on platter. Arrange fruit around Brie. Cover and refrigerate any remaining Brie.

HIGH ALTITUDE (3500-6500 FT): Heat oven to 375°F. Unroll dough and separate crosswise into 2 sections; press dough into 2 squares, firmly pressing perforations to seal. Place 1 square on ungreased cookie sheet and cut off corners with a sharp knife. (Cutouts will have a leaf appearance.) Set cutouts aside. Continue with Step 2. With sharp knife, cut off corners of remaining dough square. Set cutouts aside. Place the remaining dough on top of cheese round. Press around cheese, folding bottom edges over top edges. Press to seal completely. Brush dough with egg. Arrange cutouts over top and edges; brush with egg. Bake 25 to 30 minutes.

NUTRITION INFORMATION PER SERVING: Calories 170 • Total Fat 10g • Saturated Fat 5g • Cholesterol 35mg • Sodium 270mg • Total Carbohydrate 15g • Dietary Fiber 0g • Protein 6g. DIETARY EXCHANGES: 1/2 Starch • 1/2 Other Carbohydrate • 1/2 High-Fat Meat • 1 Fat • 1 Carb Choice.

garlic, cheese and tomato bread bites

PREP TIME: 30 Minutes ✳ READY IN: 50 Minutes ✳ SERVINGS: 10

- 10 Pillsbury® frozen soft white dinner rolls (from 12.4-oz. bag)
- 1 container (6.5 oz.) garlic-and-herbs spreadable cheese

- 1 tablespoon diced sun-dried tomatoes
- 1 tablespoon diced pitted kalamata olives
- 1 jar (8 oz.) marinara sauce, warmed

1 Heat oven to 375°F. Remove rolls from bag; thaw 10 minutes. With thumb, make indentation in center of each roll.

2 In medium bowl, mix cheese, sundried tomatoes and olives. Place 1 tablespoon cheese mixture in each indentation. Place on ungreased cookie sheet. Bake 12 to 17 minutes or until tops are light golden brown. Serve with warmed marinara sauce.

NUTRITION INFORMATION PER SERVING: Calories 210 • Total Fat 11g • Saturated Fat 5g • Cholesterol 20mg • Sodium 370mg • Total Carbohydrate 22g • Dietary Fiber 1g • Protein 4g. DIETARY EXCHANGES: 1 Starch • 1/2 Other Carbohydrate • 2 Fat • 1-1/2 Carb Choices.

Pillsbury
Bake-Off®

JILL DITMIRE
Indianapolis, Indiana
Bake-Off® Contest 39, 2000

focaccia dipping sticks

PREP TIME: 15 Minutes ✶ READY IN: 35 Minutes ✶ SERVINGS: 28

1 can (13.8 oz.) Pillsbury® refrigerated classic pizza crust

1 tablespoon extra-virgin olive oil

1/3 cup red bell pepper strips (1x1/8 inch)

3 tablespoons thinly slivered pitted ripe olives

1 tablespoon chopped fresh rosemary

1/4 teaspoon kosher (coarse) salt

1 cup tomato pasta sauce, heated

1 Heat oven to 400°F. Grease cookie sheet with shortening or cooking spray. Unroll dough onto cookie sheet into 14x9-inch rectangle. With fingertips, make indentations over surface of dough.

2 Drizzle oil over dough. Top with remaining ingredients except pasta sauce; press lightly into dough.

3 Bake 13 to 18 minutes or until golden brown. Cut focaccia in half lengthwise; cut each half crosswise into 14 sticks. Serve warm sticks with warm pasta sauce for dipping.

NUTRITION INFORMATION PER SERVING: Calories 50 • Total Fat 1.5g • Saturated Fat 0g • Cholesterol 0mg • Sodium 170mg • Total Carbohydrate 8g • Dietary Fiber 0g • Protein 1g. DIETARY EXCHANGES: 1/2 Starch • 1/2 Carb Choice.

bean and bacon fiesta dip

PREP TIME: 20 Minutes ✱ **READY IN:** 35 Minutes ✱ **SERVINGS:** 22

8 slices bacon

1 can (16 oz.) Old El Paso® refried beans

1 can (4.5 oz.) Old El Paso® chopped green chiles, drained

1 cup Green Giant® Valley Fresh Steamers™ Niblets® frozen corn

1 can (15 oz.) Progresso® black beans, drained, rinsed

1 jar (16 oz.) Old El Paso® thick 'n chunky salsa

1-1/2 cups shredded Mexican cheese blend (6 oz.)

Sour cream, if desired

Tortilla chips

MADELEINE BERGQUIST
Syracuse, New York
Bake-Off® Contest 41, 2004

cook's notes

Eight slices of precooked bacon from a 2.1-ounce package, chopped, can be substituted for the cooked bacon.

1 Cook bacon until crisp; drain on paper towel. Set 2 slices of bacon aside; crumble remaining 6 slices.

2 Spray 8-inch square (2-quart) microwavable dish with cooking spray. In medium bowl, mix refried beans, green chiles and crumbled bacon. Spread mixture evenly in dish. Sprinkle frozen corn and black beans evenly over refried bean mixture. Pour salsa over top. Sprinkle cheese over salsa. Crumble remaining 2 slices of bacon; sprinkle over cheese.

3 Microwave uncovered on High 10 to 15 minutes or until cheese is bubbly and mixture is thoroughly heated. Garnish with spoonfuls of sour cream. Serve warm dip with tortilla chips.

NUTRITION INFORMATION PER SERVING: Calories 100 • Total Fat 4g • Saturated Fat 2g • Cholesterol 10mg • Sodium 420mg • Total Carbohydrate 11g • Dietary Fiber 3g • Protein 6g. DIETARY EXCHANGES: 1/2 Starch • 1/2 Very Lean Meat • 1 Fat • 1 Carb Choice.

baked artichoke squares

PREP TIME: 15 Minutes ✶ READY IN: 35 Minutes ✶ SERVINGS: 60

2 cans (8 oz. each) Pillsbury® refrigerated crescent dinner rolls

1 can (14 oz.) artichoke hearts, drained, chopped

1 box (9 oz.) Green Giant® frozen spinach, thawed, squeezed to drain

3/4 cup grated Parmesan cheese

2/3 cup mayonnaise

2/3 cup sour cream

1/8 teaspoon garlic powder

1 Heat oven to 375°F. Unroll dough into 4 long rectangles. Place crosswise in ungreased 15x10x1-inch pan; press over bottom and 1 inch up sides to form crust. Press perforations to seal.

2 Bake 10 to 12 minutes or until light golden brown. Meanwhile, in medium bowl, mix remaining ingredients. Spread evenly over partially baked crust. Bake 8 to 10 minutes longer or until the topping is hot. Cut into 1-1/2-inch squares. Serve warm.

HIGH ALTITUDE (3500-6500 FT): Bake 12 to 14 minutes.

NUTRITION INFORMATION PER SERVING: Calories 60 • Total Fat 4.5g • Saturated Fat 1.5g • Cholesterol 0mg • Sodium 115mg • Total Carbohydrate 4g • Dietary Fiber 0g • Protein 1g. DIETARY EXCHANGES: 1/2 Other Carbohydrate • 1 Fat.

layered reuben spread

PREP TIME: 15 Minutes ✶ READY IN: 40 Minutes ✶ SERVINGS: 4

2/3 cup mayonnaise

1/3 cup Thousand Island dressing

1 can (8 oz.) sauerkraut, well drained

1 bag (8 oz.) shredded Swiss cheese (2 cups)

1 package (6 oz.) thinly sliced corned beef, chopped

2 tablespoons sliced green onions (2 medium)

1 box (8 oz.) toasted wheat crackers (about 72 crackers)

1 Heat oven to 350°F. In small bowl, mix mayonnaise and dressing until well blended. In ungreased 9-inch pie pan, layer sauerkraut, half of the cheese, the corned beef and mayonnaise mixture. To remaining half of cheese in bag, add onions; toss to mix. Sprinkle over top. Bake 20 to 25 minutes or until bubbly around edge. Serve spread with crackers.

NUTRITION INFORMATION PER SERVING: Calories 150 • Total Fat 11g • Saturated Fat 3.5g • Cholesterol 15mg • Sodium 350mg • Total Carbohydrate 7g • Dietary Fiber 0g • Protein 5g. DIETARY EXCHANGES: 1/2 Starch • 1/2 High-Fat Meat • 1-1/2 Fat • 1/2 Carb Choice.

baked artichoke squares

easy pesto pinwheels

PREP TIME: 10 Minutes ✳ **READY IN:** 30 Minutes ✳ **SERVINGS:** 24

1 can (8 oz.) Pillsbury® refrigerated crescent dinner rolls

1/4 cup basil pesto

1/4 cup chopped roasted red bell peppers (from a jar)

1 Heat oven to 350°F. Unroll dough and separate into 4 rectangles; firmly press perforations to seal. Spread the pesto over each rectangle to within 1/4 inch of edges. Sprinkle with the roasted peppers.

2 Starting with 1 short side, roll up each rectangle; press edge to seal. With serrated knife, cut each roll into 6 slices. On ungreased cookie sheet, place slices cut side down.

3 Bake 13 to 17 minutes or until edges are golden brown. Immediately remove from cookie sheet. Serve warm.

NUTRITION INFORMATION PER SERVING: **Calories** 50 • **Total Fat** 3.5g • **Saturated Fat** 1g • **Cholesterol** 0mg • **Sodium** 95mg • **Total Carbohydrate** 4g • **Dietary Fiber** 0g • **Protein** 1g. DIETARY EXCHANGE: 1 Fat.

camembert with cranberry caramelized onions

READY IN: 35 Minutes ✳ SERVINGS: 12

1 tablespoon butter	1/4 teaspoon salt
1 small sweet onion, halved, thinly sliced	2 tablespoons sweet or dry sherry
1 (8 oz.) round Camembert cheese	2 tablespoons chopped fresh marjoram or 1 teaspoon dried marjoram leaves
1/4 cup sweetened dried cranberries	
2 teaspoons brown sugar	Assorted crackers or small cocktail breads

1 Heat oven to 350°F. Melt butter in large nonstick skillet over medium heat. Add onion; cook 8 to 10 minutes or until very tender, stirring frequently.

2 Meanwhile, place cheese in ungreased decorative ovenproof shallow baking dish or plate. Bake at 350°F for 10 to 12 minutes or until cheese is soft.

3 Add cranberries, brown sugar, salt and sherry to onion; mix well. Cook 5 minutes or until sugar is dissolved, stirring frequently. Stir in marjoram; cook and stir 1 minute.

4 To serve, spoon warm onion mixture over cheese. Serve with assorted crackers and small cocktail bread slices. Store in refrigerator.

NUTRITION INFORMATION PER SERVING: Calories 90 • Total Fat 6g • Saturated Fat 3g • Cholesterol 15mg • Sodium 210mg • Total Carbohydrate 4g • Dietary Fiber 0g • Protein 4g. DIETARY EXCHANGES: 1/2 Fruit • 1/2 Other Carbohydrate • 1/2 High-Fat Meat.

kitchen tip

Camembert cheese is a round French cheese covered with a soft, white edible rind. When ripe, this smooth, fragrant cheese oozes slightly.

three-cheese spread

PREP TIME: 15 Minutes ✳ **READY IN:** 2 Hours 15 Minutes ✳ **SERVINGS:** 18

- 1 package (8 oz.) cream cheese
- 1 package (6 oz.) chèvre (goat) cheese
- 1 cup shredded Parmesan cheese (4 oz.)
- 1/3 cup chopped fresh basil
- 1/4 cup diced red bell pepper
- Sourdough cocktail bread slices or crackers

1 In food processor, process all cheeses until well blended. Add basil and bell pepper; process with quick on-and-off motions until finely chopped and well blended. Cover; refrigerate at least 2 hours or until firm. Spoon the cheese mixture into 3 (1-cup) ramekins or 1 (3-cup) bowl. Serve with bread slices.

NUTRITION INFORMATION PER SERVING: Calories 180 • Total Fat 9g • Saturated Fat 5g • Cholesterol 20mg • Sodium 350mg • Total Carbohydrate 16g • Dietary Fiber 0g • Protein 8g. DIETARY EXCHANGES: 1 Starch • 1/2 Medium-Fat Meat • 1 Fat • 1 Carb Choice.

olive-cheese bites

PREP TIME: 25 Minutes ✳ **READY IN:** 35 Minutes ✳ **SERVINGS:** 24

1 can (11 oz.) Pillsbury® refrigerated breadsticks

48 large pimiento-stuffed green olives (from two 10-oz. jars), well drained

1 egg, beaten

3 tablespoons sesame seed, if desired

1 cup pasteurized process cheese sauce (from a jar)

3 tablespoons tomato juice

1/8 teaspoon ground red pepper (cayenne)

1 Heat oven to 375°F. Spray cookie sheets with cooking spray. Remove dough from can; separate into 12 breadsticks. Cut each into 4 pieces; flatten each piece.

2 For each appetizer, place 1 olive in center of each piece of dough. Wrap dough around olive to completely cover, stretching dough to fit if necessary and pressing edges firmly to seal. Dip tops into beaten egg, then into sesame seed; place seam side down on cookie sheets. Bake 11 to 14 minutes or until golden brown.

3 Meanwhile, in 1-quart saucepan, mix cheese sauce, tomato juice and ground red pepper. Cook over low heat 3 to 4 minutes, stirring constantly, until cheese sauce melts and mixture is well blended. Serve as dip with warm appetizers.

NUTRITION INFORMATION PER SERVING: Calories 80 • Total Fat 4.5g • Saturated Fat 2g • Cholesterol 15mg • Sodium 430mg • Total Carbohydrate 8g • Dietary Fiber 0g • Protein 3g. DIETARY EXCHANGES: 1/2 Starch • 1 Fat • 1/2 Carb Choice.

cook's notes

This recipe requires two cookie sheets. Both sheets of the "bites" may be baked at one time if the sheets are rearranged front to back and top to bottom halfway through the baking process. However, baking one batch at a time ensures a steady supply of hot appetizers.

frosty mocha

READY IN: 10 Minutes ✱ **SERVINGS:** 4

1-1/2 cups milk

1/3 cup chocolate-flavored syrup

2 tablespoons instant malted milk powder, if desired

2 tablespoons instant coffee (dry)

3-1/2 cups small ice cubes

1 In blender container, place all ingredients except ice; blend until well mixed. Add ice cubes a few at a time, blending well after each addition until smooth.

NUTRITION INFORMATION PER SERVING: **Calories** 120 • **Total Fat** 2g • **Saturated Fat** 1.5g • **Cholesterol** 5mg • **Sodium** 55mg • **Total Carbohydrate** 22g • **Dietary Fiber** 0g • **Protein** 4g. DIETARY EXCHANGES: 1 Other Carbohydrate • 1/2 Low-Fat Milk • 1-1/2 Carb Choices.

avocado-corn salsa

READY IN: 10 Minutes ✱ **SERVINGS:** 24

1 cup Old El Paso® thick 'n chunky salsa

1 medium avocado, pitted, peeled and coarsely chopped

1 can (11 oz.) Green Giant® Mexicorn® whole kernel corn with red and green peppers, drained

2 tablespoons chopped fresh cilantro

24 oz. tortilla chips

1 In medium bowl, mix all ingredients except tortilla chips. Serve immediately, or cover and refrigerate until serving time.

NUTRITION INFORMATION PER SERVING: **Calories** 170 • **Total Fat** 8g • **Saturated Fat** 1g • **Cholesterol** 0mg • **Sodium** 290mg • **Total Carbohydrate** 22g • **Dietary Fiber** 2g • **Protein** 2g. DIETARY EXCHANGES: 1 Starch • 1/2 Other Carbohydrate • 1-1/2 Fat • 1-1/2 Carb Choices.

fajita chicken wings

PREP TIME: 20 Minutes ✱ **READY IN:** 5 Hours ✱ **SERVINGS:** 24

12 chicken wings, tips removed

MARINADE

1/4 cup lime juice

2 tablespoons vegetable oil

3 tablespoons chopped fresh cilantro

1 teaspoon ground cumin

1/2 teaspoon salt

1/2 teaspoon dried oregano leaves

1/4 teaspoon crushed red pepper flakes

1 clove garlic, finely chopped

1 Cut each chicken wing in half; place in large resealable food-storage plastic bag. Add marinade ingredients; seal bag. Turn bag to coat wings. Refrigerate at least 4 hours but no longer than 24 hours, turning bag occasionally.

2 Heat oven to 375°F. Drain the chicken wings, reserving the marinade. Place chicken on the broiler pan.

3 Bake 45 to 60 minutes or until juice of chicken is clear when thickest part is cut to bone (180°F), brushing occasionally with reserved marinade. Discard any remaining marinade. Serve warm.

NUTRITION INFORMATION PER SERVING: **Calories** 50 • **Total Fat** 4g • **Saturated Fat** 1g • **Cholesterol** 15mg • **Sodium** 40mg • **Total Carbohydrate** 0g • **Dietary Fiber** 0g • **Protein** 4g. DIETARY EXCHANGE: 1/2 High-Fat Meat.

frosty mocha

cook's notes

Shredded Cheddar or Colby-Monterey Jack cheese can be used in place of the Mexican cheese blend.

mini tostadas

PREP TIME: 20 Minutes ✳ **READY IN:** 35 Minutes ✳ **SERVINGS:** 40

1 package (11.5 oz.) Old El Paso® flour tortillas for burritos (8 tortillas)	8 medium green onions, sliced (1/2 cup)
Cooking spray	2 cups finely shredded Mexican cheese blend (8 oz.)
1 can (16 oz.) Old El Paso® refried beans	2/3 cup sour cream

1 Place oven rack in lowest rack position; heat oven to 400°F. Spray one side of each tortilla with cooking spray. With 2-1/2-inch round cutter, cut 5 rounds from each tortilla (if desired, stack 2 tortillas to cut).

2 On ungreased large cookie sheets, place tortilla rounds with sprayed sides down. Spread each round with beans. Set aside 1 tablespoon of the onions. Sprinkle rounds with remaining onions and cheese.

3 Bake on lowest oven rack 11 to 13 minutes or until bottoms are crisp and cheese is melted and bubbly. Top each with about 1 teaspoon sour cream and some of the reserved onions.

HIGH ALTITUDE (3500-6500 FT): Bake on lowest oven rack 9 to 11 minutes.

NUTRITION INFORMATION PER SERVING: Calories 50 • Total Fat 3g • Saturated Fat 1.5g • Cholesterol 10mg • Sodium 110mg • Total Carbohydrate 4g • Dietary Fiber 0g • Protein 2g. DIETARY EXCHANGES: 1/2 Starch • 1/2 Fat.

smoky bean dip

READY IN: 35 Minutes ✳ **SERVINGS:** 8

2   dried chipotle chiles

2   cans (15.5 or 15 oz. each) pinto beans, drained, rinsed

1/8   teaspoon Liquid Smoke, if desired

1   large garlic clove, minced

2   tablespoons chopped fresh cilantro

1/2   each of green, yellow and red bell pepper

2   Italian plum tomatoes, chopped

1   cup shredded Mexican cheese blend (4 oz.)

8   oz. tortilla chips

1   Heat oven to 375°F. Place chiles in small bowl; cover with boiling water. Let stand 10 minutes or until soft. Drain chiles, reserving 3 tablespoons of soaking water. Remove and discard seeds from chiles; coarsely chop chiles.

2   In food processor bowl with metal blade or blender container, place beans, chiles, reserved water, Liquid Smoke and garlic; process on high speed until well combined. Stir in cilantro. Place mixture in ungreased shallow 9-inch glass pie pan. Cover with foil.

3   Bake 15 to 20 minutes or until mixture is thoroughly heated. Meanwhile, cut bell peppers with cactus, coyote and moon-shaped cookie cutters; set aside.

4   Uncover dip; sprinkle with tomatoes and cheese. Bake 2 to 3 minutes longer or until cheese is melted. Garnish top of dip with bell pepper cutouts. Serve with tortilla chips.

NUTRITION INFORMATION PER SERVING: Calories 340 • Total Fat 12g • Saturated Fat 3.5g • Cholesterol 15mg • Sodium 270mg • Total Carbohydrate 45g • Dietary Fiber 9g • Protein 14g. DIETARY EXCHANGES: 3 Starch • 1/2 Very Lean Meat • 2 Fat • 3 Carb Choices.

cook's notes

If you use canned chipotle chiles, it is not necessary to soak them as directed in the recipe. Add the canned chiles directly to the beans in the food processor, along with 3 tablespoons of the adobo sauce from the can in place of the soaking liquid.

holiday appetizer wreath

PREP TIME: 20 Minutes ✱ **READY IN:** 55 Minutes ✱ **SERVINGS:** 16

6	slices bacon
1/2	cup chive-and-onion cream cheese spread (from 8-oz. container)
2	cans (8 oz. each) Pillsbury® refrigerated crescent dinner rolls
2	cups Green Giant Select® frozen broccoli florets (from 14-oz. bag), thawed, finely chopped and patted dry with paper towel
1/3	cup diced red bell pepper
1	egg, beaten
1	teaspoon sesame seed
	Fresh rosemary, if desired

1 Heat oven to 375°F. Cook bacon as desired until crisp. Drain on paper towel; crumble bacon and set aside.

2 Unroll both cans of dough; separate into 16 triangles. On ungreased large cookie sheet, arrange triangles with shortest sides toward center, overlapping in wreath shape and leaving 4-inch round circle open in center. Crescent dough points may overlap edge of cookie sheet. Press overlapping dough to flatten.

3 Spread cream cheese spread on dough to within 1 inch of points. In small bowl, mix crumbled bacon, broccoli and bell pepper; spoon onto widest part of dough. Pull end points of triangles over broccoli mixture and tuck under dough to form ring (filling will be visible). Carefully brush dough with beaten egg; sprinkle with sesame seed.

4 Bake 25 to 30 minutes or until deep golden brown. Cool 5 minutes. With broad spatula, carefully loosen wreath from cookie sheet; slide onto serving platter. Garnish with fresh rosemary. Serve warm. Store in refrigerator.

HIGH ALTITUDE (3500-6500 FT): Heat oven to 350°F. Use 1/3 cup cheese spread. Bake 30 to 35 minutes.

NUTRITION INFORMATION PER SERVING: Calories 100 • Total Fat 7g • Saturated Fat 3g • Cholesterol 25mg • Sodium 210mg • Total Carbohydrate 7g • Dietary Fiber 0g • Protein 3g. DIETARY EXCHANGES: 1/2 Starch • 1-1/2 Fat • 1/2 Carb Choice.

roasted vegetables with spicy aïoli dip

PREP TIME: 25 Minutes ✳ **READY IN:** 50 Minutes ✳ **SERVINGS:** 24

AÏOLI DIP
1 cup mayonnaise or salad dressing
1/2 cup sour cream
1/2 cup garlic ranch dressing
Fresh chives, if desired

VEGETABLES
4 medium red bell peppers, cut into
1-1/2-inch squares

2 medium red onions, cut into wedges
4 small yellow summer squash, cut into
1-inch-thick slices
1/2 lb. fresh green beans, trimmed
24 fresh whole mushrooms
2 tablespoons olive or vegetable oil
2 teaspoons seasoned salt

1 In medium bowl, mix mayonnaise, sour cream and dressing until smooth. Refrigerate at least 30 minutes to blend flavors. Garnish with chives.

2 Meanwhile, heat oven to 450°F. In large bowl, toss vegetables with oil and seasoned salt to coat evenly. Arrange vegetables in ungreased large shallow roasting pan, at least 16x12 inches.

3 Bake 15 to 20 minutes or until crisp-tender. Refrigerate vegetables at least 8 hours or overnight, and serve cold with dip.

GRILLING DIRECTIONS: Heat gas or charcoal grill. In large bowl, toss vegetables with oil and seasoned salt to coat evenly. Place vegetables, cut side down, on gas grill over medium-low heat or charcoal grill over medium-high coals. Cover grill. Cook 14 to 18 minutes or until crisp-tender, turning once and brushing with additional oil to keep surfaces moist. (Cooking time will vary according to size of vegetables.)

NUTRITION INFORMATION PER SERVING: Calories 130 • Total Fat 12g • Saturated Fat 2.5g • Cholesterol 10mg • Sodium 210mg • Total Carbohydrate 5g • Dietary Fiber 1g • Protein 2g. DIETARY EXCHANGES: 1 Vegetable • 2-1/2 Fat • 1/2 Carb Choice.

cook's notes

Aïoli is traditionally a garlic sauce. This version uses garlic ranch dressing for an easy shortcut.

cheese fondue with roasted vegetable dippers

cheese fondue with roasted vegetable dippers

READY IN: 30 Minutes ✳ **SERVINGS:** 12

DIPPERS

- 2 cups fresh cauliflower florets
- 1 medium green bell pepper, cut into 1-1/2-inch pieces
- 1 medium red bell pepper, cut into 1-1/2-inch pieces
- 1 medium yellow summer squash, cut into 1/2-inch slices
- 1 package (8 oz.) fresh whole mushrooms
- 2 cups French bread cubes
- 1 tablespoon olive oil

FONDUE

- 4 oz. Havarti cheese, shredded (1 cup)
- 1 cup shredded sharp Cheddar cheese (4 oz.)
- 1 cup shredded American cheese (4 oz.)
- 2 tablespoons all-purpose flour
- 1 cup dry white wine
- 1/4 teaspoon garlic powder

1 Heat oven to 450°F. In large bowl, toss dippers with oil to coat evenly; arrange in ungreased 15x10x1-inch pan. Bake 15 to 20 minutes or until vegetables are crisp-tender and bread cubes are toasted.

2 In medium bowl, toss cheeses and flour to mix. Place wine in 2-quart saucepan; cook over medium heat about 1 minute or until very hot. Do not boil. Add cheese mixture 1/2 cup at a time, stirring each time until melted. Cook until very warm. Pour into fondue pot. Stir in garlic powder. Keep warm over medium-low heat.

3 To serve, skewer roasted vegetables and bread cubes with fondue forks to be dipped into warm cheese.

NUTRITION INFORMATION PER SERVING: Calories 170 • Total Fat 11 g • Saturated Fat 6g • Cholesterol 30mg • Sodium 320mg • Total Carbohydrate 8g • Dietary Fiber 1g • Protein 8g. DIETARY EXCHANGES: 1/2 Starch • 1 Vegetable • 1/2 High-Fat Meat • 1-1/2 Fat • 1/2 Carb Choice.

special touch

Sprinkle chopped fresh chives over the mixture in the fondue pot. Garnish the platter of roasted vegetables and bread with long strands of chives or sprigs of another fresh herb.

spicy fire roasted cream cheese dip

READY IN: 10 Minutes ✳ **SERVINGS:** 12

DIP

- 1 package (8 oz.) cream cheese, softened
- 1 can (14.5 oz.) Muir Glen® organic fire roasted crushed tomatoes with medium green chiles, drained
- 1 teaspoon crushed red pepper flakes
- 1/8 teaspoon ground red pepper (cayenne)

DIPPERS

- Assorted raw vegetables and crackers, as desired

1 In medium bowl, stir together dip ingredients. Serve with dippers. Cover and refrigerate any remaining dip.

NUTRITION INFORMATION PER SERVING: Calories 70 • Total Fat 7g • Saturated Fat 4g • Cholesterol 20mg • Sodium 70mg • Total Carbohydrate 2g • Dietary Fiber 0g • Protein 2g. DIETARY EXCHANGES: 1/2 High-Fat Meat • 1/2 Fat.

pastry-wrapped cranberry brie

PREP TIME: 20 Minutes ✳ **READY IN:** 1 Hour 20 Minutes ✳ **SERVINGS:** 12

1 can (8 oz.) Pillsbury® refrigerated crescent dinner rolls

1 round (8 oz.) Brie cheese (do not use triple crème Brie)

3 tablespoons whole berry cranberry sauce

1 tablespoon apricot preserves

1/2 teaspoon dried rosemary leaves, crushed

2 ripe medium unpeeled pears, thinly sliced

1 Heat oven to 350°F. Unroll dough and separate crosswise into 2 sections. Press dough into 2 (7-inch) squares, firmly pressing perforations to seal.

2 Cut cheese round horizontally to make 2 rounds. Place 1 cheese round, rind side down, on center of 1 dough square. (Do not remove rind from cheese.) In small bowl, mix cranberry sauce and preserves. Spread over top of cheese; sprinkle with rosemary. Top with remaining cheese round, rind side up.

3 With small cookie or canapé cutter or sharp knife, make 1/2- to 1-inch cutouts to look like poinsettia petals from each corner of remaining dough square. Roll 3 small pieces of dough into 3 small balls; set cutouts and dough balls aside. Place remaining dough on top of cheese round. Press dough evenly around cheese, folding top edges over bottom edges; press to seal completely. Place on ungreased cookie sheet.

4 On 7-inch square sheet of foil, arrange dough petals to look like a poinsettia. Place balls in center on top of arranged petals. Lift foil square with poinsettia and place on cookie sheet next to wrapped cheese.

5 Bake poinsettia 8 to 11 minutes or until light golden brown around edges. Lift with foil from cookie sheet; cool. Continue baking wrapped cheese 25 to 30 minutes longer or until golden brown. Remove from cookie sheet; place on serving plate. Place poinsettia on top of wrapped cheese. Let stand 15 minutes before serving. Serve warm with pears.

NUTRITION INFORMATION PER SERVING: Calories 160 • Total Fat 9g • Saturated Fat 4.5g • Cholesterol 20mg • Sodium 270mg • Total Carbohydrate 15g • Dietary Fiber 1g • Protein 5g. DIETARY EXCHANGES: 1/2 Starch • 1/2 Other Carbohydrate • 1/2 High-Fat Meat • 1 Fat • 1 Carb Choice.

game-time nachos

READY IN: 15 Minutes ✳ **SERVINGS:** 8

- 6 oz. light prepared cheese product, cut into cubes (from 16-oz. loaf)
- 1/4 cup shredded reduced-fat sharp Cheddar cheese (1 oz.)
- 3 tablespoons fat-free (skim) milk
- 1-1/2 teaspoons Old El Paso® 40% less-sodium taco seasoning mix (from 1-oz. pkg.)

- 3 oz. baked bite-size tortilla chips (about 64 chips)
- 1-1/2 cups finely chopped plum (Roma) tomatoes (about 5 medium)
- 1/4 cup chopped fresh cilantro

1 In 1-quart saucepan, heat cheese product, Cheddar cheese, milk and taco seasoning mix over medium-low heat, stirring frequently, until cheeses are melted and mixture is smooth.

2 Meanwhile, arrange chips on large serving platter. Pour warm cheese mixture over chips. Top with tomatoes and cilantro. Serve immediately.

NUTRITION INFORMATION PER SERVING: Calories 120 • Total Fat 4g • Saturated Fat 2g • Cholesterol 10mg • Sodium 440mg • Total Carbohydrate 14g • Dietary Fiber 1g • Protein 7g. DIETARY EXCHANGES: 1 Starch • 1/2 Medium-Fat Meat • 1 Carb Choice.

special touch

For a fun presentation, vary the color of tortilla chips you use. Choose red, green, white, blue or yellow tortilla chips.

cook's notes

Blanching turns the pea pods a

bright green color and makes

them pliable to wrap around

the shrimp.

pea pod wrap-ups

READY IN: 1 Hour 20 Minutes ✳ SERVINGS: 35

1 lb. cooked deveined peeled large shrimp
(about 35)

1 cup (8 oz.) Asian ginger dressing

6 oz. fresh snow pea pods (about 35)

Toothpicks or appetizer picks

1 In medium bowl, place shrimp. Pour dressing evenly over shrimp; stir to coat. Cover; refrigerate
1 hour. Meanwhile, remove stem and strings from pea pods. To partially cook pea pods, place in
boiling water about 1 minute or until pea pods turn bright green. Drain; rinse with cold water and
dry with paper towels.

2 Drain dressing from shrimp. Wrap 1 pea pod around each shrimp; secure with toothpick. Cover;
refrigerate until serving time.

NUTRITION INFORMATION PER SERVING: Calories 35 • Total Fat 2g • Saturated Fat 0g • Cholesterol 25mg • Sodium 60mg •
Total Carbohydrate 1g • Dietary Fiber 0g • Protein 3g. DIETARY EXCHANGES: 1/2 Very Lean Meat • 1/2 Fat.

crusty bread boat with crab and artichoke spread

PREP TIME: 20 Minutes ✹ READY IN: 1 Hour 20 Minutes ✹ SERVINGS: 6

- 1 can (11 oz.) Pillsbury® refrigerated crusty French loaf
- 1 package (3 oz.) cream cheese, softened
- 2 tablespoons mayonnaise or salad dressing
- 1 tablespoon white wine Worcestershire sauce
- 1/4 teaspoon crushed red pepper flakes
- 1 small garlic clove, finely chopped

- 1 cup shredded Asiago cheese (4 oz.)
- 1 can (14 oz.) artichoke hearts, drained, chopped
- 1 can (6 oz.) crabmeat, well drained
- 1 jar (2 oz.) diced pimientos, drained
- 1 tablespoon chopped fresh parsley

1 Heat oven to 350°F. Bake French loaf as directed on can. Cool 30 minutes. In medium microwavable bowl, mix remaining ingredients except parsley. Set aside.

2 Cut 1 inch from top of cooled loaf. Cut top into 1-inch pieces; place in serving basket. With sharp knife, cut around inside of loaf, leaving 1/2-inch-thick sides. Remove bread, leaving inside of loaf hollow. Cut removed bread into 1-inch pieces; place in serving basket.

3 Microwave cream cheese mixture on Medium 3 to 4 minutes, stirring twice, until hot. Spoon hot mixture into hollowed out loaf. Sprinkle with parsley. Serve spread with bread pieces and/or crackers.

NUTRITION INFORMATION PER SERVING: (excluding hollowed loaf): Calories 350 • Total Fat 16g • Saturated Fat 7g • Cholesterol 55mg • Sodium 990mg • Total Carbohydrate 32g • Dietary Fiber 4g • Protein 20g. DIETARY EXCHANGES: 2 Starch • 2 Lean Meat • 2 Fat • 2 Carb Choices.

cook's notes

White wine Worcestershire sauce is milder in flavor and lighter in color than regular Worcestershire sauce. In a pinch, the regular variety will work in this recipe.

cranberry fizz

cranberry fizz

READY IN: 10 Minutes ✻ SERVINGS: 16

1 quart (4 cups) cranberry juice cocktail, chilled	1 cup orange juice, chilled
1 cup grapefruit juice, chilled	1/2 cup sugar
	2 cups ginger ale, chilled

1 In large nonmetal pitcher or punch bowl, mix cranberry juice cocktail, grapefruit juice, orange juice and sugar until well blended. Just before serving, stir in ginger ale.

NUTRITION INFORMATION PER SERVING: Calories 90 • Total Fat 0g • Saturated Fat 0g • Cholesterol 0mg • Sodium 5mg • Total Carbohydrate 22g • Dietary Fiber 0g • Protein 0g. DIETARY EXCHANGES: 1-1/2 Other Carbohydrate • 1-1/2 Carb Choices

cook's notes

You can combine the juice ingredients and sugar several hours ahead and chill. Just before serving, add the ginger ale. For festive ice cubes, add cranberries, orange zest and fresh thyme to the water in the ice cube trays and freeze.

onion-bacon crescent bites

PREP TIME: 25 Minutes ✻ READY IN: 45 Minutes ✻ SERVINGS: 32

3 slices bacon, cut into pieces	1/2 teaspoon paprika
1/2 cup chopped onion	1/4 teaspoon caraway seed, crushed
1 package (3 oz.) cream cheese, softened	1 can (8 oz.) Pillsbury® refrigerated crescent dinner rolls or 1 can (8 oz.) Pillsbury® Crescent Recipe Creations® refrigerated seamless dough sheet
1/3 cup shredded Cheddar cheese	
1 tablespoon finely chopped fresh parsley	

1 Heat oven to 375°F. Spray cookie sheet with cooking spray. In 6-inch skillet, cook bacon over medium heat 3 minutes. Add onion; cook 3 to 5 minutes or until tender. Remove from heat. Drain if necessary.

2 In small bowl, stir cream cheese until smooth. Add bacon mixture, Cheddar cheese, parsley, paprika and caraway seed; mix well. Set aside.

3 If using crescent rolls: Unroll dough; separate into 4 rectangles. Press perforations to seal. If using dough sheet: Unroll dough; cut into 4 rectangles.

4 Spoon 1/4 of bacon mixture onto each rectangle; spread to within 1/2 inch from 1 long side. Roll up each rectangle, starting with topped long side and rolling to untopped side. Press edge to seal. With serrated knife, cut each roll into 8 slices. Place cut down side on cookie sheet. Bake 15 to 20 minutes or until golden brown. Serve warm.

NUTRITION INFORMATION PER SERVING: Calories 45 • Total Fat 3g • Saturated Fat 1.5g • Cholesterol 0mg • Sodium 90mg • Total Carbohydrate 3g • Dietary Fiber 0g • Protein 1g. DIETARY EXCHANGES: 1/2 Other Carbohydrate • 1/2 Fat.

Blissful Breads
& Baked Goods

Fill your home with the enticing aroma of freshly baked coffee cakes, cinnamon rolls, quick breads and more. It's a scrumptious way to celebrate the Yuletide.

p. 42

p. 46

p. 49

p. 44

p. 57

crescent angel wings p. 51

cook's notes

After the coffee cake is cooled completely, place in an air-tight container or plastic bag and keep at room temperature for 2 to 3 days.

sour cream chocolate swirl coffee cake

PREP TIME: 25 Minutes ✳ **READY IN:** 1 Hour 25 Minutes ✳ **SERVINGS:** 16

COFFEE CAKE

- 1/4 cup finely chopped pecans
- 3 oz. semisweet chocolate, chopped
- 1 cup sugar
- 1/2 cup butter or margarine, softened
- 1 container (8 oz.) sour cream
- 2 teaspoons vanilla
- 3 eggs
- 2 cups all-purpose flour
- 1-1/2 teaspoons baking powder
- 1/4 teaspoon salt

GLAZE

- 1 oz. semisweet chocolate, chopped
- 1/2 teaspoon oil

1 Heat oven to 350°F. Generously grease 12-cup fluted tube pan. Sprinkle with pecans, tilting pan to coat sides with some of the nuts. Set pan aside. In 1-quart microwavable bowl, place 3 ounces chocolate. Microwave on High 30 seconds; stir. If necessary, microwave in 10-second increments, stirring each time, until melted. Set aside to cool.

2 In large bowl, beat sugar and butter with electric mixer on medium speed 1 to 2 minutes or until light and fluffy. Beat in 1/2 cup of the sour cream, the vanilla and eggs until smooth. On low speed, beat in 1 cup of the flour, the baking powder and salt until dry ingredients are moistened. Beat in remaining sour cream and flour just until blended.

3 Spoon 2 cups of the batter into cooled chocolate; stir until mixed. Spoon half of the remaining batter into pan. Drop half of the chocolate batter over the vanilla batter. With table knife, gently swirl. Spoon remaining vanilla batter into pan. Top with remaining chocolate batter. Gently swirl; smooth top.

4 Bake 38 to 45 minutes or until toothpick inserted in center comes out clean. Cool in pan 15 minutes. Invert onto serving platter.

5 Place 1 ounce chocolate and the oil in small microwavable bowl. Microwave on High 20 seconds; stir until smooth. Drizzle over coffee cake. Serve warm or cool.

HIGH ALTITUDE (3500-6500 FT): Decrease baking powder to 1-1/4 teaspoons. In Step 2, add 1/4 cup water with the sour cream, vanilla and eggs. Bake 45 to 52 minutes.

NUTRITION INFORMATION PER SERVING: Calories 250 • Total Fat 13g • Saturated Fat 7g • Cholesterol 65mg • Sodium 140mg • Total Carbohydrate 30g • Dietary Fiber 1g • Protein 4g. DIETARY EXCHANGES: 1 Starch • 1 Other Carbohydrate • 2-1/2 Fat • 2 Carb Choices.

buttermilk banana bread

PREP TIME: 10 Minutes ✱ **READY IN:** 3 Hours 40 Minutes ✱ **SERVINGS:** 16 Slices

2	cups Fiber One® Honey Clusters® cereal	1	egg
3/4	cup sugar	1	cup mashed very ripe bananas (2 medium)
1/4	cup canola or vegetable oil	2	cups all-purpose flour
1	cup buttermilk	1	teaspoon baking soda
2	teaspoons vanilla	1/4	teaspoon salt

1 Heat oven to 350°F. Grease bottom only of 9x5-inch loaf pan. Place cereal in resealable food-storage plastic bag; seal bag and crush with rolling pin or meat mallet (or crush in food processor).

2 In large bowl, beat sugar and oil with electric mixer on medium speed until well mixed. On low speed, beat in buttermilk, vanilla and egg until smooth. Beat in bananas. Beat in flour, baking soda and salt until will blended.

3 Stir in cereal just until mixed. Spread in pan. Bake 1 hour 10 minutes to 1 hour 20 minutes or until toothpick inserted in center comes out clean. Cool 10 minutes. Remove from pan to cooling rack. Cool completely, about 2 hours, before slicing.

HIGH ALTITUDE (3500-6500 FT): Heat oven to 375°F.

NUTRITION INFORMATION PER SERVING: Calories 180 • Total Fat 4.5g • Saturated Fat 0g • Cholesterol 15mg • Sodium 170mg • Total Carbohydrate 31g • Dietary Fiber 2g • Protein 3g. DIETARY EXCHANGES: 1 Starch • 1 Other Carbohydrate • 1 Fat • 2 Carb Choices.

kitchen tip

Give any homemade banana bread a flavor and fiber boost with Fiber One® Honey Clusters® cereal.

Kitchen tip

Serve this crescent ring with cut-up fresh fruit, crisp slices of bacon and glasses of freshly squeezed orange juice.

caramel chai crescent ring

PREP TIME: 35 Minutes ✳ **READY IN:** 1 Hour 10 Minutes ✳ **SERVINGS:** 12

1/4 cup butter (do not use margarine)	1/2 teaspoon ground nutmeg
1/2 cup packed brown sugar	1/4 teaspoon ground cloves
2 tablespoons maple syrup or corn syrup	2 cans (8 oz. each) Pillsbury® refrigerated reduced-fat crescent dinner rolls
2 tablespoons whipping cream	2 tablespoons butter, melted
2 tablespoons granulated sugar	16 large marshmallows
1 tablespoon ground cinnamon	1/4 cup chopped nuts
1/2 teaspoon ground ginger	

1 Heat oven to 350°F. In 1-quart saucepan, melt 1/4 cup butter. With 1 to 2 tablespoons of the melted butter, grease bottom and side of 12-cup fluted tube cake pan. To remaining melted butter, stir in brown sugar and maple syrup. Heat just to boiling, stirring occasionally. Remove from heat; stir in whipping cream.

2 In small bowl, mix granulated sugar, cinnamon, ginger, nutmeg and cloves. Unroll dough from both cans and separate into 16 triangles. Brush triangles with 2 tablespoons melted butter. Sprinkle about 1/2 teaspoon granulated sugar mixture onto each triangle to within 1/4 inch of edges. Top each with marshmallow. Roll up, starting at shortest side of triangle, and rolling to opposite point. Completely cover marshmallow with dough; firmly pinch edges to seal. Arrange 8 balls in buttered pan. Sprinkle with nuts; spoon half of brown sugar mixture over dough. Place remaining 8 balls alternately over bottom layer. Spoon remaining brown sugar mixture over balls.

3 Bake 25 to 28 minutes or until golden brown. Cool 3 minutes. Place heatproof serving platter upside down over pan; turn pan and platter over. Remove pan. Serve warm.

HIGH ALTITUDE (3500-6500 FT): Bake 27 to 30 minutes.

NUTRITION INFORMATION PER SERVING: Calories 290 • Total Fat 14g • Saturated Fat 7g • Cholesterol 20mg • Sodium 350mg • Total Carbohydrate 38g • Dietary Fiber 0g • Protein 3g. DIETARY EXCHANGES: 1 Starch • 1-1/2 Other Carbohydrate • 2-1/2 Fat • 2-1/2 Carb Choices.

poinsettia coffee cake

PREP TIME: 15 Minutes ✳ **READY IN:** 30 Minutes ✳ **SERVINGS:** 8

1 can (13.9 oz.) Pillsbury® refrigerated orange sweet rolls	1/4 cup sweetened dried cranberries

1 Heat oven to 400°F. Grease cookie sheet. Remove dough and icing from can. Place 1 sweet roll in center of cookie sheet; press to 2-1/2 inches in diameter. Place remaining rolls around center roll, seams toward center; press each to 2-1/2 inches.

2 Pinch outside edge of each roll into a point. (Exaggerate points, as they tend to shrink into original shape during baking.)

3 Bake 11 to 14 minutes or until golden brown. Carefully spread with icing; sprinkle with cranberries except on center roll. Cool 1 minute. With broad metal spatula, carefully loosen coffee cake from cookie sheet and slide onto serving plate.

NUTRITION INFORMATION PER SERVING: Calories 180 • Total Fat 7g • Saturated Fat 1.5g • Cholesterol 0mg • Sodium 340mg • Total Carbohydrate 28g • Dietary Fiber 0g • Protein 2g. DIETARY EXCHANGES: 1 Starch • 1 Other Carbohydrate • 1 Fat • 2 Carb Choices.

caramel chai crescent ring

banana-cranberry spice muffins

PREP TIME: 15 Minutes ✳ **READY IN:** 40 Minutes ✳ **SERVINGS:** 12

1 cup Fiber One® original bran cereal	1/2 cup sugar
1 egg	3 teaspoons baking powder
3/4 cup fat-free (skim) milk	1 teaspoon ground cinnamon
3 tablespoons vegetable oil	1/4 teaspoon ground nutmeg
1 cup mashed ripe bananas (about 2 medium)	1/4 teaspoon salt
1-1/4 cups all-purpose flour	1/2 cup sweetened dried cranberries

1 Heat oven to 400°F. Grease bottoms only of 12 regular-size muffin cups with shortening or cooking spray, or use paper baking cups. Place cereal in resealable food-storage plastic bag; seal bag and crush with rolling pin or meat mallet (or crush in food processor).

2 In medium bowl, beat egg, milk and oil with fork or wire whisk until well mixed; beat in bananas. Stir in cereal; let stand 5 minutes.

3 Stir in remaining ingredients except cranberries until blended. Stir in cranberries. Divide batter evenly among muffin cups.

4 Bake 20 to 25 minutes or until light golden brown. Immediately remove from pan to cooling rack. Serve warm.

NUTRITION INFORMATION PER SERVING: Calories 180 • Total Fat 4.5g • Saturated Fat 0.5g • Cholesterol 20mg • Sodium 200mg • Total Carbohydrate 32g • Dietary Fiber 3g • Protein 3g. DIETARY EXCHANGES: 1 Starch • 1 Other Carbohydrate • 1 Fat • 2 Carb Choices.

lemony carrot-walnut bread

PREP TIME: 15 Minutes ✳ **READY IN:** 2 Hours 40 Minutes ✳ **SERVINGS:** 16 Slices

1-1/2 cups Fiber One® original bran cereal

1 can (14.5 oz.) sliced carrots, drained, 1/2 cup liquid reserved

1 teaspoon grated lemon peel

1/3 cup lemon juice

1/4 cup vegetable oil

2 eggs

2-2/3 cups all-purpose flour

3/4 cup sugar

2 teaspoons baking powder

2 teaspoons pumpkin pie spice

1/2 teaspoon baking soda

1/4 teaspoon salt

1/2 cup chopped walnuts

1 Heat oven to 350°F. Grease bottom only of 9x5-inch loaf pan with shortening or cooking spray. Place cereal in resealable food-storage plastic bag; seal bag and crush with rolling pin or meat mallet (or crush in food processor). Set aside.

2 In large bowl, mash carrots with fork. With electric mixer on low speed, beat in reserved carrot liquid, lemon peel, lemon juice, oil and eggs until blended.

3 Beat in flour, sugar, baking powder, pumpkin pie spice, baking soda and salt until blended. Stir in crushed cereal and walnuts. Spoon batter into pan.

4 Bake about 1 hour 10 minutes or until toothpick inserted in center comes out clean. Cool 15 minutes; remove from pan to cooling rack. Cool completely, about 1 hour, before slicing.

HIGH ALTITUDE (3500-6500 FT): Bake about 1 hour 20 minutes.

NUTRITION INFORMATION PER SERVING: Calories 210 • Total Fat 7g • Saturated Fat 1g • Cholesterol 25mg • Sodium 210mg • Total Carbohydrate 32g • Dietary Fiber 4g • Protein 4g, DIETARY EXCHANGES: 1-1/2 Starch • 1/2 Other Carbohydrate • 1 Fat • 2 Carb Choices.

kitchen tip

Grease only the bottoms of loaf pans for quick breads. Ungreased sides allow the batter to cling while rising during baking, which helps form a gently rounded top. If sides are greased, the edges of the loaf may have ridges.

apple-cranberry-pistachio bread

apple-cranberry-pistachio bread

PREP TIME: 20 Minutes　✳　**READY IN:** 3 Hours　✳　**SERVINGS:** 16 Slices

BREAD

1-1/2	cups all-purpose flour
3/4	cup granulated sugar
2	teaspoons baking powder
1/2	teaspoon salt
1/4	cup vegetable oil
1/3	cup apple cider or apple juice
2	eggs, beaten

1	cup shredded peeled apple (1 medium)
1/2	cup sweetened dried cranberries
1/3	cup chopped pistachios

TOPPING

1/2	cup powdered sugar
2 to 3	teaspoons apple cider or apple juice
2	tablespoons finely chopped pistachios

1 Heat oven to 350°F. Grease and flour bottom only of 8x4-inch loaf pan. In large bowl with wooden spoon, mix flour, granulated sugar, baking powder and salt. Beat in oil, 1/3 cup cider and eggs until smooth. Stir in apple, cranberries and 1/3 cup pistachios. Spoon and spread evenly in pan.

2 Bake 50 to 60 minutes or until toothpick inserted in center comes out clean. Cool in pan 10 minutes. Remove from pan. Cool completely, about 1 hour 30 minutes.

3 In small bowl, mix powdered sugar and enough of the 2 to 3 teaspoons cider for desired glaze consistency. Spread over top of bread. Sprinkle with 2 tablespoons pistachios.

HIGH ALTITUDE (3500-6500 FT): Decrease baking powder to 1-1/2 teaspoons.

NUTRITION INFORMATION PER SERVING: Calories 180 • Total Fat 6g • Saturated Fat 1g • Cholesterol 25mg • Sodium 140mg • Total Carbohydrate 28g • Dietary Fiber 1g • Protein 3g. DIETARY EXCHANGES: 1/2 Starch • 1-1/2 Other Carbohydrate • 1 Fat • 2 Carb Choices.

easy stromboli

PREP TIME: 15 Minutes　✳　**READY IN:** 35 Minutes　✳　**SERVINGS:** 6

1/2	lb. lean ground beef
1	can (13.8 oz.) Pillsbury® refrigerated classic pizza crust
1/4	cup pizza sauce

1	cup shredded mozzarella cheese (4oz.)
1/4	cup chopped green and/or red bell pepper, if desired
1/4	teaspoon dried Italian seasoning

1 Heat oven to 400°F. Spray cookie sheet with nonstick cooking spray. Brown ground beef in medium skillet over medium-high heat until thoroughly cooked, stirring frequently. Drain. Set aside.

2 Unroll dough; place on sprayed cookie sheet. Starting at center, press out dough with hands to form 12x8-inch rectangle.

3 Spread sauce over dough to within 2 inches of long sides and 1/2 inch of short sides. Place cooked ground beef lengthwise down center, forming 3-inch-wide strip and to within 1/2 inch of short sides. Top with cheese, bell pepper and Italian seasoning.

4 Fold long sides of dough over filling; press edges to seal. Bake at 400°F for 15 to 20 minutes or until crust is golden brown.

NUTRITION INFORMATION PER SERVING: Calories 290 • Total Fat 10g • Saturated Fat 4.5g • Cholesterol 35mg • Sodium 630mg • Total Carbohydrate 33g • Dietary Fiber 0g • Protein 17g. DIETARY EXCHANGES: 1-1/2 Starch • 1/2 Other Carbohydrate • 1-1/2 Medium-Fat Meat • 1/2 Fat • 2 Carb Choices.

cook's notes

Wrap the cooled loaf and store at room temperature overnight for easier slicing. Most quick breads slice better the second day. A sharp serrated knife or an electric knife works well for slicing quick breads.

kitchen tip

For a delicious variation on pizza, roll up your favorite ingredients with an Italian flair in a Pillsbury® pizza crust.

cream cheese-raspberry coffee cake

PREP TIME: 30 Minutes ✳ READY IN: 1 Hour ✳ SERVINGS: 12

COFFEE CAKE

- 2 cans (8 oz. each) Pillsbury® refrigerated crescent dinner rolls
- 1 package (8 oz.) cream cheese, softened
- 1/4 cup granulated sugar
- 2 teaspoons grated orange peel
- 1 teaspoon vanilla
- 1 egg
- 1 pint (2 cups) fresh raspberries
- 1 teaspoon granulated sugar

GLAZE

- 1/2 cup powdered sugar
- 1 tablespoon butter or margarine, softened
- 2 teaspoons orange juice

1 Heat oven to 350°F. Spray large cookie sheet or 14-inch pizza pan with cooking spray. Unroll both cans of dough; separate into 16 triangles. Reserve 4 triangles for topping.

2 On cookie sheet, arrange 12 triangles in circle with points toward center, leaving 3-inch hole in center. Press dough to form 14-inch ring; press seams together to seal. Fold outer and center edges up 1/4 inch.

3 In medium bowl, mix cream cheese, 1/4 cup granulated sugar, the orange peel, vanilla and egg until well blended. Gently stir in raspberries. (Mixture will be thin.)

4 Spoon raspberry mixture evenly over dough. With scissors or pizza cutter, cut each reserved dough triangle lengthwise into thirds. Place 1 teaspoon granulated sugar on work surface. Press each dough strip into sugar. Arrange sugared dough strips, sugar side up, evenly in spoke pattern over filling. Press ends to seal at center and outer edges.

5 Bake 25 to 30 minutes or until golden brown. Cool 10 minutes. In small bowl, mix powdered sugar, butter and orange juice until smooth. Drizzle over coffee cake. Serve warm.

NUTRITION INFORMATION PER SERVING: Calories 280 • Total Fat 16g • Saturated Fat 8g, • Cholesterol 40mg • Sodium 360mg • Total Carbohydrate 27g • Dietary Fiber 2g • Protein 5g. DIETARY EXCHANGES: 1/2 Starch • 1-1/2 Other Carbohydrate • 1/2 High-Fat Meat • 2-1/2 Fat • 2 Carb Choices.

cook's notes

Pat the maraschino cherries dry with a paper towel to prevent the juice from bleeding.

sugarplum brunch ring

PREP TIME: 20 Minutes ✳ READY IN: 2 Hours ✳ SERVINGS: 16

- 3/4 cup sugar
- 1 teaspoon ground cinnamon
- 18 frozen bread dough rolls, thawed (1/2 of 48-oz. pkg.)
- 4 tablespoons butter or margarine, melted
- 1/2 cup chopped pecans
- 1/2 cup maraschino cherries, chopped
- 1/3 cup dark corn syrup

1 Grease 12-cup fluted tube pan. In small bowl, mix sugar and cinnamon. Cut each roll in half. Dip in butter; roll in sugar mixture. Place half of rolls in pan. Sprinkle with half of pecans and half of cherries. Drizzle with half of corn syrup. Repeat with remaining half of ingredients.

2 Drizzle any remaining butter over top; sprinkle with any remaining sugar mixture. Cover with greased plastic wrap and cloth towel. Let rise in warm place (80 to 85°F) until light and doubled in size, about 1 hour.

3 Heat oven to 350°F. Uncover dough. Bake 30 to 35 minutes or until top is deep golden brown. Cool in pan 5 minutes. Invert onto serving plate; remove pan. Serve warm to pull apart, or cool completely and slice.

HIGH ALTITUDE (3500-6500 FT): Bake 35 to 40 minutes.

NUTRITION INFORMATION PER SERVING: Calories 240 • Total Fat 8g • Saturated Fat 3g • Cholesterol 10mg • Sodium 240mg • Total Carbohydrate 38g • Dietary Fiber 2g • Protein 4g. DIETARY EXCHANGES: 1 Starch • 1-1/2 Other Carbohydrate • 1-1/2 Fat • 2-1/2 Carb Choices.

crescent angel wings

PREP TIME: 25 Minutes ✳ READY IN: 1 Hour 5 Minutes ✳ SERVINGS: 16

3 tablespoons gold decorator sugar crystals

1 can (8 oz.) Pillsbury® refrigerated crescent dinner rolls

1 teaspoon grated lemon peel

2 tablespoons butter or margarine, melted

1 Line cookie sheets with cooking parchment paper. Sprinkle cutting board with half of sugar crystals. Unroll dough and separate into 4 rectangles; place on sugar-sprinkled board, firmly pressing perforations to seal. Lightly press dough into sugar. In small bowl, mix remaining half of sugar and the lemon peel. Brush rectangles with 1 tablespoon of the melted butter; sprinkle with sugar mixture.

2 Place 1 rectangle on top of another. Starting with both of the shortest sides, roll up each side jelly roll fashion until rolls meet in center. Repeat with remaining 2 rectangles. Cover; refrigerate dough rolls about 30 minutes or until dough is firm.

3 Heat oven to 375°F. With serrated knife, cut each roll into 8 slices, making 16 slices total. Place slices, cut side down, 2 inches apart on cookie sheets. Brush with remaining tablespoon melted butter.

4 Bake 9 to 13 minutes or until golden brown. If necessary, gently reroll cookies. Immediately remove from cookie sheets to cooling rack. Cool completely. Store in airtight container.

HIGH ALTITUDE (3500-6500 FT): Bake 7 to 11 minutes.

NUTRITION INFORMATION PER SERVING: Calories 80 • Total Fat 4.5g • Saturated Fat 2g • Cholesterol 0mg • Sodium 120mg • Total Carbohydrate 8g • Dietary Fiber 0g • Protein 1g. DIETARY EXCHANGES: 1/2 Starch • 1 Fat • 1/2 Carb Choice.

special touch

For a slightly different look, use silver decorator sugar crystals instead of the gold.

easy cherry-almond coffee cake

PREP TIME: 10 Minutes ✳ **READY IN:** 50 Minutes ✳ **SERVINGS:** 6

1 can (12.4 oz.) Pillsbury® refrigerated cinnamon rolls with icing

1 cup cherry pie filling (from 21-oz. can)

1 tablespoon slivered almonds

1 Heat oven to 375°F. Spray 9-inch round cake pan with cooking spray. Separate dough into 8 rolls. Cut each into 4 pieces; place rounded side down in pan. Spoon pie filling over dough. Sprinkle with almonds.

2 Bake 25 to 35 minutes or until deep golden brown. Cool in pan 3 minutes. Place wire rack upside down over pan; turn rack and pan over. Remove pan. Place heatproof plate upside down over coffee cake; turn over.

3 Remove cover from icing; microwave on High 3 to 7 seconds. Stir icing; drizzle desired amount over warm coffee cake. Cut into wedges; serve warm.

NUTRITION INFORMATION PER SERVING: Calories 250 • Total Fat 8g • Saturated Fat 2g • Cholesterol 0mg • Sodium 450mg • Total Carbohydrate 43g • Dietary Fiber 2g • Protein 3g. DIETARY EXCHANGES: 1 Starch • 2 Other Carbohydrate • 1-1/2 Fat • 3 Carb Choices.

european walnut, hazelnut and golden raisin wheat rolls

PREP TIME: 40 Minutes ✳ **READY IN:** 3 Hours 35 Minutes ✳ **SERVINGS:** 18

5-1/2 to 6-1/2 cups bread flour

1 package active dry yeast

2-1/2 cups water heated to 100 to 105°F, divided

3/4 cup golden raisins

3/4 cup whole wheat flour

2-1/2 teaspoons salt

3/4 cup coarsely chopped, toasted walnuts

3/4 cup coarsely chopped hazelnuts (filberts)

Water

1 Lightly spoon flour into measuring cup; level off. In medium bowl, combine 2 cups of the bread flour and yeast; mix well. Stir in 1-1/2 cups of the warm water to form a loose starter dough. Let rest 15 to 30 minutes. In small bowl, combine raisins and remaining 1 cup warm water. Let stand 15 minutes.

2 Meanwhile, grease cookie sheets. In large bowl, combine 3-1/2 cups of the remaining bread flour, whole wheat flour and salt; mix well.

3 Stir raisins with water into starter dough until well mixed. Add starter mixture to whole wheat flour mixture; stir until soft dough forms. Turn dough out onto floured surface; knead 10 to 12 minutes, adding 1/2 to 1 cup flour until dough is smooth and elastic. Dough will be slightly sticky. Knead walnuts and hazelnuts into dough.

4 Spray large bowl with nonstick cooking spray. Place dough in sprayed bowl; cover loosely with sprayed plastic wrap and cloth towel. Let rise in warm place (80 to 85°F) until doubled in size, about 1-1/2 hours.

5 Punch down dough several times to remove all air bubbles. Divide dough into 18 pieces. Shape each piece into ball; place on greased cookie sheets. Cover; let rise until doubled in size, about 1 hour.

6 Heat oven to 425°F. Uncover dough; brush tops of rolls lightly with water. Bake at 425°F for 17 to 22 minutes or until golden brown.

NUTRITION INFORMATION PER SERVING: Calories 280 • Total Fat 7g • Saturated Fat 1g • Cholesterol 0mg • Sodium 300mg • Total Carbohydrate 46g • Dietary Fiber 3g • Protein 8g. DIETARY EXCHANGES: 3 Starch • 3 Other Carbohydrate • 1 Fat.

easy cherry-almond coffee cake

kitchen tip

When melted butter is called

for in a recipe, the butter is

measured first, then melted.

The convenient markings on

the wrappers make it easy to

slice off the amount you need

and melt it.

easy caramel sticky buns

PREP TIME: 10 Minutes ✱ READY IN: 35 Minutes ✱ SERVINGS: 10

TOPPING

- 1/4 cup butter or margarine, melted
- 1/4 cup packed brown sugar
- 2 tablespoons light corn syrup
- 1/4 cup chopped pecans

BUNS

- 1-1/2 tablespoons butter or margarine, melted
- 1/3 cup granulated sugar
- 1/2 teaspoon ground cinnamon
- 1 can (7.5 oz.) Pillsbury® Flaky Layer refrigerated buttermilk biscuits

1 Heat oven to 375°F. In ungreased 8-inch round pan, place 1/4 cup melted butter. Stir in brown sugar and corn syrup until well blended. Sprinkle with pecans.

2 In small bowl, place 1-1/2 tablespoons melted butter. In another small bowl, mix granulated sugar and cinnamon.

3 Separate dough into 10 biscuits. Dip biscuits into melted butter in bowl to coat all sides; dip into sugar mixture, coating well. Arrange biscuits, sides touching, over topping in pan.

4 Bake 18 to 22 minutes or until golden brown. Cool 2 minutes; turn upside down onto heatproof serving plate. Let pan remain 1 minute so caramel can drizzle over rolls. Serve warm.

NUTRITION INFORMATION PER SERVING: Calories 210 • Total Fat 12g • Saturated Fat 5g • Cholesterol 15mg • Sodium 250mg • Total Carbohydrate 25g • Dietary Fiber 0g • Protein 1g. DIETARY EXCHANGES: 1 Starch • 1/2 Other Carbohydrate • 2 Fat • 1-1/2 Carb Choices.

savory nutty crescents

PREP TIME: 10 Minutes ❋ **READY IN:** 25 Minutes ❋ **SERVINGS:** 8

- 2 tablespoons butter or margarine, softened
- 1 teaspoon dried sage leaves
- 1 can (8 oz.) Pillsbury® refrigerated crescent dinner rolls
- 1/4 cup chopped pecans

1 Heat oven to 375°F. In small bowl, mix butter and sage. Separate dough into 8 triangles. Reserve 1 tablespoon butter mixture for topping. Spread remaining butter mixture evenly over triangles. Sprinkle with pecans.

2 Roll up, starting at shortest side of each triangle, rolling to opposite point. Place on ungreased cookie sheet; curve each into crescent shape. Spread reserved butter mixture over tops of rolls. Bake 11 to 13 minutes or until golden brown. Serve warm.

NUTRITION INFORMATION PER SERVING: Calories 155 • Total Fat 10g • Saturated Fat 3g • Cholesterol 10mg • Sodium 360mg • Total Carbohydrate 14g • Dietary Fiber 0g • Protein 2g. DIETARY EXCHANGES: 1 Starch • 1 Other Carbohydrate • 2 Fat.

chocolate-banana bread

PREP TIME: 15 Minutes ❋ **READY IN:** 3 Hours 45 Minutes ❋ **SERVINGS:** 16 Slices

BREAD
- 2 cups Banana Nut Cheerios® cereal
- 3/4 cup sugar
- 1/4 cup canola or vegetable oil
- 3/4 cup buttermilk
- 2 teaspoons vanilla
- 1 egg
- 1 cup mashed very ripe bananas (2 medium)

- 2 cups all-purpose flour
- 1/4 cup unsweetened baking cocoa
- 1 teaspoon baking soda
- 1/4 teaspoon salt
- 1/3 cup miniature semisweet chocolate chips

TOPPING
- 1/2 cup Banana Nut Cheerios® cereal

1 Heat oven to 350°F. Spray bottom only of 9x5-inch loaf pan with cooking spray. Place 2 cups cereal in resealable food-storage plastic bag or between sheets of waxed paper; crush with rolling pin to make 3/4 cup. Set aside.

2 In large bowl, beat sugar and oil with electric mixer on low speed until well mixed. Beat in buttermilk, vanilla and egg just until blended; beat in bananas. Stir in flour, cocoa, baking soda and salt until well mixed. Stir in 3/4 cup crushed cereal and chocolate chips. Spoon into pan; spread evenly.

3 Place 1/2 cup cereal in resealable food-storage plastic bag or between sheets of waxed paper; coarsely crush with rolling pin. Sprinkle over batter in pan; press lightly.

4 Bake 1 hour 10 minutes to 1 hour 20 minutes or until toothpick inserted in center comes out clean. Cool 10 minutes. Remove from pan to cooling rack. Cool completely, about 2 hours.

NUTRITION INFORMATION PER SERVING: Calories 200 • Total Fat 6g • Saturated Fat 1.5g • Cholesterol 15mg • Sodium 170mg • Total Carbohydrate 33g • Dietary Fiber 1g • Protein 3g. DIETARY EXCHANGES: 1 Starch • 1 Other Carbohydrate • 1 Fat • 2 Carb Choices.

cook's notes

Mini chips are used in this recipe because the larger ones can sink to the bottom.

fruit-nut breakfast bread

fruit-nut breakfast bread

PREP TIME: 10 Minutes ✳ **READY IN:** 50 Minutes ✳ **SERVINGS:** 10 Slices

1 can (11 oz.) Pillsbury® refrigerated crusty French loaf	1/2 cup slivered almonds
1 cup dried apricots, chopped	1/2 cup powdered sugar
1/2 cup chopped dates	1 to 2 teaspoons milk

1 Heat oven to 350°F. Spray cookie sheet with nonstick cooking spray. Carefully unroll dough onto cookie sheet. Sprinkle apricots, dates and almonds evenly over dough. Starting with long side, roll up; seal edges. Fold ends under; seal.

2 Bake 26 to 30 minutes or until deep golden brown. Immediately remove loaf from cookie sheet; place on serving plate or cutting board. Cool 10 minutes.

3 Meanwhile, in small bowl, blend powdered sugar and enough milk for desired drizzling consistency; stir until smooth. Drizzle icing over slightly cooled loaf. To serve, cut diagonally into slices with serrated knife.

NUTRITION INFORMATION PER SERVING: Calories 200 • Total Fat 4.5g • Saturated Fat 0.5g • Cholesterol 0mg • Sodium 190mg • Total Carbohydrate 35g • Dietary Fiber 3g • Protein 4g. DIETARY EXCHANGES: 1 Starch • 1-1/2 Other Carbohydrate • 1 Fat • 2 Carb Choices.

cook's notes

Try a different combination of dried fruits instead of the apricots and dates. Dried tropical fruits such as papaya or mango, or dried cherries would also be delicious.

apricot scones with white chocolate drizzle

PREP TIME: 25 Minutes ✳ **READY IN:** 45 Minutes ✳ **SERVINGS:** 12

2 cups self-rising flour	1/3 cup milk
1/2 cup powdered sugar	2 eggs
1/4 cup butter, chilled, cut into 1/2-inch pieces	3 tablespoons milk
1/2 cup finely chopped dried apricots	2 oz. white chocolate baking bar, melted

1 Heat oven to 400°F. Lightly spray cookie sheet with nonstick cooking spray. Lightly spoon flour into measuring cup; level off. In medium bowl, combine 1-3/4 cups of the flour and powdered sugar. With pastry blender or fork, cut in butter until mixture resembles coarse crumbs.

2 Reserve 2 tablespoons of the apricots for topping; stir remaining apricots into flour mixture. In small bowl, combine 1/3 cup milk and eggs; beat well. Add to flour mixture; stir just until soft dough forms.

3 Sprinkle work surface with remaining 1/4 cup flour. Place dough on floured surface. With lightly floured hands, turn dough to coat with flour. Gently knead dough 8 to 10 times, working just enough flour into dough to prevent sticking. Divide dough in half. Flatten each half into 7-inch round. Cut each into 6 wedges; place on sprayed cookie sheet. Brush with 3 tablespoons milk.

4 Bake at 400°F for 12 to 16 minutes or until light golden brown. Remove scones from cookie sheet; place on wire rack.

5 Place melted white chocolate in small resealable food storage plastic bag. Cut off small corner of bag. Pipe small amount of white chocolate over scones. Sprinkle with reserved 2 tablespoons apricots. Pipe with remaining white chocolate. Serve warm or cool.

NUTRITION INFORMATION PER SERVING: Calories 190 • Total Fat 7g • Saturated Fat 4g • Cholesterol 50mg • Sodium 60mg • Total Carbohydrate 28g • Dietary Fiber 1g • Protein 4g. DIETARY EXCHANGES: 1 Starch • 1 Fruit • 2 Other Carbohydrate • 1-1/2 Fat.

Seasonal Soups, Sides & Salads

A holiday meal shines when the main dish is matched with super recipes. These sensational side dishes, salads and soups help to create a beautifully balanced meal.

p. 60

p. 77

p. 84

p. 62

p. 61

green beans with colored peppers p. 67

cook's notes

To make your own Italian seasoning, combine 1/4 teaspoon each of basil, thyme, rosemary and oregano for each teaspoon of Italian Seasoning called for in the recipe.

easy italian sausage-vegetable soup

PREP TIME: 15 Minutes ✳ **READY IN:** 9 Hours 45 Minutes ✳ **SERVINGS:** 7

1/2 lb. bulk Italian pork sausage

1 cup sliced fresh carrots

1 large baking potato, peeled, cut into 1/2-inch cubes

1 garlic clove, minced

2 cans (14 oz. each) beef broth

1 can (15 oz.) garbanzo beans or chickpeas, drained

1 can (14.5 oz.) pasta-style chunky tomatoes, undrained

1-1/2 cups water

1/2 teaspoon dried Italian seasoning

1 bay leaf

1 cup julienne-cut (2x1/8x1/8-inch) zucchini

1/4 cup grated fresh Parmesan cheese, if desired

1 Cook sausage in large skillet until no longer pink, stirring frequently. Drain. In 3-1/2- or 4-quart slow cooker, combine cooked sausage and all remaining ingredients except zucchini and cheese; stir gently to mix. Cover; cook on Low setting for 7 to 9 hours.

2 About 30 minutes before serving, remove and discard bay leaf from soup. Gently stir in zucchini. Cover; cook an additional 30 minutes or until zucchini is tender. To serve, ladle soup into individual bowls. Sprinkle with cheese.

NUTRITION INFORMATION PER SERVING: Calories 220 • Total Fat 9g • Saturated Fat 3g • Cholesterol 20mg • Sodium 1000mg • Total Carbohydrate 27g • Dietary Fiber 6g • Protein 14g. DIETARY EXCHANGES: 1-1/2 Starch • 1-1/2 Medium-Fat Meat • 1-1/2 Carb Choices.

tortilla taco salad

READY IN: 20 Minutes ✳ SERVINGS: 6

- 6 Old El Paso® flour tortillas for burritos, (8 inch) (from 11-oz. pkg.)
- 1 container (18 oz.) refrigerated taco sauce with seasoned ground beef
- 1 can (15 oz.) pinto beans, drained
- 2 tablespoons sweet-spicy French dressing

- 1-1/2 cups shredded lettuce
- 3/4 cup chopped tomato (1 medium)
- 3/4 cup shredded Mexican or taco-seasoned cheese blend (3 oz.)
- Old El Paso® taco sauce, if desired

1 Heat oven to 400°F. To make tortilla bowls, cut 6 (25x12-inch) sheets of foil. Slightly crush each sheet to make 4-inch ball; flatten balls slightly with palm of hand.

2 On ungreased large cookie sheet, place tortillas in single layer; cover completely with another sheet of foil. Heat in oven 1 minute or just until warm. Remove tortillas from cookie sheet; place foil balls on same sheet. Top each ball with 1 warm tortilla, shaping tortilla gently to fit around ball.

3 Bake 6 to 8 minutes or until tortillas are crisp and lightly browned. Remove tortilla bowls from foil balls; place on wire rack. Cool 2 minutes.

4 Meanwhile, in medium microwavable bowl, mix taco sauce with ground beef, pinto beans and dressing. Cover with microwavable plastic wrap, folding back one edge 1/4 inch to vent steam. Microwave on High 4 to 6 minutes or until hot.

5 Place tortilla bowls on plates. Spoon about 1/2 cup hot beef mixture into each tortilla bowl. Top each with 1/4 cup lettuce, 2 tablespoons tomato and 2 tablespoons cheese. Serve with taco sauce.

NUTRITION INFORMATION PER SERVING: Calories 420 • Total Fat 17g • Saturated Fat 6g • Cholesterol 35mg • Sodium 1170mg • Total Carbohydrate 47g • Dietary Fiber 6g • Protein 21g. DIETARY EXCHANGES: 3 Starch • 1-1/2 Medium-Fat Meat • 1-1/2 Fat • 3 Carb Choices.

refreshing ginger fruit salad

PREP TIME: 20 Minutes ✳ **READY IN:** 1 Hour 20 Minutes ✳ **SERVINGS:** 8

1/3 cup ginger ale	1/2 cup seedless green grapes, halved
1 tablespoon honey or light brown sugar	1/2 cup seedless red grapes, halved
1/2 teaspoon grated lime peel	1/2 cup fresh raspberries
2 teaspoons fresh lime juice	1/2 cup fresh blackberries
2 nectarines, halved, pitted and sliced	

1 In large bowl, mix ginger ale, honey, lime peel and lime juice. Add remaining ingredients; stir gently to combine. Cover; refrigerate at least 1 hour before serving.

NUTRITION INFORMATION PER SERVING: Calories 50 • Total Fat 0g • Saturated Fat 0g • Cholesterol 0mg • Sodium 0mg • Total Carbohydrate 12g • Dietary Fiber 2g • Protein 0g. DIETARY EXCHANGES: 1 Fruit • 1 Carb Choice.

SUSAN TRUEBLOOD
Rolla, Missouri
Bake-Off® Contest 39, 2000

honey-nut snap peas

READY IN: 10 Minutes ✳ **SERVINGS:** 4

4 cups Green Giant Select® frozen sugar snap peas	1 tablespoon margarine or butter
1/2 cup peanuts or pine nuts	1 tablespoon honey
	1 teaspoon prepared mustard

1 In 1-1/2-quart microwavable casserole, combine sugar snap peas and 2 tablespoons water. Cover. Microwave on High for 6 to 9 minutes or until crisp-tender, stirring once halfway through cooking. Drain. Add peanuts, margarine, honey and mustard; toss gently to mix. Serve warm.

NUTRITION INFORMATION PER SERVING: Calories 210 • Total Fat 12g • Saturated Fat 2g • Cholesterol 0mg • Sodium 130mg • Total Carbohydrate 18g • Dietary Fiber 5g • Protein 8g. DIETARY EXCHANGES: 1/2 Fruit • 1/2 Other Carbohydrate • 2 Vegetable • 1/2 High-Fat Meat • 2 Fat.

red and green tossed salad

READY IN: 10 Minutes ✳ **SERVINGS:** 6

1 bag (10 oz.) torn mixed salad greens (about 7 cups)	1/2 cup walnuts
1 large apple, cubed (1-1/2 cups)	1/3 cup sweetened dried cranberries
	1/3 cup raspberry vinaigrette dressing

1 In large bowl, gently mix all ingredients except dressing. Just before serving, toss the salad with the vinaigrette dressing.

NUTRITION INFORMATION PER SERVING: Calories 160 • Total Fat 11g • Saturated Fat 1.5g • Cholesterol 0mg • Sodium 40mg • Total Carbohydrate 14g • Dietary Fiber 3g • Protein 2g. DIETARY EXCHANGES: 1/2 Other Carbohydrate • 1 Vegetable • 2 Fat • 1 Carb Choice.

refreshing ginger fruit salad

orange-glazed carrots and sugar snap peas

READY IN: 15 Minutes ✳ SERVINGS: 6

2 cups ready-to-eat baby-cut carrots
1 cup Green Giant Select® frozen sugar snap peas (from 1-lb. bag)

2 tablespoons orange marmalade
1/4 teaspoon salt
Dash pepper

1 In 2-quart saucepan, heat 1 cup water to boiling. Add carrots; return to boiling. Reduce heat to low; cover and simmer 8 to 10 minutes or until carrots are tender, adding sugar snap peas during last 5 minutes of cook time. Drain; return to saucepan.

2 Stir in marmalade, salt and pepper. Cook and stir over medium heat until marmalade is melted and vegetables are glazed.

NUTRITION INFORMATION PER SERVING: Calories 50 • Total Fat 0g • Saturated Fat 0g • Cholesterol 0mg • Sodium 130mg • Total Carbohydrate 10g • Dietary Fiber 2g • Protein 1g. DIETARY EXCHANGES: 1/2 Starch • 1/2 Carb Choice.

swiss vegetable casserole

PREP TIME: 20 Minutes ✳ **READY IN:** 50 Minutes ✳ **SERVINGS:** 8

2 tablespoons butter or margarine	1-1/2 cups milk
6 green onions, cut into 1/2-inch pieces (1/2 cup)	1 cup shredded Swiss cheese (4 oz.)
2 tablespoons all-purpose flour	1 bag (1 lb.) frozen broccoli, carrots & cauliflower, cooked, drained
1/4 teaspoon salt	1/4 cup crushed round buttery crackers
1/8 teaspoon pepper	

1 Heat oven to 350°F. Spray 1- to 1-1/2-quart casserole with cooking spray. In 2-quart saucepan, melt butter over medium heat. Add onions; cook and stir 2 to 3 minutes or until tender.

2 Stir in flour, salt and pepper. Gradually add milk, stirring constantly. Cook and stir until mixture is bubbly and thickened. Remove from heat.

3 Add 3/4 cup of the cheese; stir until melted. Stir in the cooked vegetables. Spoon mixture into the casserole.

4 Sprinkle with crushed crackers and remaining 1/4 cup cheese. Bake 25 to 30 minutes or until topping is golden brown and casserole is bubbly.

NUTRITION INFORMATION PER SERVING: Calories 140 • Total Fat 9g • Saturated Fat 5g • Cholesterol 25mg • Sodium 170mg • Total Carbohydrate 9g • Dietary Fiber 2g • Protein 7g. DIETARY EXCHANGES: 1/2 Other Carbohydrate • 1 Vegetable • 1/2 High-Fat Meat • 1 Fat • 1/2 Carb Choice.

cook's notes

To make ahead, prepare this casserole as directed, reserving the crushed crackers. Cover and refrigerate up to one day. Then, sprinkle the casserole with the crackers and bake it for 30 to 40 minutes.

taco-topped potatoes

READY IN: 25 Minutes ❋ **SERVINGS:** 4

4 medium baking potatoes	1/2 cup shredded Cheddar cheese (2 oz.)
1 container (18 oz.) refrigerated taco sauce with seasoned ground beef	1 medium Italian plum tomato, chopped
	2 tablespoons sliced green onions

1 Pierce potatoes with fork. Arrange in spoke pattern on microwavable paper towel in microwave. Microwave on High for 12 to 14 minutes or until tender, turning potatoes and rearranging halfway through cooking. Cool 3 minutes.

2 Meanwhile, heat taco sauce with seasoned ground beef as directed on package. To serve, cut potatoes in half lengthwise; mash slightly with fork. Spoon about 1/2 cup ground beef mixture over each potato. Top with Cheddar cheese, tomato and green onions.

NUTRITION INFORMATION PER SERVING: Calories 340 • Total Fat 17g • Saturated Fat 8g • Cholesterol 50mg • Sodium 770mg • Total Carbohydrate 35g • Dietary Fiber 2g • Protein 21g. DIETARY EXCHANGES: 2 Starch • 2 Medium-Fat Meat • 1 Fat • 2 Carb Choices.

green beans with colored peppers

READY IN: 30 Minutes ✴ **SERVINGS:** 18

1 bag (22 oz.) Green Giant® Select® frozen whole green beans

1 tablespoon lemon juice

2 teaspoons Dijon mustard

1 tablespoon chopped fresh or 1 teaspoon dried basil leaves

2 teaspoons chopped fresh or 3/4 teaspoon dried thyme leaves

1 tablespoon olive or vegetable oil

1 medium red bell pepper, cut into strips

1 medium yellow bell pepper, cut into strips

1/2 teaspoon salt

  Freshly ground black pepper, if desired

1 In 12-inch skillet, cook green beans on stovetop as directed on bag. Drain; place beans on plate and loosely cover to keep warm. Meanwhile, in small bowl, mix lemon juice, mustard, basil and thyme; set aside.

2 Add oil to same skillet; heat over medium-high heat. Add bell peppers; cook 6 to 8 minutes, stirring frequently, just until tender.

3 Add green beans and lemon mixture to peppers; toss to coat. Sprinkle with salt; cook 2 to 3 minutes, stirring frequently. Serve sprinkled with freshly ground black pepper.

NUTRITION INFORMATION PER SERVING: Calories 20 • Total Fat 1g • Saturated Fat 0g • Cholesterol 0mg • Sodium 80mg • Total Carbohydrate 3g • Dietary Fiber 1g • Protein 0g. DIETARY EXCHANGE: Free.

sweet corn potluck pudding

PREP TIME: 5 Minutes ✴ **READY IN:** 6 Hours 5 Minutes ✴ **SERVINGS:** 14

1 bag (1 lb.) Green Giant® Niblets® frozen corn

2 cans (11 oz. each) Green Giant® Mexicorn® whole kernel corn, red and green peppers

1 can (14.75 oz.) Green Giant® cream-style sweet corn

1 package (6.5 oz.) corn muffin and bread mix

3/4 cup water

1/4 cup butter or margarine, melted

1 teaspoon salt

1 In 3- to 4-quart slow cooker, combine all ingredients; mix well. Cover; cook on Low setting 3 hours. Stir the mixture; cover and cook 2 to 3 hours longer or until pudding is slightly puffed in the center.

NUTRITION INFORMATION PER SERVING: Calories 180 • Total Fat 5g • Saturated Fat 3g • Cholesterol 10mg • Sodium 470mg • Total Carbohydrate 30g • Dietary Fiber 2g • Protein 4g. DIETARY EXCHANGES: 2 Starch • 1 Fat • 2 Carb Choices.

cook's notes

This sweet corn pudding goes perfectly with ham, green beans and biscuits.

confetti yellow pea soup
vegetable-beef-barley soup

confetti yellow pea soup

PREP TIME: 10 Minutes ✻ **READY IN:** 9 Hours 40 Minutes ✻ **SERVINGS:** 6

- 1 bag (16 oz.) dried yellow split peas, rinsed
- 1 quart (4 cups) water
- 1 can (10-1/2 oz.) condensed chicken broth
- 1 cup julienne-cut (2x1/8x1/8-inch) carrots
- 6 oz chorizo sausage, casing removed, cut into 1/4-inch slices
- 1/4 teaspoon salt
- 1/4 teaspoon pepper
- 1/2 cup sliced green onions
- 1 can (11 oz.) Green Giant® Mexicorn® whole kernel corn, red and green peppers

1 In a 3-1/2- to 4-quart slow cooker, combine all ingredients except the green onions and corn; stir gently to mix.

2 Cover; cook on Low setting 7 to 9 hours or until peas are soft. Stir in onions and corn. Cover; cook 30 minutes longer or until corn is thoroughly heated.

NUTRITION INFORMATION PER SERVING: Calories 430 • Total Fat 10g • Saturated Fat 3g • Cholesterol 20mg • Sodium 970mg • Total Carbohydrate 59g • Dietary Fiber 21g • Protein 27g. DIETARY EXCHANGES: 4 Starch • 4 Other Carbohydrate • 2 Very Lean Meat • 1 Fat.

kitchen tip

Yellow peas are low in fat and a good source of protein. One cup of cooked yellow peas has about 16 grams of protein and 1 gram of fat.

vegetable-beef-barley soup

READY IN: 35 Minutes ✻ **SERVINGS:** 4

- 1/2 lb. extra-lean (at least 90%) ground beef
- 1 can (14.5 oz.) stewed tomatoes, undrained, cut up
- 1 can (14 oz.) beef broth
- 1 can (8 oz.) no-salt-added tomato sauce
- 1 cup Green Giant® frozen mixed vegetables (from 1-lb. bag)
- 1/3 cup uncooked quick-cooking barley

1 In 3-quart saucepan, cook ground beef over medium-high heat, stirring frequently, until thoroughly cooked; drain.

2 Stir in remaining ingredients. Heat to boiling. Reduce heat to medium; cover and cook 10 to 15 minutes, stirring occasionally, until vegetables and barley are tender.

HIGH ALTITUDE (3500-6500 FT): Add up to 1/2 cup water if soup becomes too thick.

NUTRITION INFORMATION PER SERVING: Calories 230 • Total Fat 5g • Saturated Fat 2g • Cholesterol 35mg • Sodium 760mg • Total Carbohydrate 30g • Dietary Fiber 6g • Protein 16g. DIETARY EXCHANGES: 1-1/2 Starch • 1/2 Other Carbohydrate • 1-1/2 Lean Meat • 2 Carb Choices.

cook's notes

Barley can be found near the rice at your supermarket. Be sure to purchase the quick-cooking kind for this soup or it won't be tender in the 15 minute cooking time.

big bean pot

PREP TIME: 15 Minutes ✳ READY IN: 1 Hour 25 Minutes ✳ SERVINGS: 12

12 slices bacon (about 3/4 lb.), diced	1/3 cup cider vinegar
3 medium onions, chopped	1/4 cup ketchup
1 teaspoon garlic powder	2 cans (16 oz. each) baked beans
1/2 teaspoon ground mustard	1 can (15 oz.) red kidney beans, drained, rinsed
1/2 cup packed brown sugar	1 can (15 oz.) lima beans, drained, rinsed

1 Heat oven to 350°F. In Dutch oven or large saucepan over medium heat, cook and stir bacon and onions until bacon is crisp and onions are tender. Drain.

2 Stir in the remaining ingredients. Bake uncovered 60 to 70 minutes or until the beans are hot and bubbly.

NUTRITION INFORMATION PER SERVING: Calories 260 • Total Fat 4.5g • Saturated Fat 1.5g • Cholesterol 15mg • Sodium 580mg • Total Carbohydrate 41g • Dietary Fiber 9g • Protein 12g. DIETARY EXCHANGES: 1-1/2 Starch • 1 Other Carbohydrate • 1 Very Lean Meat • 1/2 Fat • 3 Carb Choices.

quick tortellini salad

READY IN: 25 Minutes ✳ **SERVINGS:** 8

DRESSING

1/3	cup olive oil
3	tablespoons red wine vinegar
1	teaspoon lemon juice
1/2	teaspoon sugar
1/2	teaspoon salt
1/4	teaspoon garlic powder
1/4	teaspoon dried oregano leaves

SALAD

1	package (9 oz.) refrigerated cheese-filled tortellini
1	cup sliced carrots
1-1/2	cups Green Giant® Valley Fresh Steamers™ frozen cut green beans
2	tablespoons sliced green onions (2 medium)

1 In a jar with a tight-fitting lid, combine all the ingredients for the dressing; shake well. Set aside.

2 Cook tortellini, carrots and green beans as directed on tortellini package until tortellini are tender and vegetables are crisp-tender. Drain; return to saucepan. Cover with cold water; let stand 5 minutes. Drain well.

3 In medium bowl, combine tortellini, carrots and green beans; add onions. Pour dressing over salad; toss gently to coat.

NUTRITION INFORMATION PER SERVING: Calories 145 • Total Fat 11g • Saturated Fat 2g • Cholesterol 25mg • Sodium 180mg • Total Carbohydrate 9g • Dietary Fiber 1g • Protein 3g. DIETARY EXCHANGES: 1/2 Starch • 1/2 Other Carbohydrate • 2 Fat.

special touch

Line a pretty platter with colorful lettuce leaves. Top it with the salad and garnish with fresh herbs.

cook's notes

A homemade apple-spiced dressing gives a boost to this coleslaw. Mix it up in only 15 minutes!

apple slaw

READY IN: 15 Minutes ✳ SERVINGS: 10

SALAD

4	cups coleslaw mix (from 16-oz. bag)
1/4	cup sliced green onions (4 medium)
2	medium Granny Smith apples, cubed

DRESSING

3	tablespoons sugar
1/4	teaspoon salt
1/4	teaspoon apple pie spice
3	tablespoons cider vinegar
2	tablespoons vegetable oil

1 In a large bowl, toss the salad ingredients to mix. In a small bowl, mix the dressing ingredients until well blended. Pour dressing over salad; toss gently to coat. Serve immediately, or refrigerate until serving time.

NUTRITION INFORMATION PER SERVING: Calories 70 • Total Fat 3g • Saturated Fat 0g • Cholesterol 0mg • Sodium 65mg • Total Carbohydrate 10g • Dietary Fiber 1g • Protein 0g. DIETARY EXCHANGES: 1/2 Other Carbohydrate • 1 Vegetable • 1/2 Fat • 1/2 Carb Choice.

cook's notes

Rinsing the sliced potatoes in water, made acidic with cream of tartar, helps keep them firm during long, slow cooking.

creamy garlic and parmesan potatoes

PREP TIME: 15 Minutes ✳ READY IN: 6 Hours 15 Minutes ✳ SERVINGS: 12

1/2	teaspoon cream of tartar
3	lb. (about 8 medium) russet potatoes, peeled, sliced
1	can (10-3/4 oz.) condensed golden mushroom soup
1/2	cup water
1/4	cup all-purpose flour

3	tablespoons butter or margarine, melted
1/2	teaspoon salt
1/4	teaspoon pepper
1/4	teaspoon garlic powder
1/3	cup shredded fresh Parmesan cheese (1-1/3 oz.), if desired

1 In large bowl, combine 1 cup water and cream of tartar. Add sliced potatoes; toss to coat. Drain, discarding water. Place potatoes in 3- to 4-quart slow cooker.

2 In medium bowl, combine soup, 1/2 cup water, flour, butter, salt, pepper and garlic powder; mix well. Pour mixture over potatoes; stir gently to coat.

3 Cover; cook on Low setting for 5 to 6 hours. Just before serving, sprinkle the Parmesan cheese over the top.

NUTRITION INFORMATION PER SERVING: Calories 160 • Total Fat 5g • Saturated Fat 3g • Cholesterol 10mg • Sodium 350mg • Total Carbohydrate 25g • Dietary Fiber 1g • Protein 4g. DIETARY EXCHANGES: 1-1/2 Starch • 1 Fat • 1-1/2 Carb Choices.

lightly lime fruit salad

READY IN: 25 Minutes ✸ **SERVINGS:** 12

SALAD

1	package (7 oz.) uncooked small shell pasta (1-3/4 cups)
1-1/2	cups seedless green grapes
1-1/2	cups cantaloupe cubes
2	bananas, sliced
2	cups halved fresh strawberries

DRESSING

1/2	cup sour cream
3	tablespoons frozen limeade concentrate, thawed
1/8	teaspoon salt

1 Cook pasta to desired doneness as directed on package. Drain; rinse with cold water to cool. Drain well.

2 Meanwhile, in large bowl, combine all remaining salad ingredients except strawberries. In small bowl, combine all dressing ingredients; blend well.

3 Add cooked pasta and dressing to fruit; mix gently to coat. Just before serving, gently stir in strawberries.

NUTRITION INFORMATION PER SERVING: Calories 150 • Total Fat 3g • Saturated Fat 1g • Cholesterol 4mg • Sodium 30mg • Total Carbohydrate 27g • Dietary Fiber 2g • Protein 3g. DIETARY EXCHANGES: 1 Starch • 1 Fruit • 2 Other Carbohydrate • 1/2 Fat.

kitchen tip

Look for plump bananas that are evenly yellow-colored. Green bananas are under-ripe, while a flecking of brown flecks indicates ripeness. If bananas are too green, place in a brown paper bag until ripe. Adding an apple to the paper bag will speed the process.

quick black bean soup

PREP TIME: 20 Minutes ✳ SERVINGS: 4

1 teaspoon oil	1/2 teaspoon garlic salt
1/2 cup chopped green bell pepper	1/2 teaspoon chili powder
1/4 cup finely chopped onion	1-1/2 cups water
1 cup finely chopped cooked ham	2 tablespoons sour cream
2 cans (15.5 oz. each) refried black beans with lime juice	2 tablespoons chopped fresh cilantro, if desired

1 Heat oil in 3-quart saucepan over medium heat until hot. Add bell pepper and onion; cook and stir 2 to 3 minutes or until crisp-tender.

2 Add all remaining ingredients except sour cream and cilantro; mix well. Cook over medium heat for about 5 minutes or until thoroughly heated, stirring frequently. Top individual servings with a dollop of sour cream. Sprinkle with cilantro.

NUTRITION INFORMATION PER SERVING: Calories 250 • Total Fat 8g • Saturated Fat 3g • Cholesterol 40mg • Sodium 1290mg • Total Carbohydrate 37g • Dietary Fiber 12g • Protein 20g. DIETARY EXCHANGES: 1-1/2 Starch • 2 Very Lean Meat • 1-1/2 Fat • 1-1/2 Carb Choices.

mashed potato gratin

PREP TIME: 20 Minutes ✳ READY IN: 1 Hour 30 Minutes ✳ SERVINGS: 8

3 lb. russet potatoes, peeled, cut into small pieces	1 teaspoon salt
1/4 cup butter or margarine	1 cup milk
3 egg yolks	1-1/2 cups shredded Swiss cheese (6 oz.)
	Chopped fresh parsley, if desired

1 Heat oven to 350°F. Spray 13x9-inch (3-quart) glass baking dish with cooking spray. In 4-quart saucepan or Dutch oven, place potatoes; add enough water to cover potatoes by 1 inch. Heat to boiling over high heat. Reduce heat to medium-low; simmer uncovered 20 minutes or until potatoes are tender and can be easily pierced with fork.

2 Drain potatoes; return to saucepan. Add butter; mash with potato masher until creamy. Stir in egg yolks, salt, milk and 1 cup of the cheese.

3 Spread potato mixture evenly in baking dish. Sprinkle with remaining 1/2 cup cheese. Bake 30 minutes or until edges are light golden brown. Sprinkle with chopped parsley.

HIGH ALTITUDE (3500-6500 FT): Heat oven to 375°F. In Step 3, do not sprinkle with remaining 1/2 cup cheese. Bake 20 minutes. Sprinkle remaining cheese over top; bake 10 minutes longer.

NUTRITION INFORMATION PER SERVING: Calories 300 • Total Fat 14g • Saturated Fat 8g • Cholesterol 115mg • Sodium 410mg • Total Carbohydrate 33g • Dietary Fiber 3g • Protein 11g. DIETARY EXCHANGES: 2 Starch • 1 High-Fat Meat • 1 Fat • 2 Carb Choices.

quick black bean soup

green beans with tomatoes and feta

READY IN: 20 Minutes ✻ **SERVINGS:** 8

2 boxes (7.4 oz. each) Cascadian Farm® frozen organic French-cut green beans with toasted almonds

1 tablespoon olive oil

1 medium onion, sliced

2 cloves garlic, finely chopped

1 can (14.5 oz.) Muir Glen® organic diced tomatoes, undrained

1 teaspoon chopped fresh oregano leaves or 1/2 teaspoon dried oregano leaves

1/8 teaspoon crushed red pepper flakes, if desired

1/4 cup crumbled feta cheese (1 oz.)

1 Cook beans as directed on boxes, reserving almonds; drain. Meanwhile, in 10-inch skillet, heat oil over medium heat. Add onion and garlic; cook 3 to 4 minutes, stirring frequently, until onion is crisp-tender.

2 Stir in tomatoes, oregano and pepper flakes. Heat to boiling. Reduce heat; simmer uncovered about 5 minutes, stirring occasionally, until thickened and most of liquid has evaporated.

3 Spoon drained beans onto serving platter; top with tomato mixture. Sprinkle with cheese and reserved almonds.

NUTRITION INFORMATION PER SERVING: Calories 80 • Total Fat 4.5g • Saturated Fat 1g • Cholesterol 0mg • Sodium 210mg • Total Carbohydrate 7g • Dietary Fiber 1g • Protein 2g. DIETARY EXCHANGES: 1 Vegetable • 1 Fat • 1/2 Carb Choice.

mexican cheesy potatoes

PREP TIME: 20 Minutes ✴ READY IN: 1 Hour 30 Minutes ✴ SERVINGS: 20

- 1 medium onion, chopped (1/2 cup)
- 1 container (16 oz.) sour cream
- 1 can (10-3/4 oz.) condensed cream of chicken soup
- 1 can (4.5 oz.) Old El Paso® chopped green chiles
- 1 bag (32 oz.) frozen southern-style diced hash-brown potatoes, thawed

- 2 cups cubed mild Mexican prepared cheese product with jalapeño peppers (12 oz. from loaf)
- 1 cup shredded pepper Jack cheese (4 oz.)
- 1 cup shredded mozzarella cheese (4 oz.)
- 2 cups crushed gold or yellow tortilla chips (about 6 oz.)

1 Heat oven to 350°F. Spray 13x9-inch (3-quart) glass baking dish with cooking spray. In large bowl, mix onion, sour cream, soup and green chiles. Stir in hash browns. Fold in cubed and shredded cheeses; pour into baking dish.

2 Bake 1 hour or until potatoes are tender and mixture is hot and bubbly. Sprinkle with crushed chips; bake 5 to 10 minutes longer or until chips are light golden brown.

HIGH ALTITUDE (3500-6500 FT): Heat oven to 375°F.

NUTRITION INFORMATION PER SERVING: Calories 250 • Total Fat 14g • Saturated Fat 7g • Cholesterol 40mg • Sodium 600mg • Total Carbohydrate 23g • Dietary Fiber 2g • Protein 8g. DIETARY EXCHANGES: 1-1/2 Starch • 1/2 High-Fat Meat • 2 Fat • 1-1/2 Carb Choices.

cook's notes

For a mild version of this recipe, use regular prepared cheese product and regular Monterey Jack cheese.

cauliflower crunch

PREP TIME: 15 Minutes ✴ READY IN: 40 Minutes ✴ SERVINGS: 4

- 3 tablespoons olive or vegetable oil
- 8 sun-dried tomatoes, cut into strips
- 2 cloves garlic, finely chopped
- 1 can (4.5 oz.) chopped green chiles, drained

- 2 boxes (10 oz. each) frozen cauliflower in a cheese-flavored sauce, thawed
- 1/4 cup unseasoned dry bread crumbs
- 1/4 cup grated Parmesan cheese

ROSEMARY LEICHT
Bethel, Ohio
Bake-Off® Contest 39, 2000

1 Heat oven to 400°F. In 8-inch skillet, heat 1 tablespoon of the oil over medium heat until hot. Cook tomatoes, garlic and green chiles in skillet 1 to 2 minutes, stirring occasionally, until hot. Spread in bottom of ungreased 9- or 10-inch quiche dish or glass pie plate. Top with cauliflower in cheese sauce.

2 In small bowl, mix bread crumbs, Parmesan cheese and remaining 2 tablespoons oil. Sprinkle over cauliflower mixture. Bake 20 to 22 minutes or until edges are bubbly and bread crumbs are golden brown.

NUTRITION INFORMATION PER SERVING: Calories 240 • Total Fat 16g • Saturated Fat 4g • Cholesterol 5mg • Sodium 1270mg • Total Carbohydrate 17g • Dietary Fiber 3g • Protein 7g. DIETARY EXCHANGES: 1 Starch • 1 Vegetable • 3 Fat • 1 Carb Choice.

cheesy green beans

READY IN: 15 Minutes ✳ SERVINGS: 4

1 teaspoon butter or margarine

2 tablespoons finely chopped onion

2 small cloves garlic, finely chopped

2 cups Green Giant® Valley Fresh Steamers™ frozen cut green beans

2 tablespoons shredded Cheddar cheese

1 In 2-quart saucepan or 10-inch skillet, melt butter over medium heat. Add onion and garlic; cook, stirring frequently, until the onion begins to brown. Remove from saucepan; cover to keep warm.

2 In same saucepan or skillet, cook beans as directed on bag; drain. Stir in onion mixture; cook until thoroughly heated. Add cheese; toss gently to mix.

NUTRITION INFORMATION PER SERVING: Calories 45 • Total Fat 2g • Saturated Fat 1.5g • Cholesterol 5mg • Sodium 35mg • Total Carbohydrate 5g • Dietary Fiber 2g • Protein 2g. DIETARY EXCHANGES: 1 Vegetable • 1/2 Fat • 1/2 Carb Choice.

three-grain salad

PREP TIME: 20 Minutes ✳ READY IN: 1 Hour 10 Minutes ✳ SERVINGS: 12

SALAD

5	cups water
4	teaspoons vegetable-flavor instant bouillon
1/2	teaspoon salt
1	cup (about 7 oz.) uncooked wheat berries, rinsed
1/3	cup uncooked medium pearl barley
1/3	cup uncooked regular long-grain brown rice
1-1/2	cups coarsely chopped unpeeled red apple (1 to 2 medium)
1/2	cup chopped red onion
1/2	cup raisins
1/2	cup pecan halves, toasted, chopped

DRESSING

1/4	cup oil
1/4	cup cider vinegar
2	tablespoons honey
3/4	teaspoon grated gingerroot

1 In 3-quart saucepan, bring water, bouillon and salt to a boil over medium-high heat. Add wheat berries; return to a boil. Reduce heat to low; cover and simmer 10 minutes.

2 Add barley and rice; cook an additional 50 minutes or until all grains are tender. Drain. In large serving bowl, combine wheat berry mixture, apple, onion and raisins; mix well.

3 In small bowl, combine all dressing ingredients; mix well. Pour dressing over salad; toss to coat. Serve immediately, or cover and refrigerate 2 to 6 hours before serving. Just before serving, fold in pecans.

HIGH ALTITUDE (3500-6500 FT): After adding wheat berries to boiling water; return to a boil. Reduce heat to medium-low; cover and simmer 10 minutes. Add barley and rice; simmer over medium-low heat 50 minutes. Continue as directed above.

NUTRITION INFORMATION PER SERVING: Calories 185 • Total Fat 9g • Saturated Fat 1g • Cholesterol 0mg • Sodium 540mg • Total Carbohydrate 29g • Dietary Fiber 3g • Protein 4g, DIETARY EXCHANGES: 1 Starch • 1 Other Carbohydrate • 1-1/2 Fat • 2 Carb Choices.

cook's notes

Instant brown rice can be used instead of the regular brown rice. Just add 1/3 cup instant brown rice 40 minutes after adding the barley.

apple-cranberry salad

apple-cranberry salad

READY IN: 15 Minutes ✳ SERVINGS: 6

- 5 cups torn romaine lettuce
- 1 medium unpeeled apple, diced (1 cup)
- 1/2 cup sweetened dried cranberries
- 1/4 cup chopped green onions (4 medium)
- 1/3 cup refrigerated poppy seed dressing

1 In large serving bowl, place lettuce, apple, cranberries and green onions. Pour dressing over salad; toss to coat.

NUTRITION INFORMATION PER SERVING: Calories 120 • Total Fat 6g • Saturated Fat 0.5g • Cholesterol 5mg • Sodium 140mg • Total Carbohydrate 17g • Dietary Fiber 2g • Protein 0g. DIETARY EXCHANGES: 1 Other Carbohydrate • 1-1/2 Fat • 1 Carb Choice.

cook's notes

Use a ripe, red or yellow-green pear instead of the apple.

beefy bean and corn chili

READY IN: 25 Minutes ✳ SERVINGS: 5

- 1 lb. lean (at least 80%) ground beef
- 2 cans (15 oz. each) spicy chili beans, undrained
- 1 can (14.5 oz.) diced tomatoes, undrained
- 1 can (11 oz.) Green Giant® Niblets® whole kernel corn, undrained
- 1 can (4.5 oz.) Old El Paso® chopped green chiles

1 In 3-quart saucepan, cook ground beef over medium-high heat, stirring frequently, until thoroughly cooked; drain well.

2 Stir in remaining ingredients. Reduce heat to medium; cook 10 to 15 minutes, stirring occasionally, until thoroughly heated and flavors are blended.

NUTRITION INFORMATION PER SERVING: Calories 380 • Total Fat 12g • Saturated Fat 4g • Cholesterol 55mg • Sodium 1030mg • Total Carbohydrate 42g • Dietary Fiber 9g • Protein 26g. DIETARY EXCHANGES: 2-1/2 Starch • 1/2 Other Carbohydrate • 2-1/2 Lean Meat • 1/2 Fat • 3 Carb Choices.

lemon dream fruit salad

READY IN: 10 Minutes ✳ SERVINGS: 6

- 1 can (11 oz.) mandarin orange segments, drained
- 1 can (8 oz.) pineapple chunks in juice, drained
- 2 bananas, halved lengthwise, cut into 1-inch chunks
- 1/4 cup halved maraschino cherries, drained
- 1 container (6 oz.) Yoplait® Thick and Creamy Lowfat lemon supreme yogurt

1 In a medium bowl, mix all of the ingredients. Serve fruit salad immediately or refrigerate until serving time.

NUTRITION INFORMATION PER SERVING: Calories 110 • Total Fat 0.5g • Saturated Fat 0g • Cholesterol 0mg • Sodium 20mg • Total Carbohydrate 27g • Dietary Fiber 2g • Protein 2g. DIETARY EXCHANGES: 1 Fruit • 1 Other Carbohydrate • 2 Carb Choices.

cook's notes

To prepare in advance, mix the fruit several hours ahead of time and refrigerate it. Fold in the yogurt just before serving.

winter fruit salad

PREP TIME: 15 Minutes ❋ **SERVINGS:** 12

2 cups cubed unpeeled red apples (2 medium)
2 cups cubed unpeeled pears (2 medium)
3/4 cup chopped dates
1 tablespoon fresh lemon juice
2 medium bananas, sliced

1/3 cup light mayonnaise or salad dressing
2 tablespoons honey
1/2 teaspoon grated lemon peel
1/8 teaspoon allspice

1 In large bowl, combine the apples, pears, dates and lemon juice; mix well. Add the bananas; stir gently to mix.

2 In small bowl, combine all remaining ingredients; blend well. Add to salad; stir gently to coat. If desired, serve in lettuce-lined bowl.

NUTRITION INFORMATION PER SERVING: Calories 120 • Total Fat 2.5g • Saturated Fat 0g • Cholesterol 0mg • Sodium 45mg • Total Carbohydrate 24g • Dietary Fiber 3g • Protein 0g. DIETARY EXCHANGES: 1 Fruit • 1/2 Other Carbohydrate • 1/2 Fat • 1-1/2 Carb Choices.

winter vegetable soup

PREP TIME: 40 Minutes ✳ **READY IN:** 10 Hours 50 Minutes ✳ **SERVINGS:** 8

- 1 lb. portobello mushroom caps
- 3 tablespoons butter or margarine
- 2 large onions, halved, sliced (3 cups)
- 2 large dark-orange sweet potatoes, peeled, cut into quarters then into 1/2-inch-thick slices (3 cups)
- 1 cup chopped celery (2-1/2 medium stalks)
- 2 cloves garlic, minced
- 1-1/2 cups Green Giant® Niblets® frozen corn (from 1-lb. bag)

- 1 can (28 oz.) diced tomatoes, undrained
- 1 can (15 or 15.5 oz.) kidney beans, drained, rinsed
- 2 cans (14 oz. each) vegetable broth
- 4 oz. fresh spinach, chopped (about 4 cups lightly packed)
- 1 teaspoon dried basil leaves
- 1/2 teaspoon salt
- 1/4 teaspoon pepper

1 With small spoon, scrape and discard gills from under side of mushroom caps. Cut caps into 1/2-inch-thick slices; set aside.

2 In 10-inch skillet, melt butter over medium heat. Add onions; cook 10 to 15 minutes, stirring occasionally, until onions are tender and have begun to caramelize.

3 Meanwhile, in 6-quart slow cooker, place mushroom slices, sweet potatoes, celery, garlic, corn, tomatoes and beans. Gently stir in broth and caramelized onions. Cover; cook on Low setting 9 to 10 hours.

4 About 10 minutes before serving, turn off heat on slow cooker. Stir in spinach, basil, salt and pepper. Cover; let stand 10 minutes or until spinach is limp.

NUTRITION INFORMATION PER SERVING: Calories 250 • Total Fat 5g • Saturated Fat 2.5g • Cholesterol 10mg • Sodium 920mg • Total Carbohydrate 42g • Dietary Fiber 9g • Protein 10g. DIETARY EXCHANGES: 1-1/2 Starch • 2 Vegetable • 1 Fat • 3 Carb Choices.

cook's notes

This delicious soup is filled with colorful vegetables important for good health. Keep extra on hand for satisfying winter meals.

marinated vegetable salad

PREP TIME: 25 Minutes ✳ **READY IN:** 4 Hours 25 Minutes ✳ **SERVINGS:** 10

1 large zucchini, quartered, very thinly sliced	1/4 cup very thinly sliced red onion, separated into rings
1 large yellow summer squash, quartered, very thinly sliced	4 radishes, very thinly sliced
1 carrot, peeled, thinly sliced	2/3 cup purchased Greek vinaigrette dressing

1 In large bowl, mix all ingredients until combined. Cover; refrigerate at least 4 hours or overnight before serving.

NUTRITION INFORMATION PER SERVING: Calories 90 • Total Fat 7g • Saturated Fat 1g • Cholesterol 0mg • Sodium 180mg • Total Carbohydrate 5g • Dietary Fiber 2g • Protein 1g. DIETARY EXCHANGES: 1 Vegetable • 1-1/2 Fat.

dilly buttered carrots and rotini

PREP TIME: 10 Minutes ✳ **READY IN:** 20 Minutes ✳ **SERVINGS:** 8

1 cup uncooked rainbow or plain rotini pasta (3 oz.)	1 teaspoon chopped fresh or 1/4 teaspoon dried dill weed
2 cups ready-to-eat baby-cut carrots, cut in half lengthwise and crosswise	1/4 teaspoon salt
1 tablespoon butter	Dash pepper

1 In 3-quart saucepan, cook pasta as directed on package, adding carrots during last 2 to 3 minutes of cooking time; cook until pasta is tender and carrots are crisp-tender. Drain; return to saucepan. Add butter, dill, salt and pepper; toss gently to coat.

NUTRITION INFORMATION PER SERVING: Calories 80 • Total Fat 2g • Saturated Fat 1g • Cholesterol 0mg • Sodium 160mg • Total Carbohydrate 14g • Dietary Fiber 2g • Protein 2g. DIETARY EXCHANGES: 1 Starch • 1 Carb Choice.

texas-style barbecued beans

PREP TIME: 15 Minutes ✳ **READY IN:** 6 Hours 15 Minutes ✳ **SERVINGS:** 24

6 slices bacon	1-1/2 cups ketchup
4 cans (15.5 oz. each) great northern beans, drained, rinsed	1/2 cup firmly packed brown sugar
4 cans (15 oz. each) black beans, drained, rinsed	1/2 cup barbecue sauce
	2 tablespoons prepared mustard
4 garlic cloves, minced	2 tablespoons Worcestershire sauce
3/4 cup finely chopped onion	3 teaspoons chili powder
	1/2 teaspoon hot pepper sauce

1 Cook bacon in large skillet over medium heat until crisp. Remove bacon from skillet; drain on paper towels.

2 In 4- to 5-quart slow cooker, combine all remaining ingredients; mix gently. Crumble bacon; sprinkle over bean mixture. Cover; cook on Low setting for 4 to 6 hours.

NUTRITION INFORMATION PER SERVING: Calories 270 • Total Fat 2g • Saturated Fat 0g • Cholesterol 5mg • Sodium 5mg • Total Carbohydrate 49g • Dietary Fiber 9g • Protein 14g. DIETARY EXCHANGES: 3 Starch • 3 Other Carbohydrate • 1/2 Very Lean Meat • 1/2 Fat.

marinated vegetable salad

Elegant Main Courses

Gathering around the table for a Yuletide feast is a precious family pastime. These entrees offer an excellent variety of showstopping recipes for your main event.

p. 94

p. 111

p. 96

p. 92

p. 99

roasted chicken with peach glaze p. 100

shrimp primavera alfredo

READY IN: 25 Minutes ✳ **SERVINGS:** 4

6 oz. uncooked linguine or spaghetti

8 oz. fresh asparagus spears, trimmed, cut into
   1-1/2-inch pieces

1 cup ready-to-eat baby-cut carrots (4 oz.),
   quartered lengthwise

1 cup sliced fresh mushrooms

1 box (9 oz.) Green Giant® frozen sugar snap
   peas

1 bag (12 oz.) frozen ready-to-cook medium
   shrimp, thawed, tail shells removed

1 container (10 oz.) refrigerated Alfredo sauce

2 tablespoons chopped fresh chives

1 teaspoon grated lemon peel

   Additional chives, if desired

1 Cook and drain linguine as directed on package; cover to keep warm. Meanwhile, in 12-inch
   skillet, place asparagus, carrots, mushrooms, sugar snap peas and 1/2 cup water. Heat to boiling.
Reduce heat to medium-low; cover and simmer 4 to 6 minutes or until vegetables are crisp-tender.

2 Add shrimp; cook and stir 2 to 3 minutes or until shrimp are pink. Drain; return the mixture
   to skillet.

3 Stir in Alfredo sauce, chives and lemon peel. Simmer uncovered 2 to 4 minutes, stirring
   occasionally, until mixture is thoroughly heated. Serve over linguine. If desired, garnish with
additional chives.

   HIGH ALTITUDE (3500-6500 FT): In Step 3, cook shrimp 3 to 5 minutes.

NUTRITION INFORMATION PER SERVING: Calories 520 • Total Fat 24g • Saturated Fat 13g • Cholesterol 190mg • Sodium 630mg • Total
Carbohydrate 48g • Dietary Fiber 6g • Protein 28g. DIETARY EXCHANGES: 3 Starch • 1 Vegetable • 2-1/2 Very Lean Meat • 4 Fat •
3 Carb Choices.

wrapped tenderloin with gorgonzola-mushroom gravy

PREP TIME: 20 Minutes ❋ **READY IN:** 35 Minutes ❋ **SERVINGS:** 2

- 2 tablespoons olive oil
- 2 beef tenderloin steaks, about 1 inch thick (4 oz. each)
- 1/2 teaspoon Montreal steak seasoning
- 4 Pillsbury® Grands® frozen buttermilk biscuits (from 25-oz. bag)
- 1 egg yolk
- 1 tablespoon water

- 1 cup crumbled gorgonzola cheese (4 oz.)
- 1/8 teaspoon pepper
- 1/2 cup whipping cream
- 1/2 teaspoon Worcestershire sauce
- 1 jar (4.5 oz.) Green Giant® sliced mushrooms, drained
- 1-1/2 teaspoons chopped fresh parsley

B_____, 2006

1 Heat oven to 400°F. In 8-inch skillet, heat oil over medium-high heat. Pat steaks dry with paper towel; sprinkle both sides with steak seasoning. Add steaks to skillet; cook 1 to 2 minutes on each side or until browned. Remove steaks from skillet; place on plate.

2 Place 2 biscuits on microwavable plate. Microwave on High 30 to 45 seconds turning biscuits over halfway through microwave time, until soft enough to press into rounds. Repeat with remaining 2 biscuits.

3 Spray cookie sheet or 13 x 9-inch baking dish with cooking spray. On cookie sheet or in baking dish, roll or press 2 of the biscuits into 5- to 6-inch rounds. Place 1 steak on center of each flattened biscuit. Press remaining 2 biscuits into 5- to 6-inch rounds; place over steaks. Flute or crimp edges with fork to seal. In small bowl, beat egg yolk and water with fork until blended; brush over top biscuits. Bake 14 to 18 minutes or until golden brown.

4 Meanwhile, in 1-quart saucepan, mix cheese, pepper, whipping cream and Worcestershire sauce. Heat to boiling. Reduce heat to medium-low; simmer uncovered, stirring constantly, until cheese is melted. Stir in mushrooms. Keep warm over low heat. Serve half of mushroom gravy over each wrapped steak; sprinkle with parsley.

NUTRITION INFORMATION PER SERVING: Calories 1130 • Total Fat 78g • Saturated Fat 34g • Cholesterol 260mg • Sodium 2300mg • Total Carbohydrate 57g • Dietary Fiber 1g • Protein 50g. DIETARY EXCHANGES: 3 Starch • 1 Other Carbohydrate • 6 Medium-Fat Meat • 9 Fat • 4 Carb Choices.

kitchen tip

Gorgonzola is an Italian cheese from the blue cheese family that is cream-yellow in color with characteristic blue veins. Like most other kinds of blue cheese, gorgonzola has a bold flavor and crumbles easily, making it a good addition to salads and other sauces.

italian classic lasagna

PREP TIME: 45 Minutes ✳ **READY IN:** 2 Hours 10 Minutes ✳ **SERVINGS:** 9

6 uncooked lasagna noodles	1/2 teaspoon dried oregano leaves
1 lb. lean (at least 80%) ground beef	1/4 teaspoon salt
1/2 lb. bulk Italian pork sausage	1/4 teaspoon garlic powder
3/4 cup chopped onions (1-1/2 medium)	2 eggs
1 can (28 oz.) Italian-style peeled tomatoes, undrained, cut up	1 container (15 oz.) ricotta cheese
1 can (6 oz.) tomato paste	1 cup cottage cheese
1 teaspoon dried basil leaves	1/2 cup grated Parmesan cheese
1/2 teaspoon sugar	1/4 cup chopped fresh parsley
	4 cups shredded mozzarella cheese (16 oz.)

1 Cook the lasagna noodles as directed on the package; drain and place the noodles in cold water to cool.

2 Meanwhile, in 4-quart saucepan or Dutch oven, cook ground beef, sausage and onions over medium-high heat 5 to 7 minutes, stirring frequently, until beef and sausage are thoroughly cooked; drain. Stir in tomatoes, tomato paste, basil, sugar, oregano, salt and garlic powder. Heat to boiling. Reduce heat to low; simmer uncovered 30 to 45 minutes, stirring occasionally, until very thick.

3 In medium bowl, beat eggs. Stir in ricotta, cottage and Parmesan cheeses and parsley; set aside.

4 Heat oven to 350°F. In ungreased 13x9-inch (3-quart) glass baking dish, spread about 1/2 cup beef mixture. Drain noodles. Top beef mixture with 3 noodles, half of the cheese mixture, half of the remaining beef mixture and half of the mozzarella cheese. Repeat layers, starting with noodles and ending with mozzarella cheese.

5 Bake 35 to 45 minutes or until lasagna is bubbly and top is golden brown. Cover with foil; let stand 10 to 15 minutes before serving.

NUTRITION INFORMATION PER SERVING: Calories 500 • Total Fat 27g • Saturated Fat 14g • Cholesterol 135mg • Sodium 1020mg • Total Carbohydrate 26g • Dietary Fiber 2g • Protein 40g. DIETARY EXCHANGES: 1 Starch • 1/2 Other Carbohydrate • 1 Vegetable • 5 Medium-Fat Meat • 2 Carb Choices.

peach-dijon pork chops

PREP TIME: 25 Minutes ✸ **SERVINGS:** 4

1/2 cup peach preserves, large pieces cut up

2 tablespoons Dijon mustard

2 tablespoons soy sauce

1/4 teaspoon dried marjoram leaves

4 (6 oz. each) pork loin chops 3/4 inch thick

1/4 teaspoon salt

1/8 teaspoon pepper

1 Heat grill. In small saucepan, combine preserves, mustard, soy sauce and marjoram; mix well. Cook over low heat until preserves are melted, stirring frequently.

2 When ready to grill, sprinkle both sides of pork chops with salt and pepper. Place chops on gas grill over medium heat or on charcoal grill 4 to 6 inches from medium coals. Cook 12 to 15 minutes or until pork is no longer pink in center, turning once and brushing with preserves mixture during last 2 minutes of cooking time. To serve, bring any remaining preserves mixture to a boil. Serve with pork chops.

NUTRITION INFORMATION PER SERVING: Calories 270 • Total Fat 7g • Saturated Fat 2g • Cholesterol 60mg • Sodium 870mg • Total Carbohydrate 29g • Dietary Fiber 1g • Protein 22g. DIETARY EXCHANGES: 2 Fruit • 2 Other Carbohydrate • 3 Very Lean Meat • 1 Fat.

cook's notes

To broil pork chops, place on broiler pan; broil 4 to 6 inches from heat using times at left as a guide, turning once and brushing occasionally with preserves mixture.

baked ziti with fire roasted tomatoes

PREP TIME: 30 Minutes ✸ **READY IN:** 55 Minutes ✸ **SERVINGS:** 6

2-1/2 cups uncooked ziti pasta (8 oz.)

1/2 lb. extra-lean (at least 90%) ground beef

1 large sweet onion, chopped (1 cup)

2 cloves garlic, finely chopped

1 medium zucchini, cut in half lengthwise, sliced 1/4 inch thick

1 can (15 oz.) Muir Glen® organic tomato sauce

1 can (14.5 oz.) Muir Glen® organic fire roasted diced tomatoes, drained

2 teaspoons chopped fresh oregano leaves

1/4 teaspoon coarse (kosher or sea) salt

1/4 teaspoon pepper

3/4 cup shredded mozzarella cheese (3 oz.)

1 Heat oven to 375°F. Cook and drain pasta as directed on box. Meanwhile, spray 12x8-inch (2-quart) glass baking dish with cooking spray. In 12-inch nonstick skillet, cook beef, onion and garlic over medium heat, stirring frequently, until beef is thoroughly cooked.

2 Stir zucchini into ground beef; cook 2 minutes. Stir in tomato sauce, tomatoes, oregano, salt and pepper. Heat to boiling. Add drained pasta; toss to coat. Spread in baking dish.

3 Cover dish tightly with foil; bake 20 minutes. Remove foil; sprinkle with cheese. Bake uncovered about 5 minutes longer or until cheese is melted.

HIGH ALTITUDE (3500-6500 FT): Increase covered bake time to 30 minutes.

NUTRITION INFORMATION PER SERVING: Calories 300 • Total Fat 7g • Saturated Fat 3g • Cholesterol 30mg • Sodium 770mg • Total Carbohydrate 41g • Dietary Fiber 5g • Protein 18g. DIETARY EXCHANGES: 1-1/2 Starch • 1/2 Other Carbohydrate • 2 Vegetable • 1-1/2 Medium-Fat Meat • 3 Carb Choices.

cook's notes

If you like, use ground turkey or chicken in place of the ground beef in this dish.

cook's notes

If fresh pea pods aren't readily available, use a package of frozen pea pods instead. Place in a colander and run under warm water to thaw them.

thai peanut beef and pea pods over noodles

READY IN: 25 Minutes ✳ **SERVINGS:** 4

8 oz. uncooked thin spaghetti	1-1/2 cups chicken broth
1 lb. lean (at least 80%) ground beef	1/4 teaspoon ground red pepper (cayenne)
4 green onions, chopped (1/4 cup)	1/4 teaspoon salt
8 oz. fresh pea pods, halved diagonally (about 3 cups)	2 teaspoons cornstarch
1 red bell pepper, cut into 3x1/4x1/4-inch thin strips	1/2 cup peanut butter
	1/4 cup chopped salted peanuts

1 Cook and drain spaghetti as directed on package; cover to keep warm. Meanwhile, in 12-inch skillet, cook ground beef over medium-high heat 5 to 7 minutes, stirring occasionally, until thoroughly cooked; drain. Add onions, pea pods and bell pepper. Cook and stir 3 to 4 minutes or until vegetables are crisp-tender.

2 In small bowl, mix broth, ground red pepper, salt and cornstarch. Stir into beef and vegetables. Add peanut butter. Cook 1 to 2 minutes, stirring frequently, until thick and bubbly. Serve over cooked spaghetti; top with peanuts.

HIGH ALTITUDE (3500-6500 FT): In Step 2, cook 2 to 3 minutes.

NUTRITION INFORMATION PER SERVING: Calories 730 • Total Fat 36g • Saturated Fat 9g • Cholesterol 70mg • Sodium 1000mg • Total Carbohydrate 60g • Dietary Fiber 8g • Protein 42g. DIETARY EXCHANGES: 3 Starch • 1/2 Other Carbohydrate • 1 Vegetable • 4-1/2 Medium-Fat Meat • 2 Fat • 4 Carb Choices.

key lime-glazed ham

PREP TIME: 20 Minutes ✳ **READY IN:** 3 Hours 5 Minutes ✳ **SERVINGS:** 8

HAM

1 fully cooked bone-in ham (6 to 7 lb.)
1 cup water

GLAZE AND SAUCE

1 cup packed brown sugar
1/2 cup Dijon mustard
1/3 cup Key lime juice

1 Heat oven to 325°F. If shallow roasting pan does not have rack, line with heavy-duty foil. Place ham, fat side up, on rack in pan or in foil-lined pan. Score ham diagonally at 1-inch intervals, cutting 1/4 inch deep; score in opposite direction to form diamond shapes. Pour water into pan. Bake 1 hour.

2 Meanwhile, in medium bowl, mix glaze ingredients. Pour half of mixture into 1-quart saucepan; set aside for sauce.

3 Remove ham from oven. Insert meat thermometer so bulb reaches center of thickest part of ham, but does not rest in fat or on bone. Brush ham with some of glaze in bowl.

4 Bake 1 hour to 1 hour 30 minutes or until thermometer reads 140°F, brushing frequently with pan drippings and remaining glaze in bowl.

5 Let ham stand in pan 15 minutes, spooning pan drippings frequently over top. Meanwhile, heat reserved sauce in saucepan over low heat; serve warm with ham.

NUTRITION INFORMATION PER SERVING: Calories 380 • Total Fat 11g • Saturated Fat 3.5g • Cholesterol 95mg • Sodium 2600mg • Total Carbohydrate 32g • Dietary Fiber 0g • Protein 39g. DIETARY EXCHANGES: 2 Other Carbohydrate • 5-1/2 Very Lean Meat • 1-1/2 Fat • 2 Carb Choices.

thai peanut beef and pea pods over noodles

cook's notes

An alternative to the plastic bag for marinating the steak would be to use a 13x9-inch (3-quart) glass baking dish. Cover with a lid or plastic wrap.

so-simple flank steak

PREP TIME: 35 Minutes ✳ READY IN: 6 Hours 35 Minutes ✳ SERVINGS: 4

1/4 cup soy sauce	1 teaspoon sugar
1/4 cup water	1 clove garlic, minced
2 tablespoons vegetable oil	1 beef flank steak (about 1-1/4 lb.)

1 In 2-gallon resealable food-storage plastic bag, mix all ingredients except steak. Add steak; seal bag and turn to coat. Refrigerate at least 6 hours or overnight to marinate, turning bag once or twice.

2 When ready to cook steak, heat gas or charcoal grill. When grill is heated, remove steak from marinade; pour marinade into measuring cup. Place steak on gas grill over medium heat or on charcoal grill over medium coals; cover grill. Cook 15 to 20 minutes, turning occasionally and brushing with marinade, until steak is desired doneness. Discard any remaining marinade.

3 Let steak stand on platter 5 minutes; cut diagonally across grain into slices. If desired, garnish with cherry tomatoes and red onion slices.

HIGH ALTITUDE (3500-6500 FT): Cook steak on covered grill over medium-low heat. Continue as directed above.

NUTRITION INFORMATION PER SERVING: Calories 290 • Total Fat 17g • Saturated Fat 5g • Cholesterol 80mg • Sodium 980mg • Total Carbohydrate 3g • Dietary Fiber 0g • Protein 31g. DIETARY EXCHANGES: 4-1/2 Lean Meat • 1 Fat.

herbed pork roast with mushroom gravy

PREP TIME: 15 Minutes ✸ **READY IN:** 1 Hour 25 Minutes ✸ **SERVINGS:** 8

1 boneless pork loin roast (2-1/2 to 3 lb.)

1 tablespoon finely chopped fresh parsley or
  1 teaspoon parsley flakes

1 tablespoon finely chopped fresh rosemary or
  1 teaspoon dried rosemary leaves, crushed

1 tablespoon finely chopped fresh thyme or
  1 teaspoon dried thyme leaves

2 cloves garlic, finely chopped

1 can (10-3/4 oz.) condensed golden
  mushroom soup

1/2 cup milk

1 jar (2.5 oz.) Green Giant® sliced mushrooms,
  drained

1 Heat oven to 350°F. In shallow roasting pan, place pork roast. In small bowl, mix parsley, rosemary, thyme and garlic; rub mixture evenly over pork. Insert meat thermometer so tip is in thickest part of pork and not resting in fat.

2 Roast uncovered about 1 hour 5 minutes to 1 hour 10 minutes or until thermometer reads 155°F. Remove pork from pan; place on cutting board. Cover with foil; let stand 10 minutes or until thermometer reads 160°F.

3 Meanwhile, in same roasting pan, stir soup into pan drippings. Stir in milk until smooth. Add mushrooms; cook and stir over medium-low heat until mixture boils. Cut pork into slices; serve with gravy.

NUTRITION INFORMATION PER SERVING: Calories 180 • Total Fat 9g • Saturated Fat 3g • Cholesterol 65mg • Sodium 190mg • Total Carbohydrate 3g • Dietary Fiber 0g • Protein 24g. DIETARY EXCHANGES: 1 Vegetable • 3 Lean Meat.

kitchen tip

To easily chop fresh herbs, place them in a measuring cup and just snip them with a kitchen scissors.

fettuccine and spinach bake

PREP TIME: 35 Minutes ✳ READY IN: 1 Hour ✳ SERVINGS: 6

1 package (12 oz.) uncooked fettuccine
2 tablespoons butter or margarine
1 medium onion, chopped (1/2 cup)
2 cloves garlic, finely chopped
1/2 teaspoon salt
1 can (14.5 oz.) stewed tomatoes, undrained

1 can (14.5 oz.) diced tomatoes with Italian-style herbs, undrained
1 bag (1 lb.) frozen cut leaf spinach, thawed, squeezed to drain
1 cup whipping cream
1 cup shredded Swiss cheese (4 oz.)

1 Heat oven to 400°F. Cook and drain fettuccine as directed on package. Meanwhile, in 10-inch skillet, melt butter over medium heat. Add onion; cook 3 to 4 minutes, stirring frequently, until tender. Stir in garlic, salt and both cans of tomatoes. Cook 5 minutes, stirring occasionally, until tomatoes are thoroughly heated.

2 In ungreased 13x9-inch (3-quart) glass baking dish, spread half of the fettuccine. Layer with all of the spinach and half of the tomato mixture. Repeat with layers of remaining fettuccine and tomato mixture.

3 Pour cream over top; sprinkle evenly with cheese. Bake uncovered 20 to 25 minutes or until thoroughly heated and cheese is melted.

HIGH ALTITUDE (3500-6500 FT): In Step 5, cover dish with sprayed foil, sprayed side down; bake covered 25 to 30 minutes.

NUTRITION INFORMATION PER SERVING: Calories 490 • Total Fat 24g • Saturated Fat 13g • Cholesterol 120mg • Sodium 1020mg • Total Carbohydrate 53g • Dietary Fiber 4g • Protein 16g. DIETARY EXCHANGES: 2-1/2 Starch • 1/2 Other Carbohydrate • 2 Vegetable • 1/2 High-Fat Meat • 3-1/2 Fat • 3-1/2 Carb Choices.

cook's notes

Look for the tomatoes with Italian-style herbs near the cans of regular diced tomatoes. Any brand with Italian flavors, such as garlic, basil and oregano, can be used.

potato-topped oven swiss steak

PREP TIME: 20 Minutes ✳ READY IN: 2 Hours 35 Minutes ✳ SERVINGS: 8

SWISS STEAK
1-1/2 lb. boneless beef round steak (1/2 inch thick), cut into pieces
3 medium carrots, sliced (1-1/2 cups)
1 large onion, cut into thin wedges (2 cups)
1 can (14.5 oz.) diced tomatoes with Italian herbs, undrained

1 jar (12 oz.) beef gravy

TOPPING
1 box (7.2 oz.) mashed potatoes seasoned with butter and herb (2 pouches)
Hot water, milk and margarine called for on potatoes box for 2 pouches
1 egg, beaten

1 Heat oven to 325°F. In ungreased 13x9-inch (3-quart) glass baking dish, arrange beef in single layer. Top with carrots and onion.

2 In medium bowl, mix tomatoes and gravy; spoon over beef and vegetables. Cover with foil; bake 2 hours.

3 In 3-quart saucepan, make both pouches of potatoes as directed on box. Stir in egg until well blended.

4 Remove the baking dish from oven. Uncover; spoon or pipe potato mixture over hot mixture. Return to oven; bake uncovered 15 to 20 minutes longer or until the potatoes are set and light golden brown.

NUTRITION INFORMATION PER SERVING: Calories 380 • Total Fat 14g • Saturated Fat 4.5g • Cholesterol 95mg • Sodium 830mg • Total Carbohydrate 32g • Dietary Fiber 3g • Protein 33g. DIETARY EXCHANGES: 1 Starch • 1 Other Carbohydrate • 1 Vegetable • 4 Lean Meat • 2 Carb Choices.

beef and chicken fondue

PREP TIME: 30 Minutes ✳ READY IN: 2 Hours 30 Minutes ✳ SERVINGS: 8

CREAMY CUCUMBER SAUCE

2 packages (3 oz. each) cream cheese, softened

2 cups sour cream

1/4 cup milk

1 cup finely chopped peeled cucumber

2 tablespoons finely chopped onion

1/2 teaspoon salt

FONDUE

1 lb. boneless beef sirloin steak

1 lb. boneless skinless chicken breasts

Lettuce

1 package (8 oz. size) whole fresh white mushrooms

2 medium bell peppers (any color), cut into 1-inch pieces

2 medium carrots, cut into 1/4-inch slices

2 cups small fresh broccoli florets (about 24)

4 cans (14 oz. each) chicken broth

2 cans (14 oz. each) beef broth

4 cloves garlic, peeled

4 teaspoons parsley flakes

2 teaspoons dried thyme leaves

1/2 teaspoon salt

1/2 teaspoon pepper

Other Purchased Dipping Sauces, if desired

Barbecue sauce

Horseradish sauce

Sweet-and-sour sauce

Teriyaki sauce

1 To make creamy cucumber sauce, in medium bowl, beat cream cheese with spoon until creamy. Stir in remaining sauce ingredients. Cover; refrigerate until chilled, about 2 hours.

2 Cut steak and chicken across grain into 1x1/2-inch pieces. Blot dry with paper towels; arrange on lettuce-lined platter. Cover; refrigerate until serving time. Arrange vegetables on separate platter; set aside.

3 At serving time, divide broth between two 3-quart electric fondue pots; add half of garlic, parsley, thyme, salt and the pepper to each fondue pot. Heat at 375°F until boiling.

4 With long-handled fondue forks, spear meats and vegetables; place in hot broth. Cook 2 to 4 minutes, keeping broth at a low boil, until beef and vegetables are desired doneness and chicken is no longer pink in center. (Because fondue forks become very hot, transfer meat and vegetables to plate and use table fork for eating.) Serve with sauces for dipping.

special touch

A lettuce-lined platter serves as an attractive way to serve the uncooked chicken and beef. Discard the lettuce leaves when the meal is over.

NUTRITION INFORMATION PER SERVING: Calories 400 • Total Fat 24g • Saturated Fat 13g • Cholesterol 125mg • Sodium 1870mg • Total Carbohydrate 11g • Dietary Fiber 2g • Protein 35g. DIETARY EXCHANGES: 1/2 Starch • 1 Vegetable • 4-1/2 Medium-Fat Meat • 1 Carb Choice.

garlic-basil chicken

PREP TIME: 20 Minutes ✳ READY IN: 35 Minutes ✳ SERVINGS: 2

3 cloves garlic, finely chopped	1 tablespoon lemon juice
1 tablespoon dried basil leaves	2 tablespoons olive oil
1/2 teaspoon pepper	2 bone-in chicken breasts (1-1/4 lb.)
1/4 teaspoon salt	

1 In shallow dish or pie pan, mix garlic, basil, pepper, salt, lemon juice and 1 tablespoon of the oil. Coat chicken with garlic-basil mixture.

2 In 10-inch skillet, heat remaining tablespoon oil over medium heat. Add chicken; cook about 5 minutes on each side or until browned.

3 Reduce heat to medium-low; cover and cook 10 to 15 minutes or until juice of chicken is clear when thickest part is cut to bone (170°F).

HIGH ALTITUDE **(3500-6500 FT):** In Step 3, cover and cook 20 to 30 minutes.

NUTRITION INFORMATION PER SERVING: Calories 400 • Total Fat 25g • Saturated Fat 5g • Cholesterol 115mg • Sodium 390mg • Total Carbohydrate 3g • Dietary Fiber 0g • Protein 42g. DIETARY EXCHANGES: 6 Lean Meat • 1-1/2 Fat.

lemony fish and tomatoes

PREP TIME: 15 Minutes ✳ **READY IN:** 35 Minutes ✳ **SERVINGS:** 4

1 lb. cod fillets	2 tablespoons olive oil
1/2 teaspoon salt	1 medium onion, chopped (1/2 cup)
1/4 teaspoon pepper	2 cloves garlic, minced
2 medium lemons, each cut into quarters	1 teaspoon parsley flakes
1 medium tomato, thinly sliced	

1 Heat oven to 400°F. Sprinkle both sides of each cod fillet with salt and pepper. In ungreased 13x9-inch (3-quart) glass baking dish, arrange fish in single layer.

2 Squeeze juice of 3 lemon quarters over fish. Arrange tomato slices on fish to cover, overlapping as necessary.

3 In 8-inch skillet, heat oil over medium heat. Add onion; cook 3 to 4 minutes, stirring frequently, until tender. Add garlic; cook and stir 1 to 2 minutes longer.

4 Remove from heat; stir in parsley. Sprinkle onion mixture evenly over tomatoes. Squeeze juice of 1 lemon quarter over onion mixture.

5 Bake uncovered 15 to 20 minutes or until fish flakes easily with fork. Serve fish with remaining lemon quarters.

NUTRITION INFORMATION PER SERVING: Calories 190 • Total Fat 8g • Saturated Fat 1.5g • Cholesterol 60mg • Sodium 390mg • Total Carbohydrate 6g • Dietary Fiber 2g • Protein 22g. DIETARY EXCHANGES: 1/2 Other Carbohydrate • 3 Very Lean Meat • 1 Fat • 1/2 Carb Choice.

cook's notes

Other mild-flavored fish fillets, such as walleye, tilapia, halibut or pike, can be substituted for the cod.

polynesian pork chops

PREP TIME: 35 Minutes ✳ READY IN: 2 Hours 35 Minutes ✳ SERVINGS: 8

1 cup ketchup	1/2 teaspoon crushed red pepper flakes
1/3 cup reduced-sodium soy sauce	4 cloves garlic, minced
2 tablespoons packed brown sugar	8 boneless pork loin chops, about 1/2 inch thick (about 1-3/4 lb.)
1 teaspoon grated gingerroot	

1　In 2-gallon resealable food-storage plastic bag, mix all ingredients except pork chops. Add pork; seal bag and turn to coat. Refrigerate 1 to 2 hours to marinate, turning bag once.

2　When ready to cook pork, heat gas or charcoal grill. When grill is heated, remove pork from marinade; reserve marinade. Place pork on gas grill over medium heat or on charcoal grill over medium coals; cover grill. Cook 15 to 20 minutes, turning occasionally and brushing with marinade, until pork is no longer pink in center. Discard any remaining marinade.

HIGH ALTITUDE (3500-6500 FT): Cook pork chops on covered grill over medium-low heat. Continue as directed above.

NUTRITION INFORMATION PER SERVING: Calories 210 • Total Fat 8g • Saturated Fat 2.5g • Cholesterol 60mg • Sodium 750mg • Total Carbohydrate 13g • Dietary Fiber 0g • Protein 22g. DIETARY EXCHANGES: 1 Other Carbohydrate • 3 Lean Meat • 1 Carb Choice.

roasted chicken with peach glaze

PREP TIME: 20 Minutes ✳ READY IN: 2 Hours 5 Minutes ✳ SERVINGS: 6

1 whole chicken (5 to 5-1/2 lb.)	1/2 cup peach or apricot preserves
1 teaspoon garlic-pepper blend	

1　Heat oven to 375°F. Spray rack in shallow roasting pan with cooking spray. Rinse chicken inside and out with cold water; drain and pat dry with paper towels.

2　Sprinkle garlic-pepper blend over chicken; place breast side up on rack in pan. Insert ovenproof meat thermometer so tip is in thickest part of inside thigh and does not touch bone.

3　Bake uncovered 1 hour. Brush chicken with preserves; bake 35 to 45 minutes longer or until thermometer reads 180°F and legs move easily when lifted or twisted. Let stand 5 to 10 minutes before serving.

NUTRITION INFORMATION PER SERVING: Calories 450 • Total Fat 22g • Saturated Fat 6g • Cholesterol 145mg • Sodium 140mg • Total Carbohydrate 19g • Dietary Fiber 0g • Protein 44g. DIETARY EXCHANGES: 1 Other Carbohydrate • 6 Lean Meat • 1 Fat • 1 Carb Choice.

cook's notes

The roasted chicken is finger-lickin' good and simple, too—only three ingredients!

honey-dijon ham

PREP TIME: 15 Minutes ✳ READY IN: 6 Hours 15 Minutes ✳ SERVINGS: 12

1 bone-in cooked ham (5 lb.)	1 tablespoon honey
1/3 cup apple juice	1 tablespoon Dijon mustard
1/4 cup packed brown sugar	

1　In 4- to 6-quart slow cooker, place ham. Add apple juice. In small bowl, mix brown sugar, honey and mustard. Spread mixture over ham.

2　Cover; cook on Low heat setting 6 to 8 hours. Remove ham from slow cooker. Cut ham into slices; place on serving platter.

NUTRITION INFORMATION PER SERVING: Calories 310 • Total Fat 10g • Saturated Fat 3.5g • Cholesterol 95mg • Sodium 2250mg • Total Carbohydrate 17g • Dietary Fiber 0g • Protein 38g. DIETARY EXCHANGES: 1 Other Carbohydrate • 5-1/2 Very Lean Meat • 1-1/2 Fat • 1 Carb Choice.

moroccan-style chicken-crescent casserole

PREP TIME: 25 Minutes ✳ **READY IN:** 50 Minutes ✳ **SERVINGS:** 6

1 tablespoon olive or vegetable oil	1-1/2 teaspoons paprika
6 boneless skinless chicken breasts (about 1-1/2 lb.), cut into bite-size pieces	1/2 teaspoon salt
1/2 cup chopped onion	1/2 teaspoon ground cumin
1/2 cup sliced carrot	1/4 to 1/2 teaspoon ground cinnamon
1 can (14.5 oz.) diced fire-roasted or regular tomatoes, undrained	1/8 teaspoon ground red pepper (cayenne)
1 tablespoon tomato paste	1 can (8 oz.) Pillsbury® refrigerated crescent dinner rolls (8 rolls)
3 tablespoons chopped fresh parsley	1 egg, beaten
3 tablespoons chopped fresh cilantro	1 tablespoon sliced almonds

1 Heat oven to 375°F. In 12-inch skillet, heat oil over medium-high heat. Add chicken, onion and carrot; cook and stir about 7 minutes or until chicken is browned and no longer pink in center. Stir in tomatoes, tomato paste, parsley, cilantro, paprika, salt, cumin, cinnamon and red pepper. Cook and stir about 5 minutes or until thoroughly heated.

2 Into ungreased 11x7-inch (2-quart) glass baking dish or 9-1/2- or 10-inch deep-dish pie plate, pour hot chicken mixture. Immediately unroll dough over chicken mixture; pinch edges and perforations to seal. Brush dough with beaten egg; sprinkle with almonds.

3 Bake 18 to 25 minutes or until deep golden brown. If desired, garnish the casserole with fresh cilantro.

NUTRITION INFORMATION PER SERVING: Calories 320 • Total Fat 13g • Saturated Fat 4g • Cholesterol 70mg • Sodium 690mg • Total Carbohydrate 23g • Dietary Fiber 2g • Protein 29g. DIETARY EXCHANGES: 1 Starch • 1 Vegetable • 3-1/2 Lean Meat • 1/2 Fat • 1-1/2 Carb Choices.

cook's notes

To add flavor and texture to the chicken mixture, add 1/4 cup of chopped, toasted and blanched almonds or raisins.

cook's notes

The chicken and pasta goes well served with a fresh salad made with baby spinach, sliced fresh strawberries and mandarin orange segments topped with poppy seed dressing.

chicken with dijon-tarragon cream sauce

READY IN: 25 Minutes ✳ SERVINGS: 4

8 oz. uncooked fettuccine
1 tablespoon butter or margarine
1 lb. boneless skinless chicken breasts, cut into 1/2-inch pieces
3/4 cup sour cream

1/2 cup milk
2 tablespoons Dijon mustard
1 tablespoon chopped fresh tarragon or 1 teaspoon dried tarragon leaves
2 tablespoons chopped fresh parsley, if desired

1 Cook and drain fettuccine as directed on package. Meanwhile, in 10-inch skillet, melt butter over medium heat. Add chicken; cook 8 to 10 minutes, stirring frequently, until no longer pink in center.

2 In small bowl, mix sour cream, milk and mustard until smooth. Stir in tarragon. Pour into skillet with chicken. Cook about 5 minutes, stirring frequently, until thoroughly heated. Serve chicken mixture over fettuccine; sprinkle with parsley.

NUTRITION INFORMATION PER SERVING: Calories 470 • Total Fat 18g • Saturated Fat 8g • Cholesterol 155mg • Sodium 310mg • Total Carbohydrate 41g • Dietary Fiber 2g • Protein 35g. DIETARY EXCHANGES: 2-1/2 Starch • 4 Lean Meat • 1 Fat • 3 Carb Choices.

cranberry-apple glazed crown pork roast with cranberry cornbread stuffing

PREP TIME: 35 Minutes ✳ **READY IN:** 3 Hours 35 Minutes ✳ **SERVINGS:** 12

STUFFING

- 3 packages (6 oz. each) one-step cornbread stuffing mix
- Butter or margarine
- Water
- 3/4 cup sweetened dried cranberries
- 3/4 cup chopped dried apples

ROAST

- 1 (12-bone) pork crown roast (about 7 lb.)
- 1/4 cup apple jelly
- 2 tablespoons jellied cranberry sauce

1 Heat oven to 350°F. In large saucepan, make stuffing as directed on package, using butter and water. Add cranberries and apples; mix well. Set aside.

2 Place pork roast on rack in shallow roasting pan. Fill cavity with as much of the stuffing as it will hold. Cover stuffing and bones loosely with foil. Spray 1-quart casserole with nonstick cooking spray. Spoon remaining stuffing into casserole. Cover; refrigerate until 45 minutes before serving time.

3 Bake roast 2-1/4 to 3 hours, allowing 25 to 30 minutes per pound, or until meat thermometer inserted in center registers 155°F.

4 Meanwhile, in small saucepan, mix apple jelly and cranberry sauce until well blended. Heat over low heat until mixture is melted and smooth. Brush roast with jelly mixture and bake any remaining stuffing during last 45 minutes of baking time.

5 Place roast on serving platter. Cover with foil; let stand 15 minutes. Remove strings from roast. To serve, slice between bones. Serve with stuffing from center of roast and additional baked stuffing.

NUTRITION INFORMATION PER SERVING: Calories 600 • Total Fat 27g • Saturated Fat 7g • Cholesterol 115mg • Sodium 890mg • Total Carbohydrate 44g • Dietary Fiber 2g • Protein 45g. DIETARY EXCHANGES: 3 Starch • 3 Other Carbohydrate • 5 Lean Meat • 2 Fat.

cook's notes

This pork roast is wonderful for holiday entertaining because it is prepared 4 hours before the meal time so you can enjoy time with your guests while it bakes. It's an attractive entree, so make sure everyone gets to see it before it is sliced!

orange zested chicken breasts

READY IN: 20 Minutes ✳ **SERVINGS:** 4

- 1/2 teaspoon seasoned salt
- 1/4 teaspoon garlic powder
- 2 tablespoons butter or margarine
- 1 teaspoon grated orange peel
- 4 boneless skinless chicken breasts (1 lb.)

1 In small bowl, mix seasoned salt and garlic powder. In 10-inch nonstick skillet, heat butter and orange peel over medium heat until butter is melted. Add chicken; sprinkle with salt mixture. Cook about 15 minutes, turning once, until juice of chicken is clear when center of thickest part is cut (170°F).

HIGH ALTITUDE (3500-6500 FT): Cook about 18 minutes.

NUTRITION INFORMATION PER SERVING: Calories 190 • Total Fat 9g • Saturated Fat 4.5g • Cholesterol 85mg • Sodium 270mg • Total Carbohydrate 0g • Dietary Fiber 0g • Protein 25g. DIETARY EXCHANGES: 3-1/2 Very Lean Meat • 1-1/2 Fat.

cook's notes

This orange chicken is super easy to prepare! Serve it with cooked fresh green beans or broccoli, warm breadsticks and a simple fruit salad.

oven-braised beef short ribs

PREP TIME: 20 Minutes ✳ **READY IN:** 2 Hours 50 Minutes ✳ **SERVINGS:** 6

3-1/2 to 4 lb. beef short ribs, trimmed of fat	1/2 teaspoon dried thyme leaves
1 (14.5 oz.) can diced tomatoes, undrained	1/2 teaspoon dried marjoram leaves
1/2 cup beef broth	1/2 teaspoon salt
1/2 cup Zinfandel wine or cranberry juice	1/2 teaspoon garlic-pepper blend
1/4 cup all-purpose flour	2 cups fresh baby carrots
1/4 cup chili sauce	1 medium onion, halved, thinly sliced

1 Heat oven to 325°F. Spray 12-inch nonstick skillet with nonstick cooking spray. Heat over medium-high heat until hot. Add short ribs; cook 6 to 8 minutes or until browned on all sides.

2 In ungreased 13x9-inch (3-quart) glass baking dish, combine tomatoes, broth, wine, flour, chili sauce, thyme, marjoram, salt and garlic-pepper blend; mix well. Add browned ribs, carrots and onion; stir gently to mix. (Baking dish will be full.) Cover with foil.

3 Bake covered at 325°F for 2 hours. Uncover baking dish, bake an additional 20 to 30 minutes or until ribs are tender and liquid is slightly thickened.

HIGH ALTITUDE (3500-6500 FT): Bake covered at 350°F for 2 hours. Uncover baking dish; bake an additional 30 to 40 minutes.

NUTRITION INFORMATION PER SERVING: Calories 285 • Total Fat 15g • Saturated Fat 6g • Cholesterol 60mg • Sodium 580mg • Total Carbohydrate 16g • Dietary Fiber 2g • Protein 22g. DIETARY EXCHANGES: 1 Starch • 1 Vegetable • 2-1/2 Medium-Fat Meat • 1/2 Fat • 1 Carb Choice.

chicken à la king pasta bake

PREP TIME: 25 Minutes ✳ **READY IN:** 1 Hour 45 Minutes ✳ **SERVINGS:** 6

2 cans (10-3/4 oz. each) condensed 98% fat-free cream of chicken soup with 30% less sodium	2 cups uncooked wide egg noodles (4 oz.)
1 can (12 oz.) evaporated fat-free milk	1 cup chopped onions (2 medium)
1/2 cup dry sherry or chicken broth	1 cup chopped green bell pepper (1 medium)
3/4 teaspoon salt	2 jars (6 oz. each) Green Giant® whole mushrooms, drained
2 cups coarsely chopped cooked chicken breast	2 jars (2 oz. each) diced pimientos, drained

1 Heat oven to 350°F. Spray 13x9-inch (3-quart) glass baking dish with cooking spray. In large bowl, mix soup, milk, sherry and salt. Stir in all remaining ingredients; pour into baking dish. Cover tightly with foil.

2 Bake 60 to 70 minutes or until noodles are tender and mixture is hot and bubbly. Let stand 10 minutes before serving.

NUTRITION INFORMATION PER SERVING: Calories 295 • Total Fat 5g • Saturated Fat 1g • Cholesterol 60mg • Sodium 1050mg • Total Carbohydrate 37g • Dietary Fiber 3g • Protein 25g. DIETARY EXCHANGES: 2-1/2 Starch • 2-1/2 Very Lean Meat • 1/2 Fat • 2-1/2 Carb Choices.

oven-braised beef short ribs

seafood manicotti

PREP TIME: 50 Minutes ✳ **READY IN:** 1 Hour 20 Minutes ✳ **SERVINGS:** 4

8 uncooked manicotti	1 can (6 oz.) crabmeat, drained, flaked
1 cup whole-milk ricotta cheese	1-1/2 cups meatless tomato pasta sauce
1 package (3 oz.) cream cheese, softened	2 oz. (1/2 cup) shredded mozzarella cheese
1/4 cup chopped green onions	
6 oz. (about 25) frozen cooked small shrimp, thawed, tails removed and shrimp cut in half crosswise	

1 Cook manicotti as directed on package. Drain; rinse with cold water to cool. Meanwhile, heat oven to 375°F. In medium bowl, combine ricotta cheese and cream cheese; mix well. Gently stir in onions, shrimp and crabmeat.

2 Spread 1/2 cup of the pasta sauce in ungreased 11x7-inch (2-quart) glass baking dish. Fill each cooked manicotti with seafood mixture; place over sauce. Spoon remaining pasta sauce over manicotti. Cover tightly with foil.

3 Bake at 375°F for 25 to 30 minutes or until bubbly. Uncover baking dish; sprinkle with mozzarella cheese. Bake uncovered an additional 5 to 8 minutes or until cheese is melted. Let stand 5 minutes before serving.

NUTRITION INFORMATION PER SERVING: Calories 535 • Total Fat 23g • Saturated Fat 12g • Cholesterol 185mg • Sodium 1020mg • Total Carbohydrate 46g • Dietary Fiber 2g • Protein 36g. DIETARY EXCHANGES: 3 Starch • 4 Lean Meat • 2 Fat • 3 Carb Choices.

pork chops with apple-sage stuffing

PREP TIME: 15 Minutes ✻ **READY IN:** 9 Hours 5 Minutes ✻ **SERVINGS:** 4

1 tablespoon butter
1/2 cup chopped onion (1 medium)
1/2 cup thinly sliced celery
1 cup chopped apple
1/2 cup raisins

1 cup apple juice
1 package (6 oz.) sage and onion-seasoned one-step stuffing mix
4 boneless smoked pork chops (4 oz. each)
2 tablespoons apple jelly

1 Spray 8-inch square (2-quart) glass baking dish with nonstick cooking spray. Melt butter in large skillet over medium heat. Add onion and celery; cook 3 to 4 minutes or until crisp-tender, stirring occasionally.

2 Add apple, raisins and apple juice; cook 2 to 3 minutes or until mixture comes to a boil. Remove from heat; stir in stuffing mix. Spread mixture in sprayed baking dish. Top with pork chops. Cover with foil; refrigerate at least 8 hours or overnight.

3 Heat oven to 350°F. Bake covered for 30 minutes. Uncover baking dish; brush pork chops with jelly. Bake uncovered 15 to 20 minutes longer or until pork chops are thoroughly heated.

NUTRITION INFORMATION PER SERVING: Calories 510 • Total Fat 14g • Saturated Fat 5g • Cholesterol 65mg • Sodium 2210mg • Total Carbohydrate 68g • Dietary Fiber 3g • Protein 28g. DIETARY EXCHANGES: 3 Starch • 1-1/2 Fruit • 2-1/2 Lean Meat • 1 Fat • 4-1/2 Carb Choices.

kitchen tip

Look for the smoked pork chops near the fresh meats. Because they are smoked, they only need to be thoroughly heated before serving.

orange chicken

PREP TIME: 1 Hour ✻ **READY IN:** 2 Hours 45 Minutes ✻ **SERVINGS:** 4

2 oranges
2 tablespoons olive oil
1 whole chicken (3 to 4 lb.)
1 teaspoon each salt and pepper

1/3 cup sugar
1/3 cup red wine vinegar
1 cup orange juice

1 Heat oven to 375°F. With vegetable peeler, remove all of outer orange portion (zest) in one long piece from oranges. Cut oranges in half. Squeeze juice from 1-1/2 oranges to measure about 1/2 cup. Stir oil into juice.

2 Sprinkle chicken, inside and out, with salt and pepper. Place orange zest from 1 orange and remaining orange half inside chicken. Tie legs together with string. Insert meat thermometer so tip does not touch bone. In 13x9-inch (3-quart) glass baking dish, pour 1/2 cup water; place chicken in dish. Pour orange juice-oil mixture over chicken.

3 Roast uncovered 1 hour 45 minutes, spooning drippings from dish over chicken every 30 minutes, until thermometer reads 180°F and legs move easily.

4 Cut remaining orange zest into thin (1-1/2x1/8-inch) strips to make about 1/4 cup. In 2-quart saucepan, place orange strips and 2 cups water. Heat to boiling. Drain and set orange strips aside. In same saucepan, heat sugar and vinegar over high heat to boiling. Reduce heat to medium; cook 5 minutes, stirring occasionally, until slightly thickened. Remove from heat; stir in orange strips and 1 cup orange juice.

5 When chicken is done, place in another shallow pan; cover to keep warm. Into small bowl, strain drippings from dish; skim off and discard fat. Add to mixture in saucepan. Cook over medium heat 20 to 25 minutes, stirring occasionally, until slightly thickened. Serve sauce with chicken.

NUTRITION INFORMATION PER SERVING: Calories 520 • Total Fat 27g • Saturated Fat 6g • Cholesterol 130mg • Sodium 710mg • Total Carbohydrate 30g • Dietary Fiber 1g • Protein 41g. DIETARY EXCHANGES: 1/2 Fruit • 1-1/2 Other Carbohydrate • 6 Lean Meat • 1-1/2 Fat • 2 Carb Choices.

cook's notes

Fresh oranges embedded into the chicken cavity while it cooks infuse fresh flavor, enhanced on the plate with luscious orange sauce.

lemon-garlic roasted pork and vegetables

PREP TIME: 10 Minutes ❋ READY IN: 50 Minutes ❋ SERVINGS: 6

PORK

2 to 3 pork tenderloins (about 1-1/2 lb.)

1 clove garlic, minced

1 teaspoon lemon-pepper seasoning

VEGETABLES

1 bag (19 oz.) Green Giant® frozen roasted potatoes with garlic & herbs, thawed

3 cups frozen broccoli, carrots and cauliflower (from 1-lb. bag), thawed

2 teaspoons lemon juice

1 Heat oven to 450°F. Spray 13x9-inch pan with cooking spray. Place pork tenderloins in pan. In small bowl, mix garlic and lemon-pepper seasoning; rub over pork. In ungreased 2-quart casserole, mix all vegetable ingredients except lemon juice; cover.

2 Bake pork and vegetables 30 to 40 minutes or until pork has slight blush of pink in center, meat thermometer inserted in center of pork reads 160°F and vegetables are tender. (If vegetables are tender before pork is done, remove casserole from oven.) Stir lemon juice into vegetables before serving.

NUTRITION INFORMATION PER SERVING: Calories 250 • Total Fat 9g • Saturated Fat 2g • Cholesterol 70mg • Sodium 320mg • Total Carbohydrate 14g • Dietary Fiber 2g • Protein 28g. DIETARY EXCHANGES: 1/2 Starch • 1 Vegetable • 3-1/2 Lean Meat • 1 Carb Choice.

make-ahead turkey tetrazzini

PREP TIME: 30 Minutes ✳ **READY IN:** 9 Hours 25 Minutes ✳ **SERVINGS:** 8

8 oz. uncooked spaghetti	1/4 cup chopped fresh parsley
1/4 cup margarine or butter	1 teaspoon salt
2 cups sliced fresh mushrooms	1/8 teaspoon nutmeg
3 tablespoons all-purpose flour	Dash pepper
2 cups chicken broth	3 cups cubed cooked turkey
3/4 cup half-and-half	1/2 cup grated Parmesan cheese
1 to 3 tablespoons dry sherry, if desired	Chopped fresh parsley, if desired

1 Cook spaghetti as directed on package. Drain. Meanwhile, melt margarine in Dutch oven over medium heat. Add mushrooms; cook 5 minutes or until tender, stirring frequently. Reduce heat to medium-low. Add flour; cook and stir until bubbly. Gradually add broth, stirring constantly, until mixture boils and thickens. Remove from heat; stir in half-and-half, sherry, 1/4 cup parsley, salt, nutmeg and pepper.

2 Add cooked spaghetti and turkey to mushroom mixture; stir gently to mix. Spoon mixture into ungreased 13x9-inch (3-quart) glass baking dish. Cover with foil; refrigerate at least 8 hours or overnight.

3 Heat oven to 350°F. Uncover baking dish; sprinkle Parmesan cheese over top. Cover; bake at 350°F for 45 to 55 minutes or until thoroughly heated, removing foil during last 10 minutes of baking time. Sprinkle with parsley.

HIGH ALTITUDE (3500-6500 FT): Increase chicken broth to 2-1/2 cups. Bake at 350°F for 50 to 60 minutes, removing foil during last 10 minutes of baking time.

NUTRITION INFORMATION PER SERVING: Calories 340 • Total Fat 15g • Saturated Fat 5g • Cholesterol 60mg • Sodium 900mg • Total Carbohydrate 27g • Dietary Fiber 1g • Protein 24g. DIETARY EXCHANGES: 2 Starch • 2-1/2 Lean Meat • 1-1/2 Fat • 2 Carb Choices.

cook's notes

The turkey tetrazzini may be baked immediately after it is assembled. Bake at 350°F for 30 to 40 minutes, or until brown and bubbly.

pepper-curry chicken

pepper-curry chicken

PREP TIME: 25 Minutes ✷ READY IN: 1 Hour 5 Minutes ✷ SERVINGS: 4

2 tablespoons olive oil	1/2 teaspoon dried thyme leaves
1 cut-up whole chicken (3-1/2 to 4 lb.)	1/2 teaspoon salt
1 medium onion, finely chopped (1/2 cup)	1/4 teaspoon ground red pepper (cayenne)
1 medium green bell pepper, cut into thin bite-size strips	1/2 cup chicken broth
2 medium tomatoes, chopped (1-1/2 cups)	2 cups water
3 cloves garlic, minced	1-1/2 cups uncooked couscous
1 tablespoon curry powder	1 medium tart red apple, cut into cubes

1 In 4- to 5-quart Dutch oven, heat oil over medium heat. Add chicken pieces; cook about 5 minutes on each side or until browned (if necessary, cook chicken a few pieces at a time). Remove chicken from Dutch oven; set aside.

2 In same Dutch oven, cook onion and bell pepper 3 to 4 minutes, stirring occasionally, until onion begins to brown; drain. Stir in tomatoes, garlic, curry powder, thyme, salt, ground red pepper and broth. Return chicken pieces to Dutch oven. Reduce heat to low; cover and simmer 30 to 40 minutes or until juice of chicken is clear when thickest piece is cut to bone (180°F).

3 In 2-quart saucepan, heat water to boiling. Stir in couscous. Remove from heat; cover and let stand 5 minutes.

4 Stir apple into chicken mixture; simmer uncovered 2 minutes longer or until apple is hot. Fluff couscous lightly with fork before serving with chicken mixture.

NUTRITION INFORMATION PER SERVING: Calories 760 • Total Fat 31g • Saturated Fat 8g • Cholesterol 150mg • Sodium 580mg • Total Carbohydrate 64g • Dietary Fiber 6g • Protein 57g. DIETARY EXCHANGES: 3-1/2 Starch • 1/2 Other Carbohydrate • 6-1/2 Lean Meat • 2 Fat • 4 Carb Choices.

Kitchen tip

Couscous can be found near the rice section of the grocery store. It comes in a variety of flavors. For this recipe, use uncooked regular couscous.

roasted herb pork tenderloins

PREP TIME: 15 Minutes ✷ READY IN: 50 Minutes ✷ SERVINGS: 6

1/2 teaspoon garlic pepper blend	1/4 teaspoon salt
1/2 teaspoon dried rosemary leaves, crushed	2 pork tenderloins (3/4 lb. each)
1/2 teaspoon dried thyme leaves, crushed	2 teaspoons olive or vegetable oil
1/2 teaspoon paprika	

1 Heat oven to 425°F. In small bowl, mix garlic pepper blend, rosemary, thyme, paprika and salt.

2 Brush pork tenderloins with oil. Sprinkle with seasoning mixture; rub in with fingers. In ungreased shallow roasting pan, place pork tenderloins.

3 Roast 25 to 35 minutes or until pork has slight blush of pink and meat thermometer inserted in center reads 160°F. Let stand 5 minutes before slicing.

NUTRITION INFORMATION PER SERVING: Calories 160 • Total Fat 6g • Saturated Fat 1.5g • Cholesterol 70mg • Sodium 150mg • Total Carbohydrate 0g • Dietary Fiber 0g • Protein 26g. DIETARY EXCHANGES: 3-1/2 Very Lean Meat • 1 Fat.

cook's notes

If you don't have garlic pepper blend, make your own with equal parts of garlic powder and black pepper.

cheesy spinach manicotti

PREP TIME: 30 Minutes ✳ **READY IN:** 1 Hour 45 Minutes ✳ **SERVINGS:** 7

1 tablespoon olive oil	1 jar (26 oz.) tomato pasta sauce
3/4 cup chopped onion (1 large)	1 can (14.5 oz.) diced tomatoes with basil, garlic and oregano, undrained
1 clove garlic, minced	
1 bag (1 lb.) frozen cut leaf spinach	1 package (8 oz.) manicotti pasta (14 manicotti)
1/4 to 1/2 teaspoon salt	
1 cup ricotta cheese	1-1/2 cups shredded mozzarella cheese (6 oz.)
1 cup finely shredded mild Cheddar cheese (4 oz.)	

1 Heat oven to 350°F. Spray 13x9-inch (3-quart) glass baking dish with cooking spray. In 10-inch nonstick skillet, heat oil over medium-high heat. Add onion and garlic; cook 2 to 3 minutes, stirring occasionally, until tender.

2 Stir in frozen spinach; sprinkle with salt to taste. Cover; cook 5 to 6 minutes, stirring occasionally, until spinach is thawed and liquid has evaporated. Remove from heat. Stir in ricotta and Cheddar cheeses.

3 In large bowl, mix pasta sauce and tomatoes; spread about 1-1/2 cups in bottom of baking dish. With table knife, push about 1/4 cup spinach mixture into each uncooked manicotti pasta, pushing filling in from both ends. Place filled pasta diagonally over sauce in dish. Pour remaining sauce mixture over top.

4 Cover tightly with foil; bake 55 to 65 minutes or until pasta around outer edge is fork-tender. Uncover dish; sprinkle with mozzarella cheese. Bake uncovered 5 to 10 minutes longer or until cheese is melted and casserole is bubbly.

HIGH ALTITUDE (3500-6500 FT): Heat oven to 375°F.

NUTRITION INFORMATION PER SERVING: Calories 480 • Total Fat 19g • Saturated Fat 9g • Cholesterol 40mg • Sodium 1000mg • Total Carbohydrate 54g • Dietary Fiber 6g • Protein 22g. DIETARY EXCHANGES: 2 Starch • 1 Other Carbohydrate • 1 Vegetable • 2 Medium-Fat Meat • 1-1/2 Fat • 3-1/2 Carb Choices.

garlic roasted chicken and potatoes

PREP TIME: 15 Minutes ✳ **READY IN:** 55 Minutes ✳ **SERVINGS:** 8

8 boneless skinless chicken breast halves	4 to 6 garlic cloves, minced
10 to 12 small red potatoes, quartered	2 tablespoons olive oil
1 teaspoon dried rosemary leaves, crushed	1/4 cup shredded fresh Parmesan cheese (1 oz.)
1/2 teaspoon peppered seasoned salt	1/4 cup chopped fresh chives

1 Heat oven to 425°F. Arrange chicken and potatoes in ungreased 15x10x1-inch baking pan. In small bowl, combine rosemary, seasoned salt, garlic and oil; mix well. Brush over chicken and potatoes. Sprinkle with cheese.

2 Bake at 425°F for about 40 minutes or until chicken is golden brown, its juices run clear, and potatoes are light golden brown. Sprinkle with chives.

NUTRITION INFORMATION PER SERVING: Calories 340 • Total Fat 8g • Saturated Fat 2g • Cholesterol 75mg • Sodium 160mg • Total Carbohydrate 36g • Dietary Fiber 3g • Protein 31g. DIETARY EXCHANGES: 2-1/2 Starch • 2-1/2 Other Carbohydrate • 3-1/2 Very Lean Meat • 1/2 Fat.

baked sonoran chicken

READY IN: 1 Hour ✳ SERVINGS: 4

4   large boneless skinless chicken breasts
    (5 to 6 oz. each)
2   cups crispy horn-shaped corn snacks, crushed
1   can (4.5 oz.) chopped green chiles, drained
6   oz. queso fresco (Mexican cheese), cut into
    4 equal slices
    Salt and pepper, if desired
1   cup frozen whole kernel corn (from
    1-lb. bag), thawed
1   tablespoon olive oil
1/3 cup roasted red bell peppers (from 4-oz. jar)

1   cup whipping cream
1/2   cup water
2   tablespoons unsalted or regular butter or
      margarine
2   teaspoons finely chopped fresh garlic
1   chicken-flavored bouillon cube
2/3   cup uncooked regular rice
1-1/3 cups water
4   flour tortillas (10 to 12 inch)
2   tablespoons chopped fresh cilantro

1 Heat oven to 425°F. Line cookie sheet with foil. Place each chicken breast, smooth side down, between pieces of plastic wrap or waxed paper; gently pound with flat side of meat mallet or rolling pin until about 1/4 inch thick.

2 Over each chicken breast, sprinkle 1/4 cup crushed corn snacks and 1/4 of the green chiles; place 1 slice cheese in center. Fold ends of chicken over and tuck in sides; secure with toothpicks. Sprinkle with salt and pepper. Place seam side down on one side of cookie sheet. In small bowl, toss thawed corn with oil. Place corn on other side of cookie sheet. Bake 20 minutes until chicken is no longer pink in center.

3 Meanwhile, in blender, place roasted peppers, whipping cream and 1/2 cup water. Cover; blend on high speed 15 seconds or until smooth. In 2-quart saucepan, melt butter over medium heat. Add garlic; cook and stir 1 minute. Add pepper mixture and bouillon cube; heat to boiling. Cook about 15 minutes, stirring constantly, until sauce is reduced and thickened.

4 Cook rice in 1-1/3 cups water as directed on package. Remove chicken from cookie sheet; place on cutting board. Let stand 5 minutes. Cut chicken into 1/4-inch-thick slices.

5 In 12-inch skillet, heat each tortilla over high heat until blistered on each side; place on individual dinner plates. Place 1/2 cup rice on one half of each tortilla; fan slices of 1 chicken breast leaning on rice. Top chicken on each evenly with roasted pepper sauce, roasted corn and cilantro.

NUTRITION INFORMATION PER SERVING: Calories 920 • Total Fat 45g • Saturated Fat 24g • Cholesterol 180mg • Sodium 1790mg • Total Carbohydrate 80g • Dietary Fiber 4g • Protein 48g. DIETARY EXCHANGES: 4 Starch • 1 Other Carbohydrate • 5 Very Lean Meat • 8 Fat • 5 Carb Choices.

TORI JOHNSON
Gilbert, Arizona
Bake-Off® Contest 42, 2006

kitchen tip

To crush corn snacks, place in resealable food-storage plastic bag; seal bag and crush with rolling pin.

cook's notes

Don't have ground mustard on hand? You can substitute 3/4 teaspoon yellow mustard for the ground mustard.

broiled lemon-pepper salmon

READY IN: 20 Minutes ✳ SERVINGS: 4

1	salmon fillet (1 lb.)	1	teaspoon lemon-pepper seasoning
2	tablespoons salad dressing or mayonnaise	1/4	teaspoon ground mustard

1 Set oven control to broil. Spray rack in broiler pan with cooking spray. Place salmon, skin side up, on rack in pan.

2 Broil 4 to 6 inches from heat 7 minutes. Turn salmon; broil 7 to 9 minutes longer or until fish flakes easily with fork.

3 Meanwhile, in small bowl, mix remaining ingredients. Spread salad dressing mixture over salmon; broil 1 to 2 minutes longer or until topping is lightly browned and bubbly.

NUTRITION INFORMATION PER SERVING: Calories 190 • Total Fat 10g • Saturated Fat 2.5g • Cholesterol 80mg • Sodium 200mg • Total Carbohydrate 1g • Dietary Fiber 0g • Protein 24g. DIETARY EXCHANGES: 3-1/2 Very Lean Meat • 1-1/2 Fat.

roasted pork tenderloins and vegetables

PREP TIME: 20 Minutes ✳ READY IN: 1 Hour 15 Minutes ✳ SERVINGS: 6

VEGETABLES AND PORK

- 6 ears Green Giant® Nibblers® frozen corn-on-the-cob
- 3 medium-size dark-orange sweet potatoes, peeled, cut into 1-1/2-inch pieces
- 1 large onion, cut into 8 to 12 wedges
- 2 pork tenderloins (3/4 lb. each)

GLAZE

- 2/3 cup apple jelly
- 2 tablespoons vegetable oil
- 2 teaspoons ground dry mustard
- 1 teaspoon dried marjoram leaves
- 1/2 teaspoon salt
- 1/4 teaspoon pepper

GARNISH

Italian parsley, if desired

1 Heat oven to 450°F. Place corn in large bowl of warm water to partially thaw. In ungreased 15x10x1-inch pan, arrange sweet potatoes and onion around sides.

2 In 1-quart saucepan, mix glaze ingredients. Cook over low heat, stirring constantly, until melted and smooth. Brush about half of glaze over vegetables. Roast uncovered 25 minutes.

3 Remove vegetables from oven. Turn vegetables in pan. Remove corn from water; place in pan with vegetables. Place pork tenderloins in center of pan. Brush pork and all vegetables with remaining glaze.

4 Return to oven; roast uncovered 25 to 30 minutes longer or until vegetables are tender, and pork has slight blush of pink in center and meat thermometer inserted in center reads 160°F. Slice pork. Arrange pork and vegetables on platter. Garnish with Italian parsley.

HIGH ALTITUDE (3500-6500 FT): In Step 2, cook glaze ingredients over medium heat.

NUTRITION INFORMATION PER SERVING: Calories 420 • Total Fat 10g • Saturated Fat 2.5g • Cholesterol 70mg • Sodium 270mg • Total Carbohydrate 54g • Dietary Fiber 5g • Protein 29g. DIETARY EXCHANGES: 1-1/2 Starch • 2 Other Carbohydrate • 3-1/2 Very Lean Meat • 1-1/2 Fat.

cook's notes

One whole pork tenderloin is usually about 1/2 to 3/4 pound. For this recipe, 2 large or 3 small tenderloins will yield the 1-1/2 pounds necessary. There's no waste with pork tenderloin because it's very lean and tender.

Cozy Casseroles

A warm, comforting hot dish makes for a hearty meal on a winter evening, and simple baked dishes are a blessing for harried cooks during the busy holiday season.

p. 124

p. 122

p. 120

p. 131

p. 119

french onion-beef-noodle bake p. 131

pork picadillo pie

PREP TIME: 30 Minutes ✳ READY IN: 1 Hour 15 Minutes ✳ SERVINGS: 6

1 box Pillsbury® refrigerated pie crusts, softened as directed on box	1/2 cup chili sauce
1 lb. boneless pork loin, cut into 1/2-inch cubes	1/4 cup sliced pimiento-stuffed green olives
1/2 cup chopped onion (1 medium)	1/4 cup raisins
1 can (14.5 oz.) diced tomatoes, undrained	1/2 teaspoon ground cumin
1 box (9 oz.) Green Giant® Niblets® frozen whole kernel corn	1/4 teaspoon salt
1 can (4.5 oz.) Old El Paso® chopped green chiles	2 teaspoons milk
	1 tablespoon cornmeal

1 Heat oven to 425°F. Make pie crusts as directed on box for two-crust pie using 9-1/2- or 10-inch deep-dish glass pie plate.

2 Spray 12-inch skillet with cooking spray; heat over medium-high heat until hot. Add pork and onion; cook 3 to 5 minutes, stirring occasionally, until pork is no longer pink.

3 Add tomatoes, corn, green chiles, chili sauce, olives, raisins, cumin and salt. Heat to boiling. Reduce heat to medium; simmer 5 minutes, stirring occasionally, until slightly thickened. Remove from heat; cool 5 minutes.

4 Spoon mixture into crust-lined pie plate. Cut 4 wide slits or small designs in second crust; place crust over pork mixture. Seal edge and flute edge. Brush crust with milk; sprinkle with cornmeal.

5 Bake 25 to 35 minutes or until deep golden brown. Cover crust edge with 2- to 3-inch-wide strips of foil after 10 to 15 minutes of baking to prevent excessive browning. Let pie stand 5 to 10 minutes before serving.

HIGH ALTITUDE (3500-6500 FT): In Step 3, add 1 tablespoon all-purpose flour with the other ingredients.

NUTRITION INFORMATION PER SERVING: Calories 550 • Total Fat 26g • Saturated Fat 9g • Cholesterol 60mg • Sodium 1240mg • Total Carbohydrate 59g • Dietary Fiber 4g • Protein 20g. DIETARY EXCHANGES: 2-1/2 Starch • 1 Other Carbohydrate • 1 Vegetable • 1-1/2 Lean Meat • 4 Fat • 4 Carb Choices.

cheesy mexican bubble bake

PREP TIME: 10 Minutes ✳ READY IN: 40 Minutes ✳ SERVINGS: 8

1 container (18 oz.) refrigerated taco sauce with seasoned ground beef or shredded chicken	1 cup shredded Cheddar-Monterey Jack cheese blend (4 oz.)
1 can (16.3 oz.) Pillsbury® Grands!® homestyle refrigerated buttermilk biscuits or 1 can (17.3 oz.) Pillsbury® Grands!® refrigerated golden corn biscuits	1/2 cup Old El Paso® thick 'n chunky salsa
	Shredded lettuce, chopped tomatoes, sour cream, sliced ripe olives and/or green onions, if desired

1 Heat oven to 375°F. Microwave ground beef as directed on container. Spoon into ungreased 13x9-inch (3-quart) glass baking dish.

2 Separate dough into 8 biscuits. Cut each into 8 pieces; add to ground beef in dish. With rubber spatula, stir gently until pieces are coated; spread evenly.

3 Bake about 20 minutes or until sauce is bubbly and biscuits are golden brown. Sprinkle cheese over top; bake 5 to 10 minutes longer or until cheese is bubbly. Top individual servings with salsa and desired toppings.

NUTRITION INFORMATION PER SERVING: Calories 330 • Total Fat 19g • Saturated Fat 8g • Cholesterol 30mg • Sodium 1270mg • Total Carbohydrate 31g • Dietary Fiber 0g • Protein 10g. DIETARY EXCHANGES: 2 Starch • 1/2 Lean Meat • 3 Fat • 2 Carb Choices.

three-cheese rotini bake

PREP TIME: 25 Minutes ❋ **READY IN:** 50 Minutes ❋ **SERVINGS:** 4

3 cups uncooked rainbow rotini (spiral pasta) (8 oz.)

3 tablespoons margarine or butter

1 garlic clove, minced

1/4 cup all-purpose flour

1/4 teaspoon pepper

2 cups milk

1 cup shredded American cheese (4 oz.)

1 cup shredded mozzarella cheese (4 oz.)

1/4 cup crumbled blue cheese (1 oz.)

1 Heat oven to 350°F. Spray 2-quart casserole with nonstick cooking spray. Cook rotini as directed on package. Drain.

2 Meanwhile, melt margarine in large saucepan over medium heat. Add garlic; cook and stir 30 to 60 seconds. Stir in flour and pepper; cook and stir until mixture is bubbly. Gradually add milk, stirring constantly, until mixture boils and thickens. Remove from heat. Reserve 1 tablespoon each American and mozzarella cheese for top. Add remaining cheeses to sauce; stir until melted.

3 Add cooked rotini to cheese sauce; stir gently to coat. Pour into sprayed casserole. Sprinkle with reserved cheeses. Bake at 350°F for 20 to 25 minutes or until bubbly around edges.

NUTRITION INFORMATION PER SERVING: Calories 595 • Total Fat 28g • Saturated Fat 13g • Cholesterol 55mg • Sodium 830mg • Total Carbohydrate 58g • Dietary Fiber 2g • Protein 28g. DIETARY EXCHANGES: 3 Starch • 1 Low-Fat Milk • 2 High-Fat Meat • 2 Fat • 4 Carb Choices.

cook's notes

This recipe easily adapts to your favorite cheese. Instead of American and mozzarella, try Cheddar, Swiss, Colby, Asiago, fontina or provolone.

KAREN HALL
Minneapolis, Minnesota
Bake-Off® Contest 40, 2002

cook's notes

For a milder tasting enchilada pie, substitute two 10-ounce cans of mild enchilada sauce instead of the 19-ounce can of hot enchilada sauce.

speedy layered chicken enchilada pie

PREP TIME: 25 Minutes ✸ **READY IN:** 1 Hour 10 Minutes ✸ **SERVINGS:** 6

1 package (11.5 oz.) Old El Paso® flour tortillas for burritos (8 tortillas)

2 cups cubed cooked chicken

1/2 cup uncooked instant rice

2 cups shredded reduced-fat Monterey Jack cheese (8 oz.)

1 can (15 oz.) black beans, rinsed and drained

1 can (19 oz.) Old El Paso® hot enchilada sauce

1 cup Green Giant® frozen shoepeg white corn, thawed

1 cup Old El Paso® thick 'n chunky salsa

2 tablespoons thinly sliced green onions (2 medium)

Reduced-fat sour cream, if desired

Chopped green onions, if desired

1 Heat oven to 350°F. Spray 9-inch round (2-quart) glass baking dish or casserole with cooking spray. Cut 5 of the tortillas in half. Cut remaining tortillas into 2-1/2-inch wide strips.

2 In large bowl, mix chicken, rice, 1 cup of the cheese, the beans and 1 cup of the enchilada sauce.

3 Layer 4 tortilla halves in bottom of baking dish. Top with 1/4 cup enchilada sauce and half of the chicken mixture. Top with 2 tortilla halves; fill in empty spaces with 3 tortilla strips. Spoon corn over tortillas. Spread salsa over corn. Layer with 2 tortilla halves and 3 strips. Top with remaining half of chicken mixture. Continue layering with remaining 2 tortilla halves and strips, enchilada sauce, cheese and 2 tablespoons green onions.

4 Bake uncovered 35 to 45 minutes or until mixture is thoroughly heated and cheese is melted. Cool 5 minutes. Top with sour cream and chopped green onions.

HIGH ALTITUDE (3500-6500 FT): Heat oven to 375°F. In Step 3, do not add remaining cheese to top of casserole. Bake uncovered 40 to 50 minutes, adding cheese during the last 5 minutes.

NUTRITION INFORMATION PER SERVING: Calories 570 • Total Fat 19g • Saturated Fat 8g • Cholesterol 65mg • Sodium 1490mg • Total Carbohydrate 66g • Dietary Fiber 5g • Protein 33g. DIETARY EXCHANGES: 3-1/2 Starch • 1 Other Carbohydrate • 3 Lean Meat • 1-1/2 Fat • 4-1/2 Carb Choices.

easy chicken with rice casserole

PREP TIME: 15 Minutes ✸ **READY IN:** 2 Hours 15 Minutes ✸ **SERVINGS:** 5

1 cup uncooked regular long-grain white rice

1 can (10-3/4 oz.) condensed cream of celery soup

1 can (10-3/4 oz.) condensed cream of chicken with herbs soup

1-1/2 cups water

5 bone-in chicken breast halves with skin

2 tablespoons butter or margarine, melted

1 teaspoon paprika

1 Heat oven to 325°F. Spray 13x9-inch (3-quart) glass baking dish with cooking spray. In large bowl, mix uncooked rice, both soups and water; pour into baking dish.

2 Arrange chicken, skin side up, over rice mixture. Brush chicken with melted butter; drizzle with any remaining butter. Sprinkle with paprika. Cover tightly with foil.

3 Bake 1-1/2 hours. Uncover; bake 20 to 30 minutes longer or until chicken is fork-tender, its juices run clear and skin is slightly crisp.

NUTRITION INFORMATION PER SERVING: Calories 475 • Total Fat 20g • Saturated Fat 7g • Cholesterol 90mg • Sodium 970mg • Total Carbohydrate 42g • Dietary Fiber 1g • Protein 32g. DIETARY EXCHANGES: 3 Starch • 3 Lean Meat • 2 Fat • 3 Carb Choices.

speedy layered chicken enchilada pie

cheeseburger biscuit pie

PREP TIME: 25 Minutes ✱ READY IN: 45 Minutes ✱ SERVINGS: 6

1   can (12 oz.) Pillsbury® Grands!® Jr. golden homestyle buttermilk biscuits

1   lb. lean (at least 80%) ground beef

1/4   cup chopped onion (1/2 medium)

1/3   cup ketchup

3   tablespoons yellow mustard

1/4   teaspoon salt

1/4   teaspoon pepper

7   slices (3/4 oz. each) American cheese

1   Heat oven to 400°F. Grease 9-inch pie pan with shortening. Separate dough into 10 biscuits. Press 6 biscuits in bottom and up side of pie pan to form crust. Cut remaining 4 biscuits into quarters; set aside.

2   In 10-inch skillet, cook ground beef and onion over medium heat, stirring frequently, until beef is thoroughly cooked; drain. Stir in ketchup, mustard, salt and pepper. Cook uncovered until bubbly. Spoon into biscuit-lined pan.

3   Arrange cheese slices on top of beef mixture. Place biscuit quarters, point side down, around edge of hot beef mixture. Bake 15 to 17 minutes or until biscuits are golden brown.

NUTRITION INFORMATION PER SERVING: Calories 410 • Total Fat 22g • Saturated Fat 9g • Cholesterol 70mg • Sodium 1340mg • Total Carbohydrate 28g • Dietary Fiber 0g • Protein 22g. DIETARY EXCHANGES: 1-1/2 Starch • 1/2 Other Carbohydrate • 2-1/2 Lean Meat • 2-1/2 Fat.

deep-dish turkey pie

PREP TIME: 20 Minutes ✳ **READY IN:** 1 Hour 20 Minutes ✳ **SERVINGS:** 6

2 tablespoons butter or margarine
1/4 cup chopped celery
1/4 cup chopped onion (1/2 medium)
1 can (10-3/4 oz.) condensed cream of chicken soup
1 cup milk
1/2 teaspoon poultry seasoning

1/4 teaspoon salt
1/4 teaspoon pepper
4 cups cubed cooked turkey or chicken
1 bag frozen broccoli, carrots and cauliflower, thawed, drained
1 Pillsbury® refrigerated pie crust, softened as directed on box

1 Heat oven to 400°F. In 3-quart saucepan or Dutch oven, melt butter over medium heat. Add celery and onion; cook and stir until tender. Stir in soup, milk, poultry seasoning, salt and pepper. Cook until thoroughly heated.

2 Gently stir in turkey and thawed vegetables. Pour into ungreased 2-quart casserole or 10-inch quiche pan.

3 Remove pie crust from pouch; unroll crust on work surface. Place crust over turkey mixture. Roll up edges of crust to fit top of casserole; flute edges. Cut slits in several places in crust. Bake 40 to 50 minutes or until golden brown. Let stand 10 minutes before serving.

NUTRITION INFORMATION PER SERVING: Calories 450 • Total Fat 24g • Saturated Fat 10g • Cholesterol 105mg • Sodium 760mg • Total Carbohydrate 29g • Dietary Fiber 3g • Protein 32g. DIETARY EXCHANGES: 1-1/2 Starch • 1 Vegetable • 3-1/2 Lean Meat • 2-1/2 Fat • 2 Carb Choices.

p
fro   uen.
Remove the bones and skin, and cut up.

chicken-biscuit bake

PREP TIME: 20 Minutes ✳ **READY IN:** 1 Hour ✳ **SERVINGS:** 8

2 cans (10-3/4 oz. each) condensed cream of chicken soup
1 cup milk
1/2 teaspoon dried thyme leaves
1/4 teaspoon pepper

4 cups cut-up cooked chicken
1 bag (1 lb.) frozen broccoli, carrots & cauliflower
1 can (16.3 oz.) Pillsbury® Grands!® homestyle refrigerated buttermilk biscuits

1 Heat oven to 350°F. In 4-quart saucepan, heat soup, milk, thyme, pepper, chicken and vegetables to boiling over medium-high heat, stirring occasionally. Boil and stir 3 to 5 minutes. Spread in ungreased 13x9-inch (3-quart) glass baking dish.

2 Separate dough into 8 biscuits; place evenly over hot chicken mixture. Bake 35 to 40 minutes or until biscuits are golden brown and no longer doughy on bottom. After 20 minutes, cover with foil if necessary to prevent excessive browning.

HIGH ALTITUDE (3500-6500 FT): Bake 40 to 45 minutes.

NUTRITION INFORMATION PER SERVING: Calories 420 • Total Fat 19g • Saturated Fat 6g • Cholesterol 70mg • Sodium 1230mg • Total Carbohydrate 35g • Dietary Fiber 2g • Protein 28g. DIETARY EXCHANGES: 1-1/2 Starch • 1/2 Other Carbohydrate • 1 Vegetable • 3 Lean Meat • 2 Fat • 2 Carb Choices.

kitchen tip

When using refrigerated biscuit dough as a topping on a casserole, be sure the mixture under the biscuits is hot, or the bottoms of the biscuits may not bake completely.

southwest nacho casserole

PREP TIME: 20 Minutes ✳ READY IN: 1 Hour 10 Minutes ✳ SERVINGS: 10

2 lb. lean (at least 80%) ground beef

1 cup water

2 packages (1 oz. each) Old El Paso® 40% less-sodium taco seasoning mix

1 can (4.5 oz.) Old El Paso® chopped green chiles

2 cans (16 oz. each) Old El Paso® fat-free refried beans

2 cups shredded reduced-fat Cheddar cheese (8 oz.)

1 cup chopped tomato (1 large)

1/2 cup chopped green onions (8 medium)

1 can (2.25 oz.) sliced ripe olives, drained

1 bag (12 oz.) gold tortilla chips (extra thick)

Sour cream, if desired

1 Heat oven to 350°F. Spray 13x9-inch (3-quart) glass baking dish with cooking spray. In 12-inch nonstick skillet, cook beef over medium-high heat, stirring frequently, until thoroughly cooked; drain.

2 Stir in water and taco seasoning mix. Heat to boiling; cook 2 to 4 minutes, stirring occasionally, until thickened. Stir in chiles.

3 Spread refried beans in baking dish. Top with beef mixture. Cover tightly with foil. Bake 30 to 40 minutes or until bubbly around edges.

4 Uncover; sprinkle with cheese, tomato, onions and olives. Arrange 18 to 20 tortilla chips around outside edges of baking dish. Bake uncovered about 10 minutes longer or until cheese is melted. If desired, top with sour cream. Serve with remaining tortilla chips for scooping.

NUTRITION INFORMATION PER SERVING: Calories 480 • Total Fat 21g • Saturated Fat 6g • Cholesterol 60mg • Sodium 1480mg • Total Carbohydrate 44g • Dietary Fiber 7g • Protein 29g. DIETARY EXCHANGES: 3 Starch • 3 Medium-Fat Meat • 1/2 Fat • 3 Carb Choices.

make-ahead philly beef strata

PREP TIME: 20 Minutes ✴ READY IN: 9 Hours 20 Minutes ✴ SERVINGS: 8

7 cups French bread cubes (1 inch)	8 eggs
1 bag (1 lb.) frozen bell pepper and onion stir-fry	2-1/4 cups milk
1/2 lb. thinly sliced cooked roast beef (from deli), cut into bite-sized strips (1-1/2 cups)	2 tablespoons Dijon mustard
	1/2 teaspoon salt
2 cups shredded Monterey Jack cheese (8 oz.)	1/2 teaspoon pepper

Use a sourdough bread, instead of bread if you prefer. We feel day-old bread works best.

1 Spray 13x9-inch (3-quart) glass baking dish or 3-quart oval casserole with cooking spray. Spread 1/3 of the bread cubes in baking dish. Top evenly with 1/3 of the bell pepper and onion stir-fry and 1/3 of the beef. Sprinkle with 1/3 of the cheese. Repeat layers twice, ending with cheese.

2 In large bowl, beat eggs. Stir in all remaining ingredients; pour evenly over cheese. Cover tightly with foil; refrigerate at least 8 hours or overnight.

3 When ready to bake, heat oven to 350°F. Uncover baking dish; bake 40 to 50 minutes or until puffed, top is golden brown and center is set. Let stand 10 minutes before serving.

HIGH ALTITUDE (3500-6500 FT): Spray sheet of foil with cooking spray; cover baking dish with foil, sprayed side down. Bake covered at 350°F 30 minutes. Uncover; bake 20 to 30 minutes longer or until top is golden brown and center is set.

NUTRITION INFORMATION PER SERVING: Calories 350 • Total Fat 17g • Saturated Fat 8g • Cholesterol 255mg • Sodium 960mg • Total Carbohydrate 25g • Dietary Fiber 1g • Protein 24g. DIETARY EXCHANGES: 1-1/2 Starch • 3 Medium-Fat Meat • 1/2 Fat • 1-1/2 Carb Choices.

...ny robust bread, such as
...baguette or Italian
...the French
...hat

warm-up beef pot pie

...0 Minutes ✳ **READY IN:** 1 Hour 20 Minutes ✳ **SERVINGS:** 6

...age Pillsbury® refrigerated pie crusts,
...ened as directed on package

...boneless beef sirloin steak, cut into
...2-inch cubes

...all onions, cut into thin wedges

...ups peeled baking potato cubes (3/4 inch)

...up cut (1x1/2x1/2-inch) carrot

...up Green Giant® frozen sweet peas

...jar (4.5 oz.) Green Giant® whole
...mushrooms, drained

1 jar (12 oz.) brown gravy

2 tablespoons cornstarch

1/2 teaspoon dried thyme leaves

1/2 teaspoon salt

1/4 teaspoon pepper

1 egg yolk

2 teaspoons water

1 teaspoon sesame seed

Serve wedges of this ...

pot pie with a tossed green

salad or a fruit-flavored gelatin

salad on lettuce leaves.

1 Heat oven to 425°F. Prepare pie crusts as directed on package for two-crust pie using 9-inch
glass pie pan.

2 In large nonstick skillet, cook beef and onions over medium-high heat for 4 to 6 minutes or
until beef is browned, stirring frequently. Stir in potatoes, carrot, peas and mushrooms.

3 In small bowl, combine gravy, cornstarch, thyme, salt and pepper; mix well. Stir into beef mixture;
cook until thoroughly heated. Pour mixture into crust-lined pan. Top with second crust; seal
edges and flute. Cut small slits in several places in top crust.

4 In another small bowl, combine egg yolk and water; blend well. Brush top crust with egg mixture;
sprinkle with sesame seed.

5 Bake at 425°F for 30 to 40 minutes or until crust is golden brown and filling is bubbly. Cover
edge of crust with strips of foil after first 15 to 20 minutes of baking to prevent excessive
browning. Cool 10 minutes before serving.

NUTRITION INFORMATION PER SERVING: Calories 490 • Total Fat 23g • Saturated Fat 9g • Cholesterol 85mg • Sodium 880mg • Total
Carbohydrate 53g • Dietary Fiber 3g • Protein 17g. DIETARY EXCHANGES: 3-1/2 Starch • 3-1/2 Other Carbohydrate • 1 Lean Meat • 3-1/2 Fat.

special touch

Add happy faces to some of the

biscuit circles. Cut smiling

mouths and eye shapes from

slices of American cheese.

Arrange the cheese "faces" on

the biscuits during the last five

minutes of baking.

biscuit-topped chili casserole

PREP TIME: 20 Minutes ✳ **READY IN:** 50 Minutes ✳ **SERVINGS:** 8

2 tablespoons olive oil

1 small onion, chopped

1/2 cup chopped green bell pepper

2 cans (15 oz. each) vegetarian chili with beans

1 can (28 oz.) diced tomatoes, drained

1 can (15 to 19 oz.) Progresso® black beans,
drained

2 teaspoons chili powder

1 can (16.3 oz.) Pillsbury® Grands!®
refrigerated buttermilk biscuits

1 Heat oven to 350°F. Spray 13x9-inch (3-quart) glass baking dish with cooking spray. In 12-inch
skillet, heat oil over medium-high heat. Add onion and bell pepper; cook 3 to 5 minutes, stirring
constantly, until vegetables are tender. Add chili, tomatoes, black beans and chili powder; mix well.
Cook 5 to 7 minutes, stirring occasionally, until bubbly. Pour mixture into baking dish.

2 Separate dough into 8 biscuits. Cut each biscuit in half; arrange in single layer over top of
mixture. Bake 22 to 29 minutes or until biscuits are deep golden brown.

NUTRITION INFORMATION PER SERVING: Calories 400 • Total Fat 12g • Saturated Fat 3g • Cholesterol 0mg • Sodium 1290mg • Total
Carbohydrate 60g • Dietary Fiber 9g • Protein 13g. DIETARY EXCHANGES: 2-1/2 Starch • 1 Fruit • 3-1/2 Other Carbohydrate • 1 Vegetable •
1/2 Very Lean Meat • 2 Fat.

broccoli-cauliflower tetrazzini

PREP TIME: 30 Minutes ✳ READY IN: 50 Minutes ✳ SERVINGS: 8

BARBARA VAN ITALLIE
Poughkeepsie, New York
Bake-Off® Contest 33, 1988

- 8 oz. uncooked spaghetti, broken into thirds
- 1 bag (1 lb.) frozen broccoli, carrots & cauliflower or 4 cups frozen cut broccoli
- 2 tablespoons butter or margarine
- 3 tablespoons Pillsbury Best® all-purpose flour

- 2 cups fat-free (skim) milk
- 1/2 cup grated Parmesan cheese
  Dash pepper
- 1 jar (4.5 oz.) sliced mushrooms, drained
- 2 tablespoons grated Parmesan cheese

1 Cook spaghetti as directed on package. Drain; rinse with hot water. Cover to keep warm; set aside. Cook vegetables until crisp-tender as directed on bag; drain.

2 Meanwhile, heat oven to 400°F. Grease 13x9-inch (3-quart) glass baking dish. In 2-quart saucepan, melt butter over medium heat. Stir in flour until smooth. Gradually add milk, cooking and stirring until well blended. Cook 6 to 10 minutes or until mixture boils and thickens, stirring constantly. Stir in 1/2 cup Parmesan cheese and the pepper.

3 Spoon cooked spaghetti into baking dish. Top with cooked vegetables and sliced mushrooms. Pour milk mixture over mushrooms. Sprinkle with 2 tablespoons Parmesan cheese. Bake 15 to 20 minutes or until mixture bubbles around edges and is hot.

HIGH ALTITUDE (3500-6500 FT): Bake 20 to 30 minutes.

NUTRITION INFORMATION PER SERVING: Calories 240 • Total Fat 6g • Saturated Fat 3.5g • Cholesterol 15mg • Sodium 350mg • Total Carbohydrate 34g • Dietary Fiber 3g • Protein 12g. DIETARY EXCHANGES: 2 Starch • 1 Vegetable • 1/2 Lean Meat • 1/2 Fat • 2 Carb Choices.

cook's notes

When cooking the spaghetti, carefully hold in boiling water and ease into the water. As it softens, push it around the edge of the pan. When the spaghetti is fully immersed in the water, stir it to separate the strands.

night-before taco bake

deep-dish turkey pie

PREP TIME: 20 Minutes ✹ READY IN: 1 Hour 20 Minutes ✹ SERVINGS: 6

- 2 tablespoons butter or margarine
- 1/4 cup chopped celery
- 1/4 cup chopped onion (1/2 medium)
- 1 can (10-3/4 oz.) condensed cream of chicken soup
- 1 cup milk
- 1/2 teaspoon poultry seasoning

- 1/4 teaspoon salt
- 1/4 teaspoon pepper
- 4 cups cubed cooked turkey or chicken
- 1 bag frozen broccoli, carrots and cauliflower, thawed, drained
- 1 Pillsbury® refrigerated pie crust, softened as directed on box

1 Heat oven to 400°F. In 3-quart saucepan or Dutch oven, melt butter over medium heat. Add celery and onion; cook and stir until tender. Stir in soup, milk, poultry seasoning, salt and pepper. Cook until thoroughly heated.

2 Gently stir in turkey and thawed vegetables. Pour into ungreased 2-quart casserole or 10-inch quiche pan.

3 Remove pie crust from pouch; unroll crust on work surface. Place crust over turkey mixture. Roll up edges of crust to fit top of casserole; flute edges. Cut slits in several places in crust. Bake 40 to 50 minutes or until golden brown. Let stand 10 minutes before serving.

NUTRITION INFORMATION PER SERVING: Calories 450 • Total Fat 24g • Saturated Fat 10g • Cholesterol 105mg • Sodium 760mg • Total Carbohydrate 29g • Dietary Fiber 3g • Protein 32g. DIETARY EXCHANGES: 1-1/2 Starch • 1 Vegetable • 3-1/2 Lean Meat • 2-1/2 Fat • 2 Carb Choices.

chicken-biscuit bake

PREP TIME: 20 Minutes ✹ READY IN: 1 Hour ✹ SERVINGS: 8

- 2 cans (10-3/4 oz. each) condensed cream of chicken soup
- 1 cup milk
- 1/2 teaspoon dried thyme leaves
- 1/4 teaspoon pepper

- 4 cups cut-up cooked chicken
- 1 bag (1 lb.) frozen broccoli, carrots & cauliflower
- 1 can (16.3 oz.) Pillsbury® Grands!® homestyle refrigerated buttermilk biscuits

1 Heat oven to 350°F. In 4-quart saucepan, heat soup, milk, thyme, pepper, chicken and vegetables to boiling over medium-high heat, stirring occasionally. Boil and stir 3 to 5 minutes. Spread in ungreased 13x9-inch (3-quart) glass baking dish.

2 Separate dough into 8 biscuits; place evenly over hot chicken mixture. Bake 35 to 40 minutes or until biscuits are golden brown and no longer doughy on bottom. After 20 minutes, cover with foil if necessary to prevent excessive browning.

HIGH ALTITUDE (3500-6500 FT): Bake 40 to 45 minutes.

NUTRITION INFORMATION PER SERVING: Calories 420 • Total Fat 19g • Saturated Fat 6g • Cholesterol 70mg • Sodium 1230mg • Total Carbohydrate 35g • Dietary Fiber 2g • Protein 28g. DIETARY EXCHANGES: 1-1/2 Starch • 1/2 Other Carbohydrate • 1 Vegetable • 3 Lean Meat • 2 Fat • 2 Carb Choices.

---

cook's notes

If you choose to use cooked chicken for this homey pot pie, purchase a rotisserie chicken from the grocery store deli. Remove the bones and skin, and cut up.

kitchen tip

When using refrigerated biscuit dough as a topping on a casserole, be sure the mixture under the biscuits is hot, or the bottoms of the biscuits may not bake completely.

southwest nacho casserole

PREP TIME: 20 Minutes ✳ READY IN: 1 Hour 10 Minutes ✳ SERVINGS: 10

2 lb. lean (at least 80%) ground beef

1 cup water

2 packages (1 oz. each) Old El Paso® 40% less-sodium taco seasoning mix

1 can (4.5 oz.) Old El Paso® chopped green chiles

2 cans (16 oz. each) Old El Paso® fat-free refried beans

2 cups shredded reduced-fat Cheddar cheese (8 oz.)

1 cup chopped tomato (1 large)

1/2 cup chopped green onions (8 medium)

1 can (2.25 oz.) sliced ripe olives, drained

1 bag (12 oz.) gold tortilla chips (extra thick)

Sour cream, if desired

1 Heat oven to 350°F. Spray 13x9-inch (3-quart) glass baking dish with cooking spray. In 12-inch nonstick skillet, cook beef over medium-high heat, stirring frequently, until thoroughly cooked; drain.

2 Stir in water and taco seasoning mix. Heat to boiling; cook 2 to 4 minutes, stirring occasionally, until thickened. Stir in chiles.

3 Spread refried beans in baking dish. Top with beef mixture. Cover tightly with foil. Bake 30 to 40 minutes or until bubbly around edges.

4 Uncover; sprinkle with cheese, tomato, onions and olives. Arrange 18 to 20 tortilla chips around outside edges of baking dish. Bake uncovered about 10 minutes longer or until cheese is melted. If desired, top with sour cream. Serve with remaining tortilla chips for scooping.

NUTRITION INFORMATION PER SERVING: Calories 480 • Total Fat 21g • Saturated Fat 6g • Cholesterol 60mg • Sodium 1480mg • Total Carbohydrate 44g • Dietary Fiber 7g • Protein 29g. DIETARY EXCHANGES: 3 Starch • 3 Medium-Fat Meat • 1/2 Fat • 3 Carb Choices.

make-ahead philly beef strata

PREP TIME: 20 Minutes ✳ READY IN: 9 Hours 20 Minutes ✳ SERVINGS: 8

7	cups French bread cubes (1 inch)		8	eggs
1	bag (1 lb.) frozen bell pepper and onion stir-fry	2-1/4	cups milk
1/2	lb. thinly sliced cooked roast beef (from deli), cut into bite-sized strips (1-1/2 cups)		2	tablespoons Dijon mustard
		1/2	teaspoon salt
2	cups shredded Monterey Jack cheese (8 oz.)		1/2	teaspoon pepper

cook's notes

Use any robust bread, such as a sourdough baguette or Italian bread, instead of the French bread if you prefer. We feel that day-old bread works best.

1 Spray 13x9-inch (3-quart) glass baking dish or 3-quart oval casserole with cooking spray. Spread 1/3 of the bread cubes in baking dish. Top evenly with 1/3 of the bell pepper and onion stir-fry and 1/3 of the beef. Sprinkle with 1/3 of the cheese. Repeat layers twice, ending with cheese.

2 In large bowl, beat eggs. Stir in all remaining ingredients; pour evenly over cheese. Cover tightly with foil; refrigerate at least 8 hours or overnight.

3 When ready to bake, heat oven to 350°F. Uncover baking dish; bake 40 to 50 minutes or until puffed, top is golden brown and center is set. Let stand 10 minutes before serving.

HIGH ALTITUDE (3500-6500 FT): Spray sheet of foil with cooking spray; cover baking dish with foil, sprayed side down. Bake covered at 350°F 30 minutes. Uncover; bake 20 to 30 minutes longer or until top is golden brown and center is set.

NUTRITION INFORMATION PER SERVING: Calories 350 • Total Fat 17g • Saturated Fat 8g • Cholesterol 255mg • Sodium 960mg • Total Carbohydrate 25g • Dietary Fiber 1g • Protein 24g. DIETARY EXCHANGES: 1-1/2 Starch • 3 Medium-Fat Meat • 1/2 Fat • 1-1/2 Carb Choices.

winter warm-up beef pot pie

PREP TIME: 40 Minutes ✱ READY IN: 1 Hour 20 Minutes ✱ SERVINGS: 6

1 package Pillsbury® refrigerated pie crusts, softened as directed on package	1 jar (12 oz.) brown gravy
3/4 lb. boneless beef sirloin steak, cut into 1/2-inch cubes	2 tablespoons cornstarch
2 small onions, cut into thin wedges	1/2 teaspoon dried thyme leaves
1-1/2 cups peeled baking potato cubes (3/4 inch)	1/2 teaspoon salt
3/4 cup cut (1x1/2x1/2-inch) carrot	1/4 teaspoon pepper
1/2 cup Green Giant® frozen sweet peas	1 egg yolk
1 jar (4.5 oz.) Green Giant® whole mushrooms, drained	2 teaspoons water
	1 teaspoon sesame seed

1 Heat oven to 425°F. Prepare pie crusts as directed on package for two-crust pie using 9-inch glass pie pan.

2 In large nonstick skillet, cook beef and onions over medium-high heat for 4 to 6 minutes or until beef is browned, stirring frequently. Stir in potatoes, carrot, peas and mushrooms.

3 In small bowl, combine gravy, cornstarch, thyme, salt and pepper; mix well. Stir into beef mixture; cook until thoroughly heated. Pour mixture into crust-lined pan. Top with second crust; seal edges and flute. Cut small slits in several places in top crust.

4 In another small bowl, combine egg yolk and water; blend well. Brush top crust with egg mixture; sprinkle with sesame seed.

5 Bake at 425°F for 30 to 40 minutes or until crust is golden brown and filling is bubbly. Cover edge of crust with strips of foil after first 15 to 20 minutes of baking to prevent excessive browning. Cool 10 minutes before serving.

NUTRITION INFORMATION PER SERVING: Calories 490 • Total Fat 23g • Saturated Fat 9g • Cholesterol 85mg • Sodium 880mg • Total Carbohydrate 53g • Dietary Fiber 3g • Protein 17g. DIETARY EXCHANGES: 3-1/2 Starch • 3-1/2 Other Carbohydrate • 1 Lean Meat • 3-1/2 Fat.

biscuit-topped chili casserole

PREP TIME: 20 Minutes ✱ READY IN: 50 Minutes ✱ SERVINGS: 8

2 tablespoons olive oil	1 can (15 to 19 oz.) Progresso® black beans, drained
1 small onion, chopped	2 teaspoons chili powder
1/2 cup chopped green bell pepper	1 can (16.3 oz.) Pillsbury® Grands!® refrigerated buttermilk biscuits
2 cans (15 oz. each) vegetarian chili with beans	
1 can (28 oz.) diced tomatoes, drained	

1 Heat oven to 350°F. Spray 13x9-inch (3-quart) glass baking dish with cooking spray. In 12-inch skillet, heat oil over medium-high heat. Add onion and bell pepper; cook 3 to 5 minutes, stirring constantly, until vegetables are tender. Add chili, tomatoes, black beans and chili powder; mix well. Cook 5 to 7 minutes, stirring occasionally, until bubbly. Pour mixture into baking dish.

2 Separate dough into 8 biscuits. Cut each biscuit in half; arrange in single layer over top of mixture. Bake 22 to 29 minutes or until biscuits are deep golden brown.

NUTRITION INFORMATION PER SERVING: Calories 400 • Total Fat 12g • Saturated Fat 3g • Cholesterol 0mg • Sodium 1290mg • Total Carbohydrate 60g • Dietary Fiber 9g • Protein 13g. DIETARY EXCHANGES: 2-1/2 Starch • 1 Fruit • 3-1/2 Other Carbohydrate • 1 Vegetable • 1/2 Very Lean Meat • 2 Fat.

broccoli-cauliflower tetrazzini

PREP TIME: 30 Minutes ✷ **READY IN:** 50 Minutes ✷ **SERVINGS:** 8

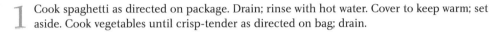

8 oz. uncooked spaghetti, broken into thirds

1 bag (1 lb.) frozen broccoli, carrots & cauliflower or 4 cups frozen cut broccoli

2 tablespoons butter or margarine

3 tablespoons Pillsbury Best® all-purpose flour

2 cups fat-free (skim) milk

1/2 cup grated Parmesan cheese
   Dash pepper

1 jar (4.5 oz.) sliced mushrooms, drained

2 tablespoons grated Parmesan cheese

1 Cook spaghetti as directed on package. Drain; rinse with hot water. Cover to keep warm; set aside. Cook vegetables until crisp-tender as directed on bag; drain.

2 Meanwhile, heat oven to 400°F. Grease 13x9-inch (3-quart) glass baking dish. In 2-quart saucepan, melt butter over medium heat. Stir in flour until smooth. Gradually add milk, cooking and stirring until well blended. Cook 6 to 10 minutes or until mixture boils and thickens, stirring constantly. Stir in 1/2 cup Parmesan cheese and the pepper.

3 Spoon cooked spaghetti into baking dish. Top with cooked vegetables and sliced mushrooms. Pour milk mixture over mushrooms. Sprinkle with 2 tablespoons Parmesan cheese. Bake 15 to 20 minutes or until mixture bubbles around edges and is hot.

HIGH ALTITUDE (3500-6500 FT): Bake 20 to 30 minutes.

NUTRITION INFORMATION PER SERVING: Calories 240 • Total Fat 6g • Saturated Fat 3.5g • Cholesterol 15mg • Sodium 350mg • Total Carbohydrate 34g • Dietary Fiber 3g • Protein 12g. DIETARY EXCHANGES: 2 Starch • 1 Vegetable • 1/2 Lean Meat • 1/2 Fat • 2 Carb Choices.

BARBARA VAN ITALLIE
Poughkeepsie, New York
Bake-Off® Contest 33, 1988

cook's notes

When cooking the spaghetti, carefully hold in boiling water and ease into the water. As it softens, push it around the edge of the pan. When the spaghetti is fully immersed in the water, stir it to separate the strands.

night-before taco bake

night-before taco bake

PREP TIME: 20 Minutes ✳ READY IN: 4 Hours 50 Minutes ✳ SERVINGS: 8

- 1 lb. lean (at least 80%) ground beef
- 2 cups frozen bell pepper and onion stir-fry (from 16-oz. bag)
- 1 can (11 oz.) Green Giant® super sweet yellow and white corn
- 1 can (4.5 oz.) Old El Paso® chopped green chiles

- 1 package (1 oz.) Old El Paso® 40% less-sodium taco seasoning mix
- 1 jar (8 oz.) Old El Paso® taco sauce
- 3 cups coarsely broken white corn chips (about 5 oz.)
- 2 cups shredded Mexican cheese blend (8 oz.)

1 Spray 12x8-inch (2-quart) glass baking dish and sheet of foil (large enough to cover dish) with cooking spray. In 12-inch nonstick skillet, cook ground beef over medium-high heat, stirring frequently, until thoroughly cooked; drain.

2 Stir in the bell pepper and onion stir-fry, corn, chiles and taco seasoning mix. Cook 5 minutes, stirring frequently, until the bell peppers and onions are tender. Stir in taco sauce. Remove from heat.

3 Spoon half of beef mixture evenly in bottom of baking dish. Cover with 2 cups of the chips. Sprinkle 3/4 cup of the cheese over chips. Spoon remaining half of beef mixture evenly over cheese. Sprinkle with 1 cup cheese. Top evenly with remaining 1 cup chips. Cover baking dish tightly with foil, sprayed side down. Refrigerate at least 4 hours or overnight.

4 When ready to bake, heat oven to 375°F. Bake casserole covered 20 minutes. Uncover; sprinkle with remaining 1/4 cup cheese. Bake uncovered 5 to 10 minutes longer or until casserole is thoroughly heated and cheese is melted. Cut into squares.

NUTRITION INFORMATION PER SERVING: Calories 370 • Total Fat 22g • Saturated Fat 9g • Cholesterol 60mg • Sodium 1030mg • Total Carbohydrate 25g • Dietary Fiber 2g • Protein 19g. DIETARY EXCHANGES: 1-1/2 Starch • 1 Vegetable • 1-1/2 Medium-Fat Meat • 2-1/2 Fat • 1-1/2 Carb Choices.

cook's notes

Fix this Mexican casserole early (or the night before) and pop it in the oven at dinnertime.

italian sausage-mashed potato pie

PREP TIME: 15 Minutes ✳ READY IN: 1 Hour 15 Minutes ✳ SERVINGS: 6

- 1 pouch (from 7.2-oz. box) roasted garlic mashed potatoes
- 3/4 cup milk
- 1/2 cup water
- 2 eggs, beaten

- 1 lb. bulk mild Italian pork sausage
- 1 medium onion, chopped (1/2 cup)
- 1 cup tomato pasta sauce
- 1 teaspoon dried basil leaves
- 1/2 cup shredded Parmesan cheese (2 oz.)

1 Heat oven to 375°F. Spray 9-inch glass pie plate. Cook 1 pouch potatoes as directed on box— except use 3/4 cup milk and 1/2 cup water; omit margarine. After 5-minute stand time, stir in eggs. Spread cooked potatoes in bottom and up sides of pie plate, forming a crust.

2 Meanwhile, in 12-inch skillet, cook sausage and onion over medium-high heat, stirring frequently, until sausage is no longer pink; drain. Stir in pasta sauce and basil. Reduce heat to low; cook about 2 minutes, stirring occasionally, until hot. Pour into potato-lined pie plate.

3 Bake about 25 minutes or until crust edges just begin to turn golden brown. Sprinkle with the cheese. Bake about 5 minutes longer or until the cheese is melted. Let stand 5 minutes before serving.

NUTRITION INFORMATION PER SERVING: Calories 360 • Total Fat 17g • Saturated Fat 6g • Cholesterol 110mg • Sodium 1010mg • Total Carbohydrate 36g • Dietary Fiber 2g • Protein 17g. DIETARY EXCHANGES: 1-1/2 Starch • 1/2 Other Carbohydrate • 1 Vegetable • 1-1/2 High-Fat Meat • 1 Fat • 2-1/2 Carb Choices.

cook's notes

If you decide to use sausage links instead of bulk sausage, be sure to remove the casings before cooking.

creamy ham and potato casserole

PREP TIME: 15 Minutes ✳ **READY IN:** 1 Hour 20 Minutes ✳ **SERVINGS:** 4

3 cups frozen potatoes O'Brien with onions
  and peppers (from 28-oz. bag)

1-1/2 cups Green Giant® frozen cut green beans

1-1/2 cups finely chopped cooked ham

3/4 cup milk

1/2 cup shredded American cheese (2 oz.)

1 can (10-3/4 oz.) condensed 98% fat-free
  cream of chicken soup with 30% less sodium

1 Heat oven to 375°F. Spray 8-inch square (2-quart) glass baking dish with cooking spray. In large
  bowl, mix all ingredients; spoon into baking dish. Bake about 1 hour or until bubbly and hot.
Let stand 5 minutes before serving.

HIGH ALTITUDE (3500-6500 FT): Thaw potatoes and green beans before mixing with other ingredients.

NUTRITION INFORMATION PER SERVING: Calories 280 • Total Fat 11 g • Saturated Fat 5g • Cholesterol 50mg • Sodium 1300mg • Total
Carbohydrate 26g • Dietary Fiber 2g • Protein 19g. DIETARY EXCHANGES: 1 Starch • 1/2 Other Carbohydrate • 1 Vegetable •
2 Medium-Fat Meat • 2 Carb Choices.

french onion-beef-noodle bake

PREP TIME: 35 Minutes ✳ **READY IN:** 1 Hour 10 Minutes ✳ **SERVINGS:** 8

5 cups uncooked wide egg noodles (8 oz.)	1/4 cup all-purpose flour
3 tablespoons butter or margarine	1 teaspoon dried rosemary leaves
2 lb. boneless beef sirloin steak, cut into 1-inch cubes	1 teaspoon salt
4 medium onions, thinly sliced (4 cups)	1 teaspoon pepper
2 cups sliced fresh mushrooms	2 cups seasoned croutons (4 oz.)
3 cups beef broth	2 cups shredded Swiss cheese (8 oz.)

1 Heat oven to 350°F. Cook and drain noodles as directed on package. Meanwhile, in 5-quart Dutch oven, melt butter over medium-high heat. Add beef, onions and mushrooms; cook about 20 minutes, stirring frequently, until beef is browned on all sides, onions are soft and mushrooms are browned.

2 Spread noodles in bottom of ungreased 13x9-inch (3-quart) glass baking dish. Spoon beef mixture over noodles.

3 In same Dutch oven, heat 2-1/2 cups of the broth to boiling over medium-high heat. In small bowl, mix remaining 1/2 cup broth and the flour until smooth. Stir flour mixture into boiling broth. Cook, stirring constantly, until bubbly and thickened. Stir in rosemary, salt and pepper. Pour over beef mixture; stir until well blended. Sprinkle with croutons, then cheese. Bake 25 to 35 minutes or until bubbly around edges and cheese is melted.

HIGH ALTITUDE (3500-6500 FT): In Step 4, do not add cheese and bake 20 minutes. Sprinkle with cheese; bake 5 to 15 minutes longer or until bubbly around edges and cheese is melted.

NUTRITION INFORMATION PER SERVING: Calories 460 • Total Fat 18g • Saturated Fat 9g • Cholesterol 125mg • Sodium 980mg • Total Carbohydrate 35g • Dietary Fiber 3g • Protein 40g. DIETARY EXCHANGES: 2 Starch • 1 Vegetable • 4-1/2 Lean Meat • 1/2 Fat • 2 Carb Choices.

cook's notes

Make sure to give the onions enough time to caramelize. It's a slow process, but the flavor is well worth it.

smoky mac 'n cheese

PREP TIME: 30 Minutes ✳ **READY IN:** 55 Minutes ✳ **SERVINGS:** 8

3 cups uncooked elbow macaroni (12 oz.)	2 cans (14.5 oz. each) Muir Glen® organic fire roasted diced tomatoes, well drained
1-1/2 cups whipping cream	1/4 cup sliced green onions (4 medium)
1 teaspoon Dijon mustard	1/3 cup grated Parmesan cheese
1/2 teaspoon coarse (kosher or sea) salt	1/3 cup plain dry bread crumbs
1/4 teaspoon ground red pepper (cayenne)	2 teaspoons olive oil
2 cups smoked Cheddar cheese, shredded (8 oz.)	

1 Cook and drain macaroni as directed on box. Return to saucepan; cover to keep warm. Meanwhile, heat oven to 375°F. Spray 13x9-inch (3-quart) glass baking dish with cooking spray.

2 In 2-quart saucepan, heat whipping cream, mustard, salt and red pepper to boiling. Reduce heat; stir in Cheddar cheese with wire whisk until smooth. Pour sauce over macaroni. Stir in tomatoes and onions. Pour into baking dish.

3 In small bowl, mix Parmesan cheese and bread crumbs. Stir in oil. Sprinkle over top of macaroni mixture. Bake uncovered 15 to 20 minutes or until edges are bubbly and top is golden brown.

HIGH ALTITUDE (3500-6500 FT): Bake 18 to 23 minutes.

NUTRITION INFORMATION PER SERVING: Calories 500 • Total Fat 27g • Saturated Fat 16g • Cholesterol 85mg • Sodium 770mg • Total Carbohydrate 47g • Dietary Fiber 4g • Protein 17g. DIETARY EXCHANGES: 2-1/2 Starch • 1/2 Other Carbohydrate • 1 Vegetable • 1 High-Fat Meat • 3-1/2 Fat • 3 Carb Choices.

cook's notes

Be sure to use whipping cream when making the sauce for this decadent mac 'n cheese. Milk or half-and-half are more likely to curdle when combined with acidic ingredients like tomatoes.

Jolly Holiday Entertaining

Festive food with a casual flair may be just what you need this Christmas season. From pizza to sandwiches, there are plenty of family-pleasing favorites to choose from.

p. 161

p. 138

p. 145

p. 150

p. 141

skillet chicken parmigiana p. 155

asian beef and broccoli

READY IN: 25 Minutes ✳ SERVINGS: 4

1 lb. lean (at least 80%) ground beef	1/2 teaspoon ground ginger
3 cups fresh broccoli florets	1 package (3 oz.) oriental-flavor ramen noodle soup mix
1 package (8 oz.) fresh mushrooms, sliced (3 cups)	Soy sauce, if desired
1 cup water	

1 In 12-inch skillet, cook beef over medium-high heat 5 to 7 minutes, stirring occasionally, until beef is thoroughly cooked; drain.

2 Stir in broccoli, mushrooms, water, ginger and contents of seasoning packet from soup mix. Heat to boiling. Cover; simmer 5 minutes, stirring occasionally.

3 Break up noodles. Add to beef mixture; cook uncovered about 5 minutes or until noodles are tender. Serve with soy sauce.

NUTRITION INFORMATION PER SERVING: Calories 340 • Total Fat 17g • Saturated Fat 6g • Cholesterol 70mg • Sodium 430mg • Total Carbohydrate 19g • Dietary Fiber 3g • Protein 25g. DIETARY EXCHANGES: 1/2 Starch • 2 Vegetable • 3 Medium-Fat Meat • 1/2 Fat • 1 Carb Choice.

slow cooker hoisin pork wraps

PREP TIME: 30 Minutes ❅ **READY IN:** 8 Hours 30 Minutes ❅ **SERVINGS:** 10

1 (2 lb.) boneless pork roast, trimmed of fat	10 flour tortillas (10 inch)
5 tablespoons hoisin sauce	3 cups shredded lettuce
1 tablespoon grated gingerroot	1/2 cup sliced green onions
1 teaspoon Chinese five-spice powder	1 can (15 oz.) mandarin orange segments, drained
2 garlic cloves, minced	

1 Place pork roast in 3- to 4-quart slow cooker. In small bowl, combine 4 tablespoons of the hoisin sauce, gingerroot, five-spice powder and garlic; mix well. Spread mixture over pork. Cover; cook on Low setting for 7 to 8 hours.

2 About 15 minutes before serving, heat oven to 300°F. Wrap tortillas in foil. Heat packet at 300°F for 10 to 15 minutes or until warm.

3 Meanwhile, remove pork from slow cooker; place on cutting board. Stir remaining tablespoon hoisin sauce into juices in slow cooker. Shred pork with 2 forks; return to slow cooker and mix well.

4 To serve, spoon about 1/2 cup pork mixture onto each warm tortilla. Top each with lettuce, onions and orange segments. Roll up.

NUTRITION INFORMATION PER SERVING: Calories 395 • Total Fat 12g • Saturated Fat 4g • Cholesterol 60mg • Sodium 490mg • Total Carbohydrate 45g • Dietary Fiber 3g • Protein 27g. DIETARY EXCHANGES: 3 Starch • 2-1/2 Lean Meat • 1/2 Fat • 3 Carb Choices.

kitchen tip

Hoisin is a thick, dark-red sauce made from soybeans, garlic and chiles. Its sweet-and-spicy flavor is great for cooking and as a table condiment. Look for hoisin sauce in the grocery store's Asian food section. Refrigerate hoisin sauce once the jar is opened.

chicken parmesan fettuccine

READY IN: 20 Minutes ✳ SERVINGS: 3

1 package (11.6 oz.) frozen breaded chicken breast tenderloins (6 pieces)

3 oz. mozzarella cheese, cut into 6 (2-1/4x1x1/4-inch) slices

1 package (9 oz.) refrigerated fettuccine

1-1/2 cups tomato pasta sauce

3 tablespoons shredded fresh Parmesan cheese

1 Bake chicken breast tenderloins as directed on package, placing mozzarella cheese slices on chicken during last 3 minutes of bake time.

2 Meanwhile, cook fettuccine as directed on package; drain. Place pasta sauce in small microwavable bowl; cover with microwavable paper towel. Microwave on High 3 to 4 minutes or until hot, stirring occasionally. Serve chicken over fettuccine. Top with sauce and Parmesan cheese.

NUTRITION INFORMATION PER SERVING: Calories 770 • Total Fat 31g • Saturated Fat 9g • Cholesterol 65mg • Sodium 1360mg • Total Carbohydrate 86g • Dietary Fiber 6g • Protein 38g. DIETARY EXCHANGES: 4 Starch • 1-1/2 Other Carbohydrate • 3-1/2 Lean Meat • 3-1/2 Fat • 6 Carb Choices.

turkey and bean cassoulet

PREP TIME: 20 Minutes ✳ **READY IN:** 18 Hours 25 Minutes ✳ **SERVINGS:** 6

1-1/2 cups dried great northern beans	2 bay leaves
1 lb. fresh turkey breast tenderloins, cut into 1-inch pieces	1/4 teaspoon pepper
1 cup sliced celery	1 can (14-1/2 oz.) ready-to-serve chicken broth
1 medium green bell pepper, chopped	1-1/2 cups water
1 medium onion, chopped	1 can (14.5 oz.) diced tomatoes, undrained
2 garlic cloves, minced	3/4 teaspoon salt

1. Place beans in medium bowl; add enough water to cover. Let stand overnight to soak. Drain beans; discard water.

2. Place beans and all remaining ingredients except tomatoes and salt in 3-1/2- to 4-quart slow cooker. Cover; cook on Low setting for 8 to 10 hours.

3. To serve, remove bay leaves. Stir in tomatoes and salt. Cover; cook on Low setting an additional 10 minutes or until thoroughly heated.

NUTRITION INFORMATION PER SERVING: Calories 280 • Total Fat 2g • Saturated Fat 0g • Cholesterol 50mg • Sodium 640mg • Total Carbohydrate 35g • Dietary Fiber 11g • Protein 31g. DIETARY EXCHANGES: 2 Starch • 2 Other Carbohydrate • 1 Vegetable • 3 Very Lean Meat.

cook's notes

Cassoulet is a classic French stew featuring white beans and a variety of meats, poultry and sausage. Our version calls only for turkey, but sliced smoked sausage can be added to the recipe.

pizza skillet hot dish

READY IN: 30 Minutes ✳ **SERVINGS:** 4

1/2 lb. lean (at least 80%) ground beef	2 cups uncooked ready-cut spaghetti (7 oz.)
2 oz. sliced pepperoni, chopped (1/2 cup)	1/4 cup sliced ripe olives
1 jar (14 oz.) tomato pasta sauce (2 cups)	1/2 green bell pepper, cut into bite-sized strips
1 cup water	1 cup shredded mozzarella cheese (4 oz.)

1. In 12-inch skillet, cook ground beef over medium-high heat 5 to 7 minutes, stirring occasionally, until thoroughly cooked. Add pepperoni; cook 1 minute. Drain.

2. Stir in pasta sauce, water and uncooked spaghetti. Heat to boiling; stir. Reduce heat to medium-low; cover and cook 10 to 15 minutes or until spaghetti is of desired doneness, stirring occasionally.

3. Gently stir in olives. Arrange pepper strips over top. Sprinkle with cheese. Remove from heat. Cover; let stand 3 to 5 minutes or until cheese is melted.

    HIGH ALTITUDE (3500-6500 FT): Cook spaghetti as directed on package. Do not overcook. In Step 2, heat sauce to boiling; stir. Reduce heat to medium-low; cover and cook 10 to 15 minutes adding pasta the last 5 minutes.

NUTRITION INFORMATION PER SERVING: Calories 600 • Total Fat 24g • Saturated Fat 9g • Cholesterol 65mg • Sodium 1130mg • Total Carbohydrate 66g • Dietary Fiber 5g • Protein 29g. DIETARY EXCHANGES: 3 Starch • 1-1/2 Other Carbohydrate • 3 Medium-Fat Meat • 1 Fat • 4-1/2 Carb Choices.

cook's notes

If your family prefers the flavor of green olives, use pimiento-stuffed green olives instead of the ripe olives.

pastrami and swiss melts

PREP TIME: 10 Minutes ✳ **READY IN:** 30 Minutes ✳ **SERVINGS:** 4

1 can (13.8 oz.) Pillsbury® refrigerated classic pizza crust	4 tablespoons Thousand Island dressing
1 teaspoon grated Parmesan cheese	1/2 lb. thinly sliced pastrami (from deli), cut into bite-sized strips
1/4 teaspoon onion powder	4 thin slices (about 1 oz. each) Swiss cheese
1/4 teaspoon caraway seed	1 cup creamy coleslaw (from deli)

1 Heat oven to 400°F. On ungreased cookie sheet, unroll dough into 14x9-inch rectangle. Sprinkle Parmesan cheese, onion powder and caraway seed over dough; press in lightly. Bake 12 to 16 minutes or until golden brown.

2 Cut crust into quarters; separate slightly. Spread each with 1 tablespoon dressing. Top each with pastrami and cheese. Bake 2 to 4 minutes longer or until thoroughly heated and cheese is melted. Top each with coleslaw.

NUTRITION INFORMATION PER SERVING: Calories 590 • Total Fat 28g • Saturated Fat 9g • Cholesterol 65mg • Sodium 1810mg • Total Carbohydrate 55g • Dietary Fiber 2g • Protein 29g. DIETARY EXCHANGES: 3-1/2 Starch • 2-1/2 Medium-Fat Meat • 3 Fat • 3-1/2 Carb Choices.

bow-ties with bacon and tomatoes

READY IN: 30 Minutes ✳ **SERVINGS:** 4

4 slices bacon, cut into 1-inch pieces	1-3/4 cups Progresso® chicken broth (from 32-oz. carton)
1 medium onion, finely chopped (1/2 cup)	3 cups uncooked bow-tie (farfalle) pasta (6 oz.)
1 can (14.5 oz.) diced tomatoes with roasted garlic and onion, undrained	1/8 teaspoon pepper

1 In 12-inch skillet, cook bacon over medium-high heat 8 to 10 minutes, stirring frequently, until bacon is brown. Reduce heat to medium. Add onion; cook 2 to 3 minutes, stirring frequently, until onion is tender.

2 Stir in tomatoes, broth, uncooked pasta and pepper. Heat to boiling over high heat. Reduce heat to medium; cook uncovered 10 to 12 minutes, stirring occasionally, until pasta is tender and mixture is as thick as you like.

HIGH ALTITUDE (3500-6500 FT): In Step 2, cook uncovered 12 to 14 minutes.

NUTRITION INFORMATION PER SERVING: Calories 260 • Total Fat 4.5g • Saturated Fat 1.5g • Cholesterol 10mg • Sodium 710mg • Total Carbohydrate 43g • Dietary Fiber 3g • Protein 12g. DIETARY EXCHANGES: 2-1/2 Starch • 1/2 Vegetable • 1/2 High-Fat Meat • 3 Carb Choices.

pastrami and swiss melts

hoagie burgers

READY IN: 40 Minutes ✳ SERVINGS: 4

1-1/2 lb. lean (at least 80%) ground beef
1/2 teaspoon salt
1/2 teaspoon pepper
2 sweet onions, halved, thinly sliced and separated into half-rings

Cooking spray
1/2 cup garlic-and-herbs spreadable cheese (from 4- to 6.5-oz. container)
4 hoagie buns (8 inch), split
4 leaves green leaf lettuce

1 Heat gas or charcoal grill. In medium bowl, mix ground beef, salt and pepper. Shape mixture into 4 oval patties, about 1/2 inch thick, to fit hoagie buns.

2 Cut 2 (18x12-inch) sheets of heavy-duty foil. Generously spray half of one side of each foil sheet with cooking spray. Place onions evenly in center of sprayed portion of foil; generously spray onions with cooking spray. Fold unsprayed half of foil over onions so edges meet; seal edges, making tight 1/2-inch fold; fold again, allowing space for heat circulation and expansion. Fold other sides to seal.

3 Place patties and packets on grill. Cover grill; cook over medium heat 11 to 13 minutes, turning patties and packets over once, until meat thermometer inserted in center of patties reads 160°F and onions are tender.

4 Spread cheese onto bottom halves of buns. Top each with lettuce leaf, patty and onions. Cover with top halves of buns.

NUTRITION INFORMATION PER SERVING: Calories 670 • Total Fat 32g • Saturated Fat 14g • Cholesterol 135mg • Sodium 1030mg • Total Carbohydrate 55g • Dietary Fiber 4g • Protein 41g. DIETARY EXCHANGES: 3-1/2 Starch • 1 Vegetable • 4 Medium-Fat Meat • 1-1/2 Fat • 3-1/2 Carb Choices.

cook's notes

Toast the buns for this hoagie burger, cut-side-down, on the grill for 1 to 2 minutes or until golden brown.

gingered pork wraps

PREP TIME: 20 Minutes ✳ READY IN: 10 Hours 20 Minutes ✳ SERVINGS: 12

1 (3-1/2 lb.) boneless rolled pork loin roast
2 tablespoons grated gingerroot
2 tablespoons dry sherry, if desired
1 garlic clove, minced
1/2 cup hoisin sauce
6 dried shiitake mushrooms

12 flour tortillas (10 to 12 inch)
2 teaspoons sesame oil
4 cups shredded Chinese (napa) cabbage
1 bunch green onions, cut into 2x1/16-inch slivers (about 3/4 cup)

1 Place pork roast in 4- to 6-quart slow cooker. In small bowl, combine gingerroot, sherry, garlic and 3 tablespoons of the hoisin sauce; mix well. Spoon mixture over roast. Snap off and discard stems from dried mushrooms; crumble the mushrooms over the roast. Cover; cook on Low setting for 8 to 10 hours.

2 About 15 minutes before serving, heat oven to 300°F. Brush tortillas with sesame oil; stack on sheet of foil. Wrap tightly. Heat packet at 300°F for 10 minutes.

3 Meanwhile, remove pork from slow cooker; place on large plate. Stir cabbage into juices in slow cooker. Increase heat setting to High; cover and cook an additional 5 minutes or until cabbage is wilted.

4 Shred pork with 2 forks; return to slow cooker. Spread each warm tortilla with 1 teaspoon remaining hoisin sauce. Top each with about 3/4 cup pork mixture and 1 tablespoon onions; roll up.

NUTRITION INFORMATION PER SERVING: Calories 500 • Total Fat 16g • Saturated Fat 5g • Cholesterol 80mg • Sodium 660mg • Total Carbohydrate 53g • Dietary Fiber 3g • Protein 36g. DIETARY EXCHANGES: 3-1/2 Starch • 3-1/2 Other Carbohydrate • 3-1/2 Lean Meat • 1/2 Fat.

cook's notes

Sesame oil has a nice nutty flavor that tastes great in this recipe, but vegetable oil can be used instead. To add a hint of sesame flavor, sprinkle the filling with toasted sesame seeds before wrapping it up.

savory crescent chicken squares

PREP TIME: 20 Minutes ✳ READY IN: 50 Minutes ✳ SERVINGS: 4

- 1 package (3 oz.) cream cheese, softened
- 1 tablespoon Land O Lakes® butter, softened
- 2 cups cubed cooked chicken
- 1 tablespoon chopped fresh chives or onion
- 1/4 teaspoon salt
- 1/8 teaspoon pepper
- 2 tablespoons milk
- 1 tablespoon chopped pimientos, if desired
- 1 can (8 oz.) Pillsbury® refrigerated crescent dinner rolls or Pillsbury® Crescent Recipe Creations® refrigerated seamless dough sheet
- 1 tablespoon Land O Lakes® butter, melted
- 3/4 cup seasoned croutons, crushed

1 Heat oven to 350°F. In medium bowl, mix cream cheese and 1 tablespoon softened butter; beat until smooth. Add chicken, chives, salt, pepper, milk and pimientos; mix well

2 Separate or cut dough into 4 rectangles. If using crescent dough, firmly press perforations to seal. Spoon 1/2 cup chicken mixture onto center of each rectangle. Pull 4 corners of dough to center of chicken mixture; twist firmly. Pinch edges to seal.

3 Place on ungreased cookie sheet. Brush tops of sandwiches with 1 tablespoon melted butter; sprinkle with crushed croutons. Bake 25 to 30 minutes or until golden brown.

NUTRITION INFORMATION PER SERVING: Calories 500 • Total Fat 32g • Saturated Fat 12g • Cholesterol 85mg • Sodium 870mg • Total Carbohydrate 28g • Dietary Fiber 1g • Protein 26g. DIETARY EXCHANGES: 1-1/2 Starch • 1/2 Other Carbohydrate • 3 Medium-Fat Meat • 3 Fat • 2 Carb Choices.

DORIS CASTLE
River Forest, Illinois
Bake-Off® Contest 25, 1974
Prize Winner

turkey caesar focaccia wedges

READY IN: 10 Minutes ✳ SERVINGS: 6

1 package (12 oz.) cheese or garlic focaccia bread (8 to 10 inch)	1/3 cup creamy Caesar dressing
3 cups torn romaine lettuce	1/4 cup grated Parmesan cheese
2 cups cooked turkey, cut into bite-size strips (9 oz.)	1/4 teaspoon coarse ground black pepper

1 Cut focaccia bread in half horizontally; set aside. In large bowl, mix remaining ingredients.
Spoon turkey mixture evenly onto bottom half of bread. Cover with top half of bread. Cut into
6 wedges to serve.

NUTRITION INFORMATION PER SERVING: Calories 320 • Total Fat 15g • Saturated Fat 4g • Cholesterol 45mg • Sodium 440mg • Total
Carbohydrate 22g • Dietary Fiber 0g • Protein 22g. DIETARY EXCHANGES: 1-1/2 Starch • 2-1/2 Lean Meat • 1-1/2 Fat • 1-1/2 Carb Choices.

chicken fajita pizza

PREP TIME: 20 Minutes ✳ READY IN: 40 Minutes ✳ SERVINGS: 8

1   can (13.8 oz.) Pillsbury® refrigerated classic pizza crust

1   tablespoon olive oil or vegetable oil

4   boneless skinless chicken breasts (about 1-1/4 lb.), cut into thin bite-size strips

1   to 2 teaspoons chili powder

1/2   to 1 teaspoon salt

1/2   teaspoon garlic powder

1   cup thinly sliced onions

1   cup green or red bell pepper strips (2x1/4 inch)

1/2   cup Old El Paso® thick 'n chunky salsa

2   cups shredded Monterey Jack cheese (8 oz.)

1   Heat oven to 425°F. Spray 12-inch pizza pan or 13x9-inch pan with cooking spray. Unroll dough; place in pan. Starting at center, press out dough to edge of pan to form crust. Bake 7 to 9 minutes or until very light golden brown.

2   Meanwhile, in 10-inch skillet, heat oil over medium-high heat. Add chicken; sprinkle with chili powder, salt and garlic powder. Cook and stir 3 to 5 minutes or until lightly browned. Add onions and bell pepper strips; cook and stir 2 to 3 minutes longer or until chicken is no longer pink in center and vegetables are crisp-tender.

3   Spoon chicken mixture evenly over crust. Spoon salsa over chicken; sprinkle with cheese. Bake 14 to 18 minutes longer or until crust is golden brown. Cut into wedges or squares to serve.

HIGH ALTITUDE (3500-6500 FT): After adding onions and bell pepper strips, cook and stir 3 to 5 minutes longer.

NUTRITION INFORMATION PER SERVING: Calories 340 • Total Fat 14g • Saturated Fat 7g • Cholesterol 70mg • Sodium 880mg • Total Carbohydrate 27g • Dietary Fiber 1g • Protein 27g. DIETARY EXCHANGES: 2 Starch • 3 Very Lean Meat • 2 Fat • 2 Carb Choices.

ELIZABETH DANIELS
Kula Maui, Hawaii
Bake-Off® Contest 34, 1990

cook's notes

Enjoy this pizza with a crisp lettuce salad tossed with fresh orange segments, cubed avocado and a vinaigrette dressing.

smoky brisket hoagies

smoky brisket hoagies

PREP TIME: 20 Minutes ✳ READY IN: 10 Hours 20 Minutes ✳ SERVINGS: 12

- 2 medium onions, sliced
- 1 medium green bell pepper, coarsely chopped
- 1 fresh beef brisket (not corned beef), trimmed of fat (4 lb.)
- 3/4 cup hickory smoke-flavored barbecue sauce
- 3/4 cup chili sauce
- 2 cloves garlic, minced
- 12 hoagie buns, split

1 In 3-1/2- to 4-quart slow cooker, place onions and bell pepper. Cut beef brisket across grain into 3 large pieces. Place beef on top of vegetables in slow cooker, overlapping pieces to fit if necessary.

2 In small bowl, mix barbecue sauce, chili sauce and garlic until blended. Pour over beef. Cover; cook on Low heat setting 10 to 11 hours.

3 To serve, remove beef from slow cooker; place on cutting board. With 2 forks, pull beef into shreds. Return beef to slow cooker; stir to mix with sauce. With slotted spoon, serve beef in hoagie buns. Garnish as desired.

NUTRITION INFORMATION PER SERVING: Calories 535 • Total Fat 14g • Saturated Fat 5g • Cholesterol 85mg • Sodium 1010mg • Total Carbohydrate 61g • Dietary Fiber 3g • Protein 41g. DIETARY EXCHANGES: 4 Starch • 4 Other Carbohydrate • 4 Lean Meat • 1/2 Fat • 4 Carb Choices.

Kitchen tip

Brisket is cut from under the first five ribs of the breast section. The beef is sold in two sections, a lean, inexpensive flat cut and a richer point cut. This recipe works best with the flat-cut brisket.

thai peanut chicken and noodles

READY IN: 30 Minutes ✳ SERVINGS: 5

- 2-3/4 cups uncooked fine egg noodles (6 oz.)
- 1/4 cup creamy peanut butter
- 1/2 teaspoon finely chopped gingerroot
- 1/4 teaspoon crushed red pepper flakes
- 1/4 cup soy sauce
- 1/4 cup water
- 1 tablespoon vegetable oil
- 2 cups small fresh broccoli florets
- 1-1/2 cups sliced fresh mushrooms (about 4 oz.)
- 1 cup ready-to-eat baby-cut carrots, quartered lengthwise
- 1 medium red bell pepper, cut into thin bite-size strips
- 1 package (9 oz.) frozen diced cooked chicken, thawed
- 1/4 cup coarsely chopped dry-roasted peanuts

1 Cook and drain the noodles as directed on package; cover to keep warm. Meanwhile, in a small bowl, beat peanut butter, gingerroot, pepper flakes and 2 tablespoons of the soy sauce with wire whisk until blended. Gradually beat in remaining 2 tablespoons soy sauce and the water until smooth. Set aside.

2 In 12-inch nonstick skillet, heat oil over medium-high heat. Cook broccoli, mushrooms, carrots and bell pepper in oil 4 to 6 minutes, stirring occasionally, until vegetables are crisp-tender. Add chicken; cook and stir until hot.

3 Reduce heat to medium. Stir peanut butter mixture; stir into mixture in skillet. Stir in cooked noodles until coated. Cook and stir until hot. Sprinkle with peanuts.

NUTRITION INFORMATION PER SERVING: Calories 410 • Total Fat 19g • Saturated Fat 3.5g • Cholesterol 70mg • Sodium 920mg • Total Carbohydrate 34g • Dietary Fiber 5g • Protein 27g. DIETARY EXCHANGES: 2 Starch • 1 Vegetable • 2-1/2 Lean Meat • 2 Fat • 2 Carb Choices.

cabbage rolls in creamy bacon sauce

PREP TIME: 45 Minutes ❋ **READY IN:** 1 Hour 15 Minutes ❋ **SERVINGS:** 6

1 large head cabbage, core removed	1/4 teaspoon pepper
1 lb. extra-lean (at least 90%) ground beef	1 cup beef broth
1/3 cup uncooked instant white rice	1/2 teaspoon caraway seed
1/3 cup milk	1/2 cup milk
1 egg	1/2 cup sour cream
1 teaspoon Worcestershire sauce	1 tablespoon all-purpose flour
1/2 teaspoon salt	1/4 cup cooked bacon pieces (from 2.1-oz. pkg.)

1 Fill 5- to 6-quart Dutch oven half full of water. Heat to boiling. Place whole cabbage in water, core side down. Cover; cook 2 to 3 minutes, turning over once, or until leaves can be removed from head. With slotted spoon remove cabbage from water. With tongs, carefully remove 6 leaves from head. Save remaining head of cabbage for later use. Shave or trim part of the thick rib from each leaf. Return leaves to water; cook 2 to 3 minutes or until wilted.

2 In medium bowl, mix ground beef, uncooked rice, 1/3 cup milk, the egg, Worcestershire sauce, 1/4 teaspoon of the salt and 1/8 teaspoon of the pepper. Spoon about 1/3 cup of the ground beef mixture on thick end of each cabbage leaf. Roll up, tucking sides in. Place filled cabbage leaves in 12-inch skillet, seam side down. Add broth and caraway seed. Cover; heat to boiling. Reduce heat; simmer 25 to 30 minutes or until thermometer inserted in center of ground beef mixture reads 160°F.

3 With slotted spoon, place cabbage rolls on serving platter; cover to keep warm. In small bowl, mix 1/2 cup milk, the sour cream, flour, remaining 1/4 teaspoon salt and 1/8 teaspoon pepper with wire whisk. Pour into skillet. Cook and stir over medium heat until thick and bubbly. Serve sauce over cabbage rolls; sprinkle with bacon.

NUTRITION INFORMATION PER SERVING: Calories 240 • Total Fat 13g • Saturated Fat 6g • Cholesterol 100mg • Sodium 530mg • Total Carbohydrate 11g • Dietary Fiber 0g • Protein 20g. DIETARY EXCHANGES: 1/2 Starch • 2-1/2 Medium-Fat Meat • 1 Carb Choice.

cranberry-turkey quesadillas

PREP TIME: 10 Minutes ✳ **READY IN:** 20 Minutes ✳ **SERVINGS:** 16

- 1 package (11 oz.) Old El Paso® flour tortillas for burritos (8 tortillas)
- 3 cups shredded pepper Jack cheese (12 oz.)
- 1 cup smoked cooked turkey, chopped (6 oz.)
- 1/2 cup sweetened dried cranberries
- 2 tablespoons butter or margarine, melted
- 1 tablespoon chopped fresh parsley

1 Heat oven to 400°F. On ungreased large cookie sheet, place 4 of the tortillas. Sprinkle 1/2 cup of the cheese over each tortilla. Top each evenly with turkey and cranberries. Sprinkle 1/4 cup remaining cheese over each. Top with remaining tortillas.

2 In small bowl, mix melted butter and parsley. Brush butter mixture over tops of filled tortillas. Bake 6 to 8 minutes or until cheese is melted and edges begin to turn light golden brown. Cut into wedges; serve warm.

NUTRITION INFORMATION PER SERVING: Calories 170 • Total Fat 9g • Saturated Fat 4.5g • Cholesterol 30mg • Sodium 450mg • Total Carbohydrate 14g • Dietary Fiber 0g • Protein 8g. DIETARY EXCHANGES: 1 Starch • 1/2 High-Fat Meat • 1 Fat • 1 Carb Choice.

cook's notes

These quesadillas could be served as appetizers or also as a light meal with a bowl of your favorite hot soup.

jerked chicken hoagies

PREP TIME: 15 Minutes ✳ **READY IN:** 6 Hours 15 Minutes ✳ **SERVINGS:** 6

- 3 tablespoons Caribbean jerk seasoning (dry)
- 3 lb. boneless skinless chicken thighs
- 1 large red or green bell pepper, chopped (1-1/2 cups)
- 1 large onion, chopped (1 cup)
- 1/2 cup chicken broth
- 1/4 cup ketchup
- 6 hoagie buns, split

1 Rub jerk seasoning generously over chicken thighs. In 3-1/2- to 4-quart slow cooker, mix bell pepper and onion. Place chicken over vegetables.

2 In small bowl, mix broth and ketchup. Pour broth mixture over chicken. Cover; cook on Low heat setting 6 to 8 hours.

3 Remove chicken from slow cooker; place on cutting board. Shred chicken with 2 forks; return to slow cooker, and mix well. To serve, with slotted spoon, spoon chicken mixture into buns.

NUTRITION INFORMATION PER SERVING: Calories 650 • Total Fat 22g • Saturated Fat 7g • Cholesterol 140mg • Sodium 1190mg • Total Carbohydrate 53g • Dietary Fiber 3g • Protein 58g. DIETARY EXCHANGES: 2-1/2 Starch • 1 Other Carbohydrate • 7 Lean Meat • 3-1/2 Carb Choices.

kitchen tip

Caribbean jerk seasoning, also known as Jamaican jerk seasoning, is generally a combination of peppers, thyme and allspice. Some blends may also contain cinnamon, ginger, cloves, garlic and onions.

easy deep-dish pizza pie

PREP TIME: 25 Minutes ✳ READY IN: 1 Hour 15 Minutes ✳ SERVINGS: 8

1 lb. lean (at least 80%) ground beef	2 cups shredded Italian cheese blend (8 oz.)
1 small onion, chopped	1 package (3 oz.) pepperoni slices
1 can (8 oz.) pizza sauce	1 egg
1 can (11 oz.) Pillsbury® refrigerated crusty French loaf	1 tablespoon water
	Pizza sauce, if desired

1 Heat oven to 350°F. Spray 9-inch glass pie plate with cooking spray. In 10-inch skillet, cook beef and onion over medium-high heat, stirring frequently, until beef is thoroughly cooked; drain. Stir in pizza sauce until well mixed.

2 Carefully unroll dough in pie plate so edges extend over sides. Pat dough in bottom and up side of pan, leaving dough extended over side. Spoon beef mixture into crust. Top with half of the cheese, pepperoni and the remaining cheese.

3 In small bowl, slightly beat egg and water. Fold extended edges of dough up and over filling; seal all edges. Brush crust with egg mixture.

4 Bake 38 to 48 minutes or until deep golden brown. Cool 15 minutes. Cut pizza into wedges; serve with additional pizza sauce.

NUTRITION INFORMATION PER SERVING: Calories 350 • Total Fat 19g • Saturated Fat 9g • Cholesterol 100mg • Sodium 780mg • Total Carbohydrate 22g • Dietary Fiber 0g • Protein 22g. DIETARY EXCHANGES: 1 Starch • 1/2 Other Carbohydrate • 2-1/2 High-Fat Meat • 1-1/2 Carb Choices.

Kitchen tip

Meaning "flute" in Spanish, a flauta is a filled tortilla rolled into a thin, flute-like tube. Enjoy the flautas with some Spanish rice.

chicken and cheese flautas

READY IN: 20 Minutes ✳ SERVINGS: 3

6 Old El Paso® flour tortillas for soft tacos & fajitas (6 inch)	1/3 cup Old El Paso® thick 'n chunky salsa
1 cup finely shredded pepper Jack cheese (4 oz.)	4 teaspoons vegetable oil
	Guacamole, if desired
3/4 cup shredded cooked chicken	Sour cream, if desired
3/4 teaspoon ground cumin	

1 Heat tortillas as directed on package. Meanwhile, in small bowl, mix cheese, chicken and cumin. Place about 1/4 cup chicken mixture on each warm tortilla. Top each with scant 1 tablespoon salsa. Roll up tightly; secure each with toothpick. Brush filled tortillas with oil.

2 In 10-inch skillet, cook filled tortillas over medium heat 4 to 6 minutes, turning occasionally, until filling is hot and the tortillas are toasted. Remove the toothpicks. Serve with guacamole and sour cream.

NUTRITION INFORMATION PER SERVING: Calories 410 • Total Fat 22g • Saturated Fat 8g • Cholesterol 65mg • Sodium 870mg • Total Carbohydrate 30g • Dietary Fiber 0g • Protein 21g. DIETARY EXCHANGES: 2 Starch • 2 Lean Meat • 3 Fat • 2 Carb Choices.

quick beef stew in bread bowls

READY IN: 35 Minutes ✳ **SERVINGS:** 4

1 can (11 oz.) Pillsbury® refrigerated crusty French loaf

1 package (17 oz.) refrigerated precooked beef tips with gravy

1 box (9 oz.) Green Giant® frozen roasted potatoes with garlic & herbs

1 box (9 oz.) Green Giant® frozen sweet peas & pearl onions

1/2 cup beef gravy (from 12-oz. jar)

1/3 cup water

1 tablespoon Worcestershire sauce

cook's notes

For bread bowls, pull cut sides of dough down to bring cut edges together forming a ball.

1 Heat oven to 350°F. Spray cookie sheet with cooking spray. Remove dough from can; do not unroll. Cut dough into 4 equal pieces. Shape each into ball, placing seam at bottom so dough is smooth on top. Place dough balls, seam side down, on cookie sheet.

2 Bake 18 to 20 minutes or until deep golden brown. Remove from cookie sheet; place on wire rack. Cool 10 minutes.

3 Meanwhile, heat beef tips with gravy, and cook potatoes and peas with onions in microwave as directed on package and boxes. In 2-quart microwavable bowl, mix beef with gravy and vegetables. Stir in remaining ingredients. Microwave on High 1 to 2 minutes or until thoroughly heated.

4 Cut top off each bread loaf. Lightly press center of bread down to form bowls. Place each bread bowl in individual shallow soup plate. Spoon about 1 cup stew into each. Place top of each bread bowl next to filled bowl.

HIGH ALTITUDE (3500-6500 FT): Bake at 375°F 18 to 20 minutes.

NUTRITION INFORMATION PER SERVING: Calories 530 • Total Fat 19g • Saturated Fat 6g • Cholesterol 50mg • Sodium 1510mg • Total Carbohydrate 62g • Dietary Fiber 5g • Protein 26g, DIETARY EXCHANGES: 4 Starch • 1 Vegetable • 1-1/2 High-Fat Meat • 1 Fat • 4 Carb Choices.

teriyaki beef and pineapple lettuce wraps

READY IN: 15 Minutes ✸ SERVINGS: 5

1 lb. lean (at least 80%) ground beef	1/4 cup teriyaki baste and glaze sauce
1/4 teaspoon salt	1 tablespoon cornstarch
1/8 teaspoon pepper	2 green onions, sliced (2 tablespoons)
1 can (8 oz.) pineapple tidbits in juice, drained, reserving liquid	1/4 cup diced red bell pepper, if desired
	5 large Bibb lettuce leaves

1 In 10-inch skillet, cook ground beef over medium-high heat 5 to 7 minutes, stirring occasionally, until thoroughly cooked; drain. Stir in salt and pepper.

2 In small bowl, mix reserved pineapple liquid, baste and glaze sauce and cornstarch. Stir mixture into ground beef. Cook and stir until thick and bubbly, stirring frequently. Stir in pineapple, green onions and bell pepper. Cook 1 to 2 minutes, stirring occasionally, until thoroughly heated. Spoon about 1/2 cup mixture into each lettuce leaf; roll up to serve.

NUTRITION INFORMATION PER SERVING: Calories 210 • Total Fat 10g • Saturated Fat 4g • Cholesterol 55mg • Sodium 490mg • Total Carbohydrate 14g • Dietary Fiber 0g • Protein 17g. DIETARY EXCHANGES: 1 Other Carbohydrate • 2-1/2 Lean Meat • 1/2 Fat • 1 Carb Choice.

lazy-day overnight lasagna

PREP TIME: 20 Minutes ✸ READY IN: 13 Hours 35 Minutes ✸ SERVINGS: 12

1 lb. mild bulk Italian pork sausage or ground beef	1/2 teaspoon dried oregano leaves
1 jar (26 to 28 oz.) tomato pasta sauce	1 egg
1 cup water	8 oz. uncooked lasagna noodles
1 container (15 oz.) ricotta cheese	1 package (16 oz.) sliced mozzarella cheese
2 tablespoons chopped fresh chives	2 tablespoons grated Parmesan cheese

1 In 12-inch skillet, cook sausage over medium-high heat, stirring occasionally, until no longer pink. Drain well. Stir in pasta sauce and water. Heat to boiling. Reduce heat to low; simmer 5 minutes. In medium bowl, mix ricotta cheese, chives, oregano and egg.

2 In ungreased 13x9-inch (3-quart) glass baking dish or lasagna pan, spread 1-1/2 cups of the meat sauce. Top with half each of the uncooked noodles, ricotta cheese mixture and mozzarella cheese. Repeat with 1-1/2 cups meat sauce and remaining noodles, ricotta cheese mixture and mozzarella cheese. Top with remaining meat sauce. Sprinkle with Parmesan cheese. Cover; refrigerate 12 hours or overnight.

3 Heat oven to 350°F. Uncover baking dish; bake 50 to 60 minutes or until noodles are tender and casserole is bubbly. Cover; let stand 15 minutes before serving.

HIGH ALTITUDE (3500-6500 FT): In Step 3, bake covered 60 minutes. Uncover and bake 10 to 20 minutes longer.

NUTRITION INFORMATION PER SERVING: Calories 380 • Total Fat 19g • Saturated Fat 9g • Cholesterol 65mg • Sodium 700mg • Total Carbohydrate 31g • Dietary Fiber 2g • Protein 22g. DIETARY EXCHANGES: 1-1/2 Starch • 1/2 Other Carbohydrate • 2-1/2 Medium-Fat Meat • 1 Fat • 2 Carb Choices.

teriyaki beef and pineapple lettuce wraps

turkey stroganoff skillet supper

PREP TIME: 25 Minutes ✹ READY IN: 35 Minutes ✹ SERVINGS: 4

1 can (14 oz.) chicken broth	1/2 cup sour cream
1 jar (12 oz.) turkey gravy	1/8 teaspoon ground nutmeg
2-1/2 cups uncooked wide egg noodles (4 oz.)	1/8 teaspoon pepper
1 cup sliced fresh carrots (2 medium)	2 cups cubed cooked turkey
1 cup Green Giant® frozen sweet peas (from 1-lb. bag)	

1 In 10-inch skillet, mix broth and gravy until well blended. Heat to boiling. Stir in noodles, carrots, peas, sour cream, nutmeg and pepper. Return to boiling. Reduce heat to low; cover and simmer 10 minutes.

2 Stir in turkey. Cook about 4 minutes, stirring occasionally, until noodles and vegetables are tender.

NUTRITION INFORMATION PER SERVING: Calories 400 • Total Fat 17g • Saturated Fat 6g • Cholesterol 105mg • Sodium 1020mg • Total Carbohydrate 32g • Dietary Fiber 3g • Protein 29g. DIETARY EXCHANGES: 1-1/2 Starch • 1/2 Other Carbohydrate • 1 Vegetable • 3 Lean Meat • 1-1/2 Fat • 2 Carb Choices.

teriyaki chicken and rice

PREP TIME: 10 Minutes ✳ **READY IN:** 1 Hour 15 Minutes ✳ **SERVINGS:** 4

2 cups fresh baby carrots, halved lengthwise

1 cup uncooked regular long-grain white rice

1 can (14 oz.) baby corn nuggets, drained

1 can (14 oz.) chicken broth

5 tablespoons teriyaki sauce

1 cut-up frying chicken, skin removed if desired (3 to 3-1/2 lb.)

1/4 cup orange marmalade

1/2 teaspoon ginger

3/4 cup cashew halves and pieces

1 Heat oven to 375°F. Spray 13x9-inch (3-quart) glass baking dish with nonstick cooking spray. In sprayed baking dish, combine carrots, rice, corn nuggets, broth and 2 tablespoons of the teriyaki sauce; mix well.

2 Arrange chicken pieces over rice mixture. In small bowl, combine remaining 3 tablespoons teriyaki sauce, orange marmalade and ginger; blend well. Spoon mixture over chicken and rice mixture. Cover with foil. Bake covered at 375°F for 45 minutes.

3 Uncover baking dish; bake an additional 15 to 30 minutes or until chicken is fork-tender and juices run clear. Sprinkle with cashews.

   HIGH ALTITUDE (3500-6500 FT): Add 1/4 cup water to carrot and rice mixture. Bake covered at 400°F for 45 minutes. Uncover baking dish; bake an additional 25 to 40 minutes.

NUTRITION INFORMATION PER SERVING: Calories 860 • Total Fat 34g • Saturated Fat 8g • Cholesterol 130mg • Sodium 1830mg • Total Carbohydrate 90g • Dietary Fiber 5g • Protein 54g. DIETARY EXCHANGES: 4-1/2 Starch • 1 Other Carbohydrate • 5-1/2 Medium-Fat Meat • 1 Fat • 5-1/2 Carb Choices.

cook's notes

To reduce the amount of fat in each serving of this recipe by about 10 grams, remove the skin from the chicken. By doing this, each serving of the lower-fat version has about 90 fewer calories than each serving of the original recipe.

hot roast beef sandwiches au jus

PREP TIME: 20 Minutes ✳ **READY IN:** 8 Hours 20 Minutes ✳ **SERVINGS:** 10

1 beef eye of round roast (2-1/2 lb.), trimmed of fat

6 cloves garlic, peeled

2 teaspoons coarsely ground black pepper

1 large onion, thinly sliced

1/2 cup condensed beef broth (from 10-1/2-oz. can)

10 kaiser rolls, split, toasted

2 large tomatoes, each cut into 5 slices

1 With sharp knife, make 6 evenly spaced slits deep into beef roast. Insert garlic into slits. Sprinkle pepper evenly over entire roast; rub pepper into roast.

2 Spray 3- to 4-qt. slow cooker with cooking spray. Place onion slices in slow cooker; pour broth over onion. Place roast over onion and broth. Cover; cook on Low heat setting 6-8 hours.

3 Remove roast from slow cooker; place on cutting board. Cut roast across grain into thin slices; return slices to slow cooker to moisten. Fill each toasted roll with beef, onion and 1 tomato slice. If desired, spoon small amount of broth from slow cooker over beef.

NUTRITION INFORMATION PER SERVING: Calories 280 • Total Fat 6g • Saturated Fat 1.5g • Cholesterol 55mg • Sodium 380mg • Total Carbohydrate 30g • Dietary Fiber 2g • Protein 27g. DIETARY EXCHANGES: 2 Starch • 3 Very Lean Meat • 1/2 Fat • 2 Carb Choices.

open-faced hamburger phillies

READY IN: 20 Minutes ✳ **SERVINGS:** 4

1   lb. lean (at least 80%) ground beef

1   medium green bell pepper, cut into 1/2-inch strips

1   medium red bell pepper, cut into 1/2-inch strips

1   small onion, cut into thin wedges

1/2 cup creamy Italian dressing

1   loaf (1 lb.) Italian bread

4   slices (1-1/2 oz. each) provolone cheese, cut into quarters

1   In 12-inch skillet, cook beef, bell peppers and onion over medium-high heat 5 to 7 minutes, stirring occasionally, until beef is thoroughly cooked; drain. Stir in 1/4 cup of the dressing.

2   Cut loaf of bread in half horizontally. Spread remaining 1/4 cup dressing on cut sides of bread. Place both halves, cut sides up, on ungreased large cookie sheet. Broil 4 to 6 inches from heat 3 to 5 minutes or until lightly toasted.

3   Remove bread from broiler. Spread beef mixture on cut halves of bread; top with cheese. Broil 2 to 3 minutes longer or until cheese is melted. Cut each half into 2 pieces.

NUTRITION INFORMATION PER SERVING: Calories 760 • Total Fat 37g • Saturated Fat 14g • Cholesterol 100mg • Sodium 1620mg • Total Carbohydrate 67g • Dietary Fiber 4g • Protein 41g. DIETARY EXCHANGES: 3-1/2 Starch • 1/2 Other Carbohydrate • 1 Vegetable • 4 Medium-Fat Meat • 3 Fat • 4-1/2 Carb Choices.

skillet chicken parmigiana

PREP TIME: 30 Minutes ✳ **READY IN:** 35 Minutes ✳ **SERVINGS:** 4

special touch

Is company coming over? Serve the chicken over steaming hot spaghetti.

4 boneless skinless chicken breasts (about 1-1/4 lb.)	1 egg
1/4 cup Progresso® plain bread crumbs	1 teaspoon olive or vegetable oil
2 tablespoons grated Parmesan cheese	1 can (19 oz.) Progresso® Vegetable Classics hearty tomato soup
1 teaspoon garlic powder	1/4 cup shredded mozzarella cheese (1 oz.)
1 teaspoon dried basil leaves	

1 Between pieces of plastic wrap or waxed paper, place each chicken breast, smooth side down; gently pound with flat side of meat mallet or rolling pin until about 1/4 inch thick.

2 In small bowl, mix bread crumbs, Parmesan cheese, garlic powder and basil. In another small bowl, beat egg with fork or wire whisk. Dip chicken into egg, then coat with crumb mixture.

3 In 12-inch nonstick skillet, heat oil over medium heat. Add chicken; cook uncovered 5 to 7 minutes, turning once, until no longer pink in center. Remove from skillet; keep warm.

4 Pour soup into same skillet; heat to boiling over medium-high heat. Boil uncovered 4 to 5 minutes, stirring occasionally, until slightly thickened.

5 Return cooked chicken to skillet. Reduce heat to low; sprinkle mozzarella cheese over chicken. Cover; cook 2 to 3 minutes or until cheese is melted.

NUTRITION INFORMATION PER SERVING: Calories 320 • Total Fat 10g • Saturated Fat 3.5g • Cholesterol 145mg • Sodium 770mg • Total Carbohydrate 19g • Dietary Fiber 2g • Protein 38g. DIETARY EXCHANGES: 1 Other Carbohydrate • 1 Vegetable • 5 Very Lean Meat • 1-1/2 Fat • 1 Carb Choice.

salsa fajita beef

salsa fajita beef

PREP TIME: 20 Minutes ✷ **READY IN:** 25 Minutes ✷ **SERVINGS:** 4

- 2 to 3 tablespoons vegetable oil
- 2 Old El Paso® flour tortillas for burritos (8 inch from 11.5-oz. pkg.), cut into 1/2-inch-wide strips
- 1 lb. boneless beef sirloin steak, cut into bite-size strips

- 1-1/2 cups frozen bell pepper and onion stir-fry (from 1-lb. bag)
- 1-1/2 cups Green Giant® Niblets® frozen corn (from 1-lb. bag)
- 1-1/2 cups Old El Paso® thick 'n chunky salsa
- 1 tablespoon sugar

1. In 10-inch skillet, heat 2 tablespoons of the oil over medium-high heat. Cook tortilla strips, a few at a time, 1 to 2 minutes, stirring occasionally, until crisp (if necessary, add additional tablespoon oil); drain tortilla strips on paper towels.

2. In same skillet, cook beef over medium-high heat 2 to 4 minutes, stirring occasionally, until browned. Stir in all remaining ingredients. Reduce heat to medium; simmer 5 minutes or until vegetables are crisp-tender. Stir in tortilla strips.

NUTRITION INFORMATION PER SERVING: Calories 380 • Total Fat 14g • Saturated Fat 3g • Cholesterol 60mg • Sodium 890mg • Total Carbohydrate 39g • Dietary Fiber 2g • Protein 26g. DIETARY EXCHANGES: 2 Starch • 1/2 Other Carbohydrate • 1 Vegetable • 2-1/2 Lean Meat • 1 Fat • 2-1/2 Carb Choices.

philly cheese steak crescent pizza

READY IN: 30 Minutes ✷ **SERVINGS:** 8

- 1 can (8 oz.) Pillsbury® refrigerated crescent dinner rolls
- 1/2 lb. thinly sliced cooked roast beef (from deli)
- 1 tablespoon Italian dressing (not creamy)
- 1 to 1-1/2 cups shredded mozzarella cheese (4 to 6 oz.)

- 2 tablespoons olive or vegetable oil
- 1 cup coarsely chopped green bell pepper
- 1 cup coarsely chopped onions
- 1/2 teaspoon beef-flavor instant bouillon

1. Heat oven to 375°F. Unroll dough into 2 long rectangles. Place in ungreased 13x9-inch pan; press over bottom and 1/2 inch up sides to form crust. Wrap beef tightly in foil. Place crescent dough and beef in oven. Bake about 10 minutes or until crust is light golden brown.

2. Arrange warm beef over crust. Brush with dressing. Sprinkle with cheese. Bake 8 to 10 minutes longer or until edges of crust are golden brown and cheese is melted.

3. Meanwhile, in 8-inch skillet, heat oil over medium heat until hot. Add bell pepper, onions and bouillon; cook 3 to 5 minutes, stirring frequently, until vegetables are tender. To serve, spoon cooked vegetables over melted cheese. Cut into squares.

NUTRITION INFORMATION PER SERVING: Calories 260 • Total Fat 17g • Saturated Fat 6g • Cholesterol 30mg • Sodium 440mg • Total Carbohydrate 15g • Dietary Fiber 1g • Protein 13g. DIETARY EXCHANGES: 1 Starch • 1-1/2 Very Lean Meat • 3 Fat • 1 Carb Choice.

JACKIE MEDLEY
Covington, Kentucky
Bake-Off® Contest 38, 1998

DEAN PHILIPP
Portland, Oregon
Bake-Off® Contest 40, 2002

smoked turkey quesadillas

READY IN: 30 Minutes ✳ SERVINGS: 4

1 ripe avocado, pitted, peeled
4 oz. cream cheese or 1/3-less-fat cream cheese (Neufchâtel), softened
1/2 teaspoon ground cumin
1/4 teaspoon garlic powder
1/4 teaspoon salt
1/8 teaspoon pepper
1/2 cup julienne-cut oil-packed sun-dried tomatoes, drained
1 can (4.5 oz.) Old El Paso® chopped green chiles, drained

1 cup shredded hot pepper Monterey Jack or Monterey Jack cheese (4 oz.)
1 package (11.5 oz.) Old El Paso® flour tortillas for burritos (8 tortillas)
8 slices (1-1/2 oz. each) smoked turkey breast
1 cup shredded Cheddar cheese (4 oz.)
2 tablespoons butter or margarine
Ripe olive slices, if desired

1 In medium bowl, mash avocado. Stir in cream cheese, cumin, garlic powder, salt and pepper until well blended. Stir in tomatoes and chiles.

2 Sprinkle 3/4 cup of the Monterey Jack cheese on 4 of the tortillas. Top each with turkey slice; spread avocado mixture over turkey. Top with remaining turkey slices; sprinkle with 3/4 cup of the Cheddar cheese. Top with remaining tortillas.

3 In 12-inch skillet, melt 1/2 tablespoon of the butter over medium heat. Add 1 quesadilla; cook 2 to 4 minutes, turning once, until golden brown. Repeat with remaining butter and quesadillas. Garnish with remaining Monterey Jack and Cheddar cheese; top each with olive slices. Cut quesadillas into quarters.

NUTRITION INFORMATION PER SERVING: Calories 840 • Total Fat 53g • Saturated Fat 25g • Cholesterol 140mg • Sodium 2740mg • Total Carbohydrate 53g • Dietary Fiber 4g • Protein 39g. DIETARY EXCHANGES: 3-1/2 Starch • 4 Medium-Fat Meat • 6 Fat • 3-1/2 Carb Choices.

havarti ham and potatoes

PREP TIME: 15 Minutes ✳ READY IN: 1 Hour 15 Minutes ✳ SERVINGS: 4

1 can (10-3/4 oz.) condensed cream of celery soup
1/2 cup sour cream with chives and onions
1 cup shredded Havarti cheese (4 oz.)
1 package (1 lb. 4 oz.) refrigerated unpeeled potato wedges

1-1/2 cups cubed cooked ham
1 cup Green Giant Select® frozen baby sweet peas
1 cup french fried onions

1 Heat oven to 350°F. Spray shallow 2-quart casserole with nonstick cooking spray. In large bowl, combine soup, sour cream and cheese; mix well. Add potatoes, ham and peas; stir gently to mix. Spoon into sprayed casserole. Cover. Bake covered at 350°F for 30 minutes.

2 Uncover casserole; sprinkle french fried onions over top. Bake uncovered an additional 25 to 30 minutes or until bubbly and thoroughly heated.

NUTRITION INFORMATION PER SERVING: Calories 550 • Total Fat 32g • Saturated Fat 15g • Cholesterol 80mg • Sodium 2020mg • Total Carbohydrate 46g • Dietary Fiber 5g • Protein 24g. DIETARY EXCHANGES: 3 Starch • 2 Medium-Fat Meat • 4 Fat • 3 Carb Choices.

smoked turkey quesadillas

SHAREE DAWN ROBERTS
Paducah, Kentucky
Bake-Off® Contest 41, 2004

orange-chicken-chipotle pizza

PREP TIME: 15 Minutes ✳ READY IN: 30 Minutes ✳ SERVINGS: 6

1 can (13.8 oz.) Pillsbury® refrigerated classic pizza crust

2 tablespoons extra-virgin olive oil

1 large onion, quartered, sliced

3 boneless skinless chicken breasts, cut into 1/2-inch pieces

1/3 cup orange marmalade

1 teaspoon seasoned salt

1 teaspoon ground cumin

1 to 3 chipotle chiles in adobo sauce (from 7-oz. can), finely chopped

1 can (11 oz.) mandarin orange segments, well drained on paper towels

1 cup shredded Monterey Jack cheese (4 oz.)

1 cup shredded sharp Cheddar cheese (4 oz.)

1 Heat oven to 425°F. Lightly spray 14-inch pizza pan with cooking spray. Unroll dough; place on pan. Starting at center, press out dough to edge of pan. Bake 6 to 8 minutes or until crust begins to brown.

2 Meanwhile, in 10-inch skillet, heat oil over medium heat until hot. Cook onion in oil 6 to 8 minutes, stirring frequently, until caramelized.

3 Reduce oven temperature to 375°F. Add chicken to skillet; cook 5 to 6 minutes, stirring frequently, until chicken is no longer pink in center. Stir in marmalade, salt, cumin, chipotle chiles and mandarin orange segments. Remove from heat; cool 1 minute.

4 Spread chicken mixture evenly over partially baked crust. Sprinkle both cheeses over top. Bake at 375°F 10 to 13 minutes or until cheese is melted and crust is deep golden brown.

NUTRITION INFORMATION PER SERVING: Calories 500 • Total Fat 21g • Saturated Fat 9g • Cholesterol 75mg • Sodium 1010mg • Total Carbohydrate 51g • Dietary Fiber 1g • Protein 28g. DIETARY EXCHANGES: 2 Starch • 1-1/2 Other Carbohydrate • 3 Very Lean Meat • 3-1/2 Fat • 3-1/2 Carb Choices.

meatballs and rice skillet dinner

PREP TIME: 10 Minutes ✳ **READY IN:** 35 Minutes ✳ **SERVINGS:** 3

1	tablespoon butter or margarine	16	frozen cooked meatballs (8 oz.)
1	package (6.8 oz.) beef-flavored rice and vermicelli mix	2	cups Green Giant® frozen broccoli cuts (from 1-lb. bag), thawed
2-1/3	cups water	1/2	cup red bell pepper strips

1 In 10-inch skillet, melt butter over medium heat. Stir in rice and vermicelli from mix; cook and stir until lightly browned. Add water, contents of seasoning packet from mix and meatballs; heat to boiling. Stir; reduce heat to medium-low. Cover; cook 15 minutes.

2 Gently stir in broccoli and bell pepper. Increase heat to medium; cover and cook 7 to 9 minutes or until broccoli is crisp-tender and rice is tender. Before serving, stir to fluff rice.

HIGH ALTITUDE (3500-6500 FT): Increase water to 2-2/3 cups.

NUTRITION INFORMATION PER SERVING: Calories 520 • Total Fat 16g • Saturated Fat 6g • Cholesterol 90mg • Sodium 1320mg • Total Carbohydrate 69g • Dietary Fiber 5g • Protein 27g. DIETARY EXCHANGES: 4 Starch • 1 Vegetable • 2 Medium-Fat Meat • 1/2 Fat • 4 Carb Choices.

cook's notes

To quickly thaw frozen broccoli, place in colander or strainer; rinse with warm water until thawed. Drain well.

italian sunday supper

PREP TIME: 30 Minutes ✳ **READY IN:** 2 Hours ✳ **SERVINGS:** 6

1	lb. lean (at least 80%) ground beef	1	bag (1 lb. 4 oz.) refrigerated sliced potatoes
1/2	lb. bulk Italian pork sausage	1	medium onion, halved, thinly sliced
1	can (19 oz.) Progresso® Vegetable Classics creamy tomato soup	1	cup shredded mozzarella cheese (4 oz.)
1	can (14.5 oz.) diced tomatoes with Italian-style herbs, undrained	1-1/2	cups shredded Gruyère cheese (6 oz.)
		3	tablespoons chopped fresh flat-leaf parsley

1 Heat oven to 350°F. Spray 13x9-inch (3-quart) glass baking dish or 3-quart oval casserole with cooking spray. Heat 12-inch nonstick skillet over medium-high heat. Add ground beef and sausage; cook, stirring frequently, until beef is thoroughly cooked and sausage is no longer pink. Drain; stir in soup and tomatoes.

2 Layer half each of the potatoes and onion in baking dish; repeat layers. Sprinkle evenly with mozzarella cheese. Pour meat mixture over cheese; stir gently to mix. Cover tightly with foil.

3 Bake 60 to 70 minutes or until potatoes are tender and mixture is hot and bubbly. Uncover; sprinkle evenly with Gruyère cheese. Bake uncovered about 10 minutes longer or until cheese is melted. Let stand 10 minutes before serving. Sprinkle with parsley.

NUTRITION INFORMATION PER SERVING: Calories 570 • Total Fat 29g • Saturated Fat 13g • Cholesterol 110mg • Sodium 990mg • Total Carbohydrate 39g • Dietary Fiber 3g • Protein 38g. DIETARY EXCHANGES: 2-1/2 Starch • 4-1/2 Medium-Fat Meat • 1 Fat • 2-1/2 Carb Choices.

cook's notes

Swiss cheese can be substituted for the Gruyère cheese.

Pillsbury

Bake-Off®

RETA M. SMITH
Libertyville, Illinois
Bake-Off® Contest 35, 1992

cook's notes

If you are unable to find fresh or canned tomatillos, you can use 2 cups of coarsely chopped green tomatoes.

white chili with salsa verde

PREP TIME: 45 Minutes ❋ READY IN: 1 Hour 15 Minutes ❋ SERVINGS: 8

SALSA VERDE

- 2 cups coarsely chopped fresh tomatillos or 2 cans (11 oz. each) tomatillos, chopped, well drained
- 1/2 cup chopped onion
- 1/2 cup chopped fresh cilantro
- 2 to 3 tablespoons lime juice
- 1/2 teaspoon lemon-pepper seasoning
- 1/2 teaspoon dried oregano leaves
- 1/2 teaspoon adobo seasoning or garlic powder
- 1 pickled jalapeño chile, chopped
- 1 clove garlic, finely chopped

CHILI

- 2-1/2 cups water
- 1 teaspoon lemon-pepper seasoning
- 1 teaspoon cumin seed
- 4 bone-in chicken breasts (about 1-1/2 lb.), skin removed
- 1 clove garlic, finely chopped
- 1 cup chopped onions
- 2 boxes (9 oz. each) frozen shoepeg white corn, thawed
- 2 cans (4.5 oz. each) chopped green chiles, undrained
- 1 teaspoon ground cumin
- 2 to 3 tablespoons lime juice
- 2 cans (15.5 oz. each) great northern beans, undrained
- 2/3 cup crushed tortilla chips
- 1/2 cup shredded reduced-fat Monterey Jack cheese (2 oz.)

1. In medium bowl, mix salsa verde ingredients. Refrigerate 30 minutes to blend flavors. Meanwhile, in 4-quart saucepan, heat water, 1 teaspoon lemon-pepper seasoning and cumin seed to boiling. Add chicken. Reduce heat to low; cover and simmer 20 to 28 minutes or until chicken is fork-tender and juices run clear. Remove chicken from bones; cut into 1-inch pieces. Return chicken to saucepan.

2. Spray 8-inch skillet with cooking spray. Heat over medium heat until hot. Add 1 clove garlic; cook and stir 1 minute. Remove from skillet; add to chicken mixture.

3. Add 1 cup onions to skillet; cook and stir until tender. Add cooked onions, corn, chiles, cumin and 2 to 3 tablespoons lime juice to chicken mixture. Heat to boiling. Add beans; cook until hot.

4. To serve, place about 1 tablespoon each of tortilla chips and cheese in each of 8 individual soup bowls; ladle soup over cheese. Serve with salsa verde.

HIGH ALTITUDE (3500-6500 FT): Add up to 1/4 cup water if chili is too thick.

NUTRITION INFORMATION PER SERVING: Calories 360 • Total Fat 7g • Saturated Fat 2g • Cholesterol 40mg • Sodium 1030mg • Total Carbohydrate 47g • Dietary Fiber 10g • Protein 27g. DIETARY EXCHANGES: 2 Starch • 1 Other Carbohydrate • 3 Very Lean Meat • 1 Fat • 3 Carb Choices.

easy glazed ham steak

READY IN: 15 Minutes ❋ SERVINGS: 4

- 2 tablespoons frozen orange juice concentrate
- 2 tablespoons packed brown sugar
- 1/8 teaspoon ground cinnamon
- 1/8 teaspoon ground cloves
- 1 slice (3/4 lb.) smoked cooked ham (3/4 inch thick)

1. In small bowl, mix orange juice concentrate, brown sugar, cinnamon and cloves. Heat 10-inch nonstick skillet over medium-high heat. Add ham; cook uncovered 4 minutes. Turn ham; brush with orange juice mixture. Cook uncovered 4 to 6 minutes longer or until thoroughly heated. Cut ham into pieces to serve.

NUTRITION INFORMATION PER SERVING: Calories 170 • Total Fat 7g • Saturated Fat 2.5g • Cholesterol 45mg • Sodium 1090mg • Total Carbohydrate 10g • Dietary Fiber 0g • Protein 17g. DIETARY EXCHANGES: 1/2 Other Carbohydrate • 2-1/2 Lean Meat • 1/2 Carb Choice.

white chili with salsa verde

Merry Christmas Morning

Rise and shine with the breakfast treats in this chapter. Hearty brunch casseroles, yummy pancakes and more make Christmas morning deliciously memorable.

p. 182

p. 175

p. 191

p. 172

p. 174

ham and eggs frittata biscuits p. 195

Kitchen tip

Hollandaise sauce from a jar won't separate when it's heated so it's a nice alternative to the traditional sauce made from scratch that often has a tendency to separate.

scrambled eggs benedict

PREP TIME: 10 Minutes ✳ READY IN: 15 Minutes ✳ SERVINGS: 4

8 eggs	1 jar (7.5 oz.) hollandaise sauce
1/2 cup milk or water	8 slices Canadian bacon (5 oz.)
1/8 teaspoon pepper	4 English muffins, split, toasted
2 tablespoons butter	Paprika, if desired

1 In medium bowl, beat eggs, milk and pepper with wire whisk or fork until well blended. In 10-inch nonstick skillet, melt butter over medium heat. Pour egg mixture into skillet. As mixture begins to set on bottom and side, gently lift cooked portion with pancake turner so thin, uncooked portion can flow to bottom of skillet (avoid constant stirring). Cook 4 to 5 minutes or until eggs are thickened throughout but still moist and fluffy.

2 In 2-cup microwavable measuring cup, microwave hollandaise sauce on High 1 minute 30 seconds to 2 minutes or until hot; cover tightly to keep warm.

3 On large microwavable plate, place Canadian bacon slices in single layer. Microwave on High 45 to 60 seconds or until warm.

4 Place 2 toasted muffin halves on each plate. Top each muffin half with slice of Canadian bacon, about 1/3 cup eggs and 2 tablespoons hollandaise sauce; sprinkle with paprika.

NUTRITION INFORMATION PER SERVING: Calories 510 • Total Fat 29g • Saturated Fat 12g • Cholesterol 480mg • Sodium 1070mg • Total Carbohydrate 34g • Dietary Fiber 2g • Protein 27g. DIETARY EXCHANGES: 2 Starch • 3 Medium-Fat Meat • 3 Fat • 2 Carb Choices.

caramel-nut breakfast biscuits

PREP TIME: 5 Minutes ✹ READY IN: 40 Minutes ✹ SERVINGS: 2

1 teaspoon butter or margarine, softened

2 tablespoons butterscotch or caramel topping

1/8 teaspoon ground cinnamon

2 tablespoons chopped walnuts

2 Pillsbury® frozen buttermilk biscuits (from 4 lb. 11-oz. bag)

1 teaspoon sugar

1 Heat oven to 350°F. Generously butter bottom and sides of 2 (6 oz.) custard cups with softened butter. In small bowl, stir together topping and cinnamon. Divide between custard cups. Sprinkle with walnuts. Place frozen biscuit in each cup. Sprinkle each biscuit with 1/2 teaspoon sugar.

2 Bake 23 to 27 minutes or until golden brown and biscuits are no longer doughy. Immediately run sharp knife around edge of cup; turn each upside down onto serving plate. Slowly lift custard cup from biscuit, releasing biscuit onto plate. Spread any topping remaining in cup over biscuit. Cool 5 minutes before serving.

HIGH ALTITUDE (3500-6500 FT): Bake 26 to 30 minutes.

NUTRITION INFORMATION PER SERVING: Calories 320 • Total Fat 16g • Saturated Fat 4g • Cholesterol 5mg • Sodium 670mg • Total Carbohydrate 39g • Dietary Fiber 0g • Protein 5g. DIETARY EXCHANGES: 1-1/2 Starch • 1 Other Carbohydrate • 3 Fat • 2-1/2 Carb Choices.

cook's notes

Vary the recipe to suit your tastes. Instead of the walnuts, use toasted almonds instead, or drizzle the finished biscuits with a little chocolate syrup.

broccoli brunch braid

D IANE T UCKER
Blackfoot, Idaho
Bake-Off® Contest 33, 1988

PREP TIME: 25 Minutes ✳ **READY IN:** 1 Hour ✳ **SERVINGS:** 8

1/2 lb. bulk pork sausage	1 cup shredded Cheddar cheese (4 oz.)
2 cups Green Giant® frozen broccoli cuts	1 jar (4.5 oz.) Green Giant® sliced mushrooms, drained
1 egg	
1 tablespoon all-purpose flour	1 can (8 oz.) Pillsbury® refrigerated crescent dinner rolls
1/4 teaspoon baking powder	
1/2 cup ricotta cheese	1 egg white, beaten
	1/4 teaspoon caraway seed, if desired

1 Brown pork sausage in medium nonstick skillet over medium heat until no longer pink, stirring frequently. Drain well. Cook broccoli as directed on package. Drain, if necessary.

2 Heat oven to 350°F. Beat 1 egg in large bowl until well blended. Add flour and baking powder; beat well. Stir in ricotta cheese, Cheddar cheese, mushrooms, cooked sausage and broccoli.

3 Separate dough into 2 long rectangles. Place on ungreased large cookie sheet with long sides overlapping 1/2 inch; firmly press perforations and edges to seal. Press or roll dough to form 14x10-inch rectangle.

4 Spoon sausage mixture in 3 1/2-inch-wide strips lengthwise down center of dough to within 1/4 inch of short sides. Form sausage mixture into mounded shape.

5 Make cuts 1 inch apart on long sides of dough rectangle just to edge of filling. For braided appearance, fold strips of dough at an angle halfway across filling, alternating from side to side with edges of strips slightly overlapping. Brush with beaten egg white. Sprinkle with caraway seed.

6 Bake at 350°F for 25 to 35 minutes or until deep golden brown. Cool 5 minutes; remove from cookie sheet. Cut into slices.

NUTRITION INFORMATION PER SERVING: Calories 265 • Total Fat 15g • Saturated Fat 6g • Cholesterol 55mg • Sodium 730mg • Total Carbohydrate 19g • Dietary Fiber 2g • Protein 13g. DIETARY EXCHANGES: 1 Starch • 1-1/2 High-Fat Meat • 1/2 Fat • 1 Carb Choice.

berry nutty breakfast muffles

PREP TIME: 25 Minutes ✳ SERVINGS: 8

1 package (15.4 oz.) Pillsbury® nut quick bread & muffin mix

1 cup sweetened dried cranberries

1 cup quick-cooking rolled oats

1-1/3 cups low-fat buttermilk

2 eggs or 3 egg whites

8 tablespoons whipped cream cheese spread (from 8-oz. container)

8 teaspoons reduced-sugar orange marmalade, if desired

MARIE GIARDINA
Harvey, Louisiana
Bake-Off® Contest 40, 2002

1 Spray 8x4-inch Belgian waffle iron with nonstick cooking spray. Heat waffle iron. In large bowl, combine quick bread mix, contents of packet from mix, cranberries and oats; mix well. Add buttermilk and eggs; stir 50 to 75 strokes with spoon until mix is moistened.

2 For each waffle, spoon about 1/2 cup batter into hot waffle iron; spread slightly. Cook 2 to 4 minutes or until steaming stops and waffle is golden brown.

3 Top each serving with 1 tablespoon cream cheese. Garnish each serving with 1 teaspoon marmalade.

HIGH ALTITUDE (3500-6500 FT): Increase low-fat buttermilk to 1-1/2 cups. Cook as directed above.

NUTRITION INFORMATION PER SERVING: Calories 400 • Total Fat 11g • Saturated Fat 4g • Cholesterol 65mg • Sodium 360mg • Total Carbohydrate 66g • Dietary Fiber 4g • Protein 9g. DIETARY EXCHANGES: 2-1/2 Starch • 2 Fruit • 4-1/2 Other Carbohydrate • 2 Fat.

cook's notes

Any waffle iron works well in this recipe. The yield may vary depending upon the size of the waffle iron.

florentine eggs on english muffins

READY IN: 15 Minutes ✳ SERVINGS: 2

1/4 cup Yoplait® original plain yogurt (from 6-oz. container)

1 tablespoon light mayonnaise

1/2 teaspoon Dijon mustard

2 eggs

1 English muffin, split, toasted

1/2 cup fresh baby spinach leaves

Dash pepper

1 In small microwavable bowl, mix yogurt, mayonnaise and mustard. Microwave on High 20 to 40 seconds or until warm. Stir; set aside.

2 In 10-inch skillet, heat 1-1/2 to 2 inches water to boiling. Reduce heat to medium-low. Break each egg into shallow dish; carefully slide egg into hot water. Quickly spoon hot water over each egg until film forms over yolk. Simmer 3 to 5 minutes or until eggs are desired doneness.

3 Meanwhile, spread about 2 tablespoons sauce on each English muffin half. Top each with half of the spinach leaves.

4 With slotted spoon, remove eggs from water; place over spinach. Top each with half of remaining sauce; sprinkle with pepper.

NUTRITION INFORMATION PER SERVING: Calories 190 • Total Fat 8g • Saturated Fat 2g • Cholesterol 215mg • Sodium 300mg • Total Carbohydrate 17g • Dietary Fiber 1g • Protein 11g. DIETARY EXCHANGES: 1 Starch • 1 Medium-Fat Meat • 1/2 Fat • 1 Carb Choice.

kitchen tip

Spinach is an excellent source of the important nutrients folic acid and vitamin C. Spinach is also a good source of iron.

breakfast hash browns, bacon and egg bake

PREP TIME: 25 Minutes ✻ READY IN: 9 Hours 25 Minutes ✻ SERVINGS: 6

4 cups frozen potatoes O'Brien with onions and peppers (from 24-oz. bag)	1/2 teaspoon salt
1-1/2 cups shredded Colby-Monterey Jack cheese blend (6 oz.)	1/2 teaspoon red pepper sauce
6 eggs	5 slices precooked bacon, cut into 1/2-inch pieces (about 1/4 cup)
1/2 cup milk	1 can (8 oz.) Pillsbury® refrigerated crescent dinner rolls
1 teaspoon salt-free garlic-herb blend	

1 Spray 11x7-inch (2-quart) glass baking dish with cooking spray. Spread potatoes evenly in baking dish. Add cheese; stir gently to mix.

2 In medium bowl, beat eggs thoroughly with wire whisk. Add milk, garlic-herb blend, salt and pepper sauce; beat until well blended. Pour over potato-cheese mixture. Top with bacon. Cover; refrigerate at least 8 hours or overnight. When ready to serve, heat oven to 350°F. Uncover baking dish; bake 30 minutes.

3 Remove baking dish from oven. Separate dough into 4 rectangles. If desired, with small canapé cutters, cut out a few shapes from each rectangle. Carefully place rectangles over hot potato mixture so corners of rectangles meet in center; do not seal seams. Carefully press edges to sides of baking dish. Place cutout shapes on top of rectangles.

4 Bake 15 to 20 minutes longer or until potatoes are tender and crust is deep golden brown. Let stand 10 minutes before serving.

HIGH ALTITUDE (3500-6500 FT): When ready to serve, bake uncovered 35 minutes. After topping with dough, bake 18 to 23 minutes longer.

NUTRITION INFORMATION PER SERVING: Calories 475 • Total Fat 23g • Saturated Fat 10g • Cholesterol 245mg • Sodium 1010mg • Total Carbohydrate 47g • Dietary Fiber 3g • Protein 20g, DIETARY EXCHANGES: 3 Starch • 1-1/2 High-Fat Meat • 2 Fat • 3 Carb Choices.

skillet eggs and rice

PREP TIME: 15 Minutes ✻ READY IN: 45 Minutes ✻ SERVINGS: 8

1/2 lb. cooked kielbasa or smoked sausage, halved lengthwise, cut into 1/2-inch pieces	1/2 cup Old El Paso® thick 'n chunky salsa
1 box (7.6 oz.) Old El Paso® Spanish rice	4 eggs
2-1/2 cups water	Old El Paso® flour tortillas for soft tacos & fajitas (6 inch), heated, if desired

1 In 10-inch nonstick skillet, cook sausage over medium heat 2 to 3 minutes, stirring occasionally, until sausage begins to brown. Stir in rice, contents of seasoning packet, water and salsa. Heat to boiling. Reduce heat to low; cover and cook 20 minutes.

2 Break 1 egg onto each quarter of rice mixture (egg will sink into rice). Cover; cook 7 to 9 minutes or until eggs are set and rice is tender. Serve with warm tortillas.

High Altitude (3500-6500 ft): After adding rice, contents of seasoning packet, water and salsa, heat to boiling. Reduce heat to medium-low; cover and cook 25 minutes. After breaking eggs onto rice mixture, cover and cook 9 to 11 minutes.

NUTRITION INFORMATION PER SERVING: Calories 450 • Total Fat 22g • Saturated Fat 7g • Cholesterol 245mg • Sodium 1440mg • Total Carbohydrate 47g • Dietary Fiber 2g • Protein 16g, DIETARY EXCHANGES: 3 Starch • 1 High-Fat Meat • 2-1/2 Fat • 3 Carb Choices.

breakfast hash browns, bacon and egg bake

sausage and cheese crescent squares

BECKY McPHERSON
Birmingham, Alabama
Bake-Off® Contest 40, 2002

PREP TIME: 20 Minutes ✳ READY IN: 1 Hour ✳ SERVINGS: 32

2 cans (8 oz. each) Pillsbury® refrigerated crescent dinner rolls or Pillsbury® Recipe Creations™ flaky dough sheet

1 lb. hot or mild bulk pork sausage
1 package (8 oz.) cream cheese
2 cups shredded sharp Cheddar cheese (8 oz.)

1 Heat oven to 375°F. Crescent Rolls: Unroll 1 can of dough into 2 long rectangles. Place in ungreased 13x9-inch (3-quart) glass baking dish; press over bottom and 1/2 inch up sides to form crust. Recipe Creations: Unroll 1 can of dough. Place in ungreased 13x9-inch (3 quart) glass baking dish; press over bottom and 1/2 inch up sides to form crust.

2 Brown sausage in large skillet over medium heat until thoroughly cooked, stirring frequently. Remove sausage from skillet; discard drippings. Add cream cheese to same skillet. Cook over low heat until melted. Add cooked sausage; stir to coat. Spoon evenly over crust in baking dish. Sprinkle with cheese.

3 Crescent Rolls: Unroll second can of dough on work surface. Press to form 13x9-inch rectangle; firmly press perforations to seal. Carefully place over cheese. Recipe Creations: Unroll second can of dough on work surface. Press to from 13x9-inch rectangle. Carefully place over cheese.

4 Bake at 375°F for 21 to 26 minutes or until golden brown. Cool 15 minutes. Cut into small squares.

NUTRITION INFORMATION PER SERVING: Calories 130 • Total Fat 10g • Saturated Fat 4g • Cholesterol 20mg • Sodium 260mg • Total Carbohydrate 6g • Dietary Fiber 0g • Protein 5g. DIETARY EXCHANGES: 1/2 Starch • 1/2 High-Fat Meat • 1 Fat.

whole-grain waffles

READY IN: 15 Minutes ✳ SERVINGS: 6 waffles

1/2 cup all-purpose flour
1/2 cup whole wheat flour
1/2 cup quick-cooking oats
1 teaspoon baking powder

1-1/4 cups fat-free (skim) milk
1/4 cup fat-free egg product or 1 egg
1 tablespoon vegetable oil
Powdered sugar, if desired

1 Heat nonstick waffle maker. In large bowl, mix all-purpose flour, whole wheat flour, oats and baking powder.

2 In small bowl, mix milk, egg product and oil until well blended. Add to flour mixture all at once; stir just until large lumps disappear.

3 Spread batter in hot waffle maker; bake until waffle is golden brown and steaming stops. Sprinkle with powdered sugar.

HIGH ALTITUDE (3500-6500 FT): Add up to 1/4 cup additional milk if batter is too thick.

NUTRITION INFORMATION PER SERVING: Calories 270 • Total Fat 6g • Saturated Fat 1g • Cholesterol 0mg • Sodium 260mg • Total Carbohydrate 45g • Dietary Fiber 5g • Protein 13g. DIETARY EXCHANGES: 3 Starch • 1 Fat • 2-1/2 Carb Choices.

cook's notes

Instead of syrup, enjoy these waffles with fresh fruit.

tropical waffle bake

PREP TIME: 25 Minutes ✳ **READY IN:** 1 Hour 10 Minutes ✳ **SERVINGS:** 6

5 frozen buttermilk waffles (from 12-oz. bag), thawed

1-1/2 cups finely chopped bananas (2 medium)

2 cans (8 oz. each) crushed pineapple in juice, drained and juice reserved

4 eggs

2/3 cup granulated sugar

5 tablespoons packed brown sugar

6 oats 'n honey crunchy granola bars (3 pouches from 8.9-oz. box), crushed (heaping 1 cup)

1/2 cup chopped macadamia nuts

3 tablespoons Pillsbury Best® all-purpose flour

1/4 cup butter or margarine, softened

1 jar (10 oz.) strawberry spreadable fruit

Whipped cream, if desired

DIANE TOOMEY
Allentown, Pennsylvania
Bake-Off® Contest 42, 2006

kitchen tip

To easily crush granola bars, do not unwrap them. Use a rolling pin to crush bars.

1 Heat oven to 350°F. Spray 8-inch square (2-quart) glass baking dish with cooking spray. Break waffles into 1- to 2-inch pieces; place in bottom of baking dish. Gently stir bananas into reserved pineapple juice to coat. With slotted spoon, place bananas evenly over waffles; discard any remaining juice.

2 In medium bowl, beat eggs, granulated sugar and 2 tablespoons of the brown sugar with wire whisk until blended. Stir in drained pineapple. Pour mixture over waffles and bananas in dish. In another medium bowl, mix crushed granola bars, nuts, flour, remaining 3 tablespoons brown sugar and the butter until crumbly; sprinkle over top. Bake 30 to 35 minutes or until knife inserted in center comes out clean. Cool 10 minutes.

3 In small microwavable bowl, microwave spreadable fruit on High 1 minute. Stir; if necessary, continue to microwave on High in 15-second increments until melted and smooth. Cut waffle bake into 6 servings. Top each serving with about 2 tablespoons warm fruit spread and 1 to 2 tablespoons whipped cream.

HIGH ALTITUDE (3500-6500 FT): Heat oven to 375°F.

NUTRITION INFORMATION PER SERVING: Calories 710 • Total Fat 24g • Saturated Fat 8g • Cholesterol 160mg • Sodium 390mg • Total Carbohydrate 114g • Dietary Fiber 7g • Protein 11g. DIETARY EXCHANGES: 3 Starch • 1 Fruit • 3-1/2 Other Carbohydrate • 4-1/2 Fat • 7-1/2 Carb Choices.

cook's notes

This recipe is the perfect make-ahead brunch dish. Make it a day ahead, cover it and then refrigerate until baking time.

baked caramel french toast

PREP TIME: 20 Minutes ✱ **READY IN:** 8 Hours 45 Minutes ✱ **SERVINGS:** 4 (2 slices each)

TOPPING

1	cup packed brown sugar
6	tablespoons butter or margarine
1/3	cup whipping (heavy) cream
1	tablespoon light corn syrup

FRENCH TOAST

3	eggs
1/2	cup milk
1	teaspoon vanilla
1/4	teaspoon salt
8	(3/4-inch-thick) diagonal cut slices French bread

1 Spray 13x9-inch (3-quart) glass baking dish with cooking spray. In 2-quart saucepan, mix topping ingredients. Cook over medium heat, stirring constantly, until smooth. Do not boil. Spread topping in baking dish.

2 In shallow bowl, beat eggs with fork. Beat in milk, vanilla and salt. Dip bread slices into egg mixture, making sure all egg mixture is absorbed; arrange over topping in dish. Cover; refrigerate at least 8 hours or overnight.

3 When ready to bake, heat oven to 400°F. Uncover baking dish; bake 20 to 25 minutes or until bubbly and toast is golden brown. Remove from oven; let stand 3 minutes.

4 Place large heatproof serving platter upside down over baking dish; turn platter and baking dish over. Remove baking dish, scraping any extra caramel topping onto toast. Serve immediately.

NUTRITION INFORMATION PER SERVING: Calories 660 • Total Fat 30g • Saturated Fat 15g • Cholesterol 230mg • Sodium 680mg • Total Carbohydrate 87g • Dietary Fiber 1g • Protein 11g. DIETARY EXCHANGES: 2 Starch • 4 Other Carbohydrate • 1/2 Medium-Fat Meat • 5 Fat • 6 Carb Choices.

tex-mex breakfast bake

PREP TIME: 20 Minutes ✳ **READY IN:** 1 Hour 10 Minutes ✳ **SERVINGS:** 6

1/4 lb. bulk lean breakfast sausage

1 can (10 oz.) red enchilada sauce

2-1/2 oz. crumbled queso fresco (Mexican cheese) or farmer's cheese

1/3 cup sour cream

4 medium green onions, chopped (1/4 cup)

1 can (16.3 oz.) Pillsbury® Grands!® refrigerated flaky biscuits

1-1/4 cups shredded Colby-Monterey Jack cheese blend (5 oz.)

1/4 cup chopped fresh cilantro

1 Heat oven to 350°F. Spray 8x8- or 11x7-inch (2-quart) glass baking dish with cooking spray. In 10-inch skillet, cook sausage over medium-high heat, stirring frequently, until no longer pink. Drain sausage on paper towels.

2 Meanwhile, in small bowl, mix 1/4 cup of the enchilada sauce, the queso fresco, sour cream and onions; set aside. Pour remaining enchilada sauce into medium bowl. Separate dough into 8 biscuits; cut each into 8 pieces. Gently stir dough pieces into enchilada sauce to coat. Spoon mixture into baking dish; spread evenly. Sprinkle sausage evenly on top of biscuit pieces. Spread sour cream mixture evenly over top.

3 Bake 30 to 35 minutes or until center is set and edges are deep golden brown. Sprinkle Colby-Monterey Jack cheese over top.

4 Bake about 10 minutes longer or until cheese is bubbly. Sprinkle with cilantro. Let stand 5 minutes before serving. Cut into squares.

HIGH ALTITUDE (3500-6500 FT): Heat oven to 375°F. Use 11x7-inch (2-quart) glass baking dish. Bake 45 to 50 minutes. Sprinkle Colby-Monterey Jack cheese over top; bake about 5 minutes longer.

NUTRITION INFORMATION PER SERVING: Calories 440 • Total Fat 26g • Saturated Fat 10g • Cholesterol 40mg • Sodium 1170mg • Total Carbohydrate 36g • Dietary Fiber 0g • Protein 15g. DIETARY EXCHANGES: 1-1/2 Starch • 1 Other Carbohydrate • 1-1/2 High-Fat Meat • 2-1/2 Fat • 2-1/2 Carb Choices.

Pillsbury
Bake-Off®

LYNNE MILLIRON
Austin, Texas
Bake-Off® Contest 41, 2004

kitchen tip

With its slightly sharp flavor, cilantro, also known as Chinese parsley, gives a distinctive taste to Mexican, Latin American and Asian dishes.

get up 'n go breakfast sandwiches

get up 'n go breakfast sandwiches

PREP TIME: 15 Minutes ✻ **READY IN:** 45 Minutes ✻ **SERVINGS:** 8

- 1 can (16.3 oz.) Pillsbury® Grands!® refrigerated buttermilk or southern-style biscuits
- 8 thin slices Canadian bacon (about 4-1/2 oz.)
- 8 slices (1 oz. each) American cheese
- 8 thin slices tomato, if desired

1 Bake biscuits as directed on can. Cool completely, about 20 minutes. Split warm biscuits. Fill each with 1 slice Canadian bacon and 1 slice cheese cut to fit. Wrap sandwiches individually in microwavable plastic wrap. Place in large resealable freezer plastic bag; seal bag and freeze. For best quality, use within 3 months.

2 To heat 1 frozen sandwich, loosen wrapping. Microwave on High 45 to 60 seconds or until thoroughly heated and cheese is melted. Let stand 30 to 60 seconds to cool slightly before serving. Add tomato slice to each sandwich.

NUTRITION INFORMATION PER SERVING: Calories 320 • Total Fat 18g • Saturated Fat 9g • Cholesterol 35mg • Sodium 1270mg • Total Carbohydrate 25g • Dietary Fiber 0g • Protein 14g. DIETARY EXCHANGES: 1-1/2 Starch • 1-1/2 Medium-Fat Meat • 2 Fat • 1-1/2 Carb Choices.

cook's notes

It works best to microwave the sandwiches one by one. Start with the minimum time and check the middle of the biscuits before adding more time.

overnight brunch egg bake

PREP TIME: 30 Minutes ✻ **READY IN:** 9 Hours 35 Minutes ✻ **SERVINGS:** 12

- 6 cups shredded Colby-Monterey Jack cheese blend (24 oz.)
- 2 tablespoons butter or margarine
- 1/3 cup sliced green onions
- 1/2 medium red bell pepper, chopped
- 1 jar (4.5 oz.) Green Giant® sliced mushrooms, drained
- 8 oz. cooked ham, cut into thin bite-sized strips
- 8 eggs
- 1/2 cup all-purpose flour
- 2 tablespoons chopped fresh parsley
- 1-3/4 cups milk

1 Spray 13x9-inch (3-quart) glass baking dish with nonstick cooking spray. Sprinkle half of cheese evenly into baking dish. Melt margarine in medium skillet over medium heat. Cook onions, bell pepper and mushrooms in margarine until tender. Arrange vegetables over cheese in baking dish. Top with ham strips. Sprinkle remaining cheese over ham.

2 Beat eggs in large bowl. Beat in flour, parsley and milk. Pour over mixture in baking dish. Cover; refrigerate 8 hours or overnight.

3 Heat oven to 350°F. Uncover baking dish; bake 55 to 65 minutes or until mixture is set and top is lightly browned. Let stand 10 minutes. Cut into squares. If desired, garnish with red bell pepper and fresh parsley.

NUTRITION INFORMATION PER SERVING: Calories 360 • Total Fat 26g • Saturated Fat 15g • Cholesterol 215mg • Sodium 730mg • Total Carbohydrate 8g • Dietary Fiber 0g • Protein 24g. DIETARY EXCHANGES: 1/2 Starch • 3 High-Fat Meat • 1/2 Fat • 1/2 Carb Choice.

kitchen tip

When a recipe calls for sliced green onions, it's easier and faster to cut them with kitchen scissors than with a knife.

crescent breakfast pizzas

PREP TIME: 25 Minutes ✳ READY IN: 40 Minutes ✳ SERVINGS: 8

- 4 slices bacon
- 1 cup sliced fresh mushrooms (about 3 oz.)
- 1 can (8 oz.) Pillsbury® refrigerated crescent dinner rolls or 1 can (8 oz.) Pillsbury® Crescent Recipe Creations® refrigerated seamless dough sheet
- 1 package (3 oz.) cream cheese, softened

- 1/4 cup basil pesto
- 1 cup shredded mozzarella cheese (4 oz.)
- 2 large plum (Roma) tomatoes, each cut into 8 slices
- 3 medium green onions, sliced (3 tablespoons)

1 Heat oven to 375°F. Spray large cookie sheet with cooking spray. In 10-inch skillet, cook bacon until crisp; drain on paper towels. Crumble bacon; set aside. Reserve 1 tablespoon bacon drippings in skillet. Cook mushrooms in bacon drippings over medium heat 4 to 5 minutes, stirring frequently, until lightly browned.

2 If using crescent rolls: Unroll dough; separate into 4 rectangles. Press each into 8x4-inch rectangle, firmly pressing perforations to seal. If using dough sheet: Unroll dough; cut into 4 rectangles. Press each into 8x4-inch rectangle. Cut each in half crosswise, making 8 squares; place 1/2 inch apart on cookie sheet.

3 Spread 2 teaspoons cream cheese and about 1/2 tablespoon pesto on each square. Top evenly with cooked mushrooms and 1/2 cup of the mozzarella cheese. Arrange tomato slices over cheese. Sprinkle with onions, crumbled bacon and remaining 1/2 cup cheese.

4 Bake 13 to 15 minutes or until crust is golden brown. Immediately remove from cookie sheet. Serve warm.

NUTRITION INFORMATION PER SERVING: Calories 260 • Total Fat 18g • Saturated Fat 7g • Cholesterol 25mg • Sodium 480mg • Total Carbohydrate 13g • Dietary Fiber 0g • Protein 9g. DIETARY EXCHANGES: 1 Starch • 1 High-Fat Meat • 2 Fat • 1 Carb Choice.

huevos rancheros casserole

PREP TIME: 20 Minutes ✹ **READY IN:** 9 Hours 10 Minutes ✹ **SERVINGS:** 6

5	corn tortillas (6 inch)	6	eggs
1-1/2	cups finely shredded Colby-Monterey Jack cheese blend (6 oz.)	1/2	cup milk
1/2	lb. smoked cooked chorizo sausage, coarsely chopped	1/2	teaspoon dried oregano leaves
		1/8	teaspoon ground red pepper (cayenne)
1	can (4.5 oz.) Old El Paso® chopped green chiles		Old El Paso® thick 'n chunky salsa

1 Spray 8-inch square (2-quart) glass baking dish with nonstick cooking spray. Place 4 of the tortillas in bottom of sprayed baking dish, overlapping as necessary, about 1/2 to 1 inch up sides. Cut remaining tortilla in half; cut into 1/2-inch-wide strips.

2 Sprinkle 1/2 cup of the cheese over tortillas in baking dish. Top with chorizo, chiles and 1/2 cup cheese. Arrange tortilla strips over cheese.

3 In medium bowl, combine eggs, milk, oregano and ground red pepper; beat well. Pour over mixture in baking dish. Sprinkle with remaining 1/2 cup cheese; press lightly into egg mixture. Cover with foil. Refrigerate at least 8 hours or overnight.

4 Heat oven to 350°F. Bake covered casserole for 30 minutes. Uncover; bake 15 to 20 minutes longer or until knife inserted in center comes out clean. Let stand 5 minutes before serving. Cut into squares. Serve with salsa.

NUTRITION INFORMATION PER SERVING: Calories 390 • Total Fat 26g • Saturated Fat 11g • Cholesterol 265mg • Sodium 920mg • Total Carbohydrate 16g • Dietary Fiber 2g • Protein 23g. DIETARY EXCHANGES: 1 Starch • 1 Other Carbohydrate • 3 High-Fat Meat • 1/2 Fat.

asparagus quiche

PREP TIME: 15 Minutes ✹ **READY IN:** 1 Hour 20 Minutes ✹ **SERVINGS:** 6

1	Pillsbury® refrigerated pie crust, softened as directed on box	2	tablespoons all-purpose flour
1	can (10.5 oz.) Green Giant® cut spears asparagus, well drained	3	eggs, slightly beaten
		1/2	cup half-and-half
1	jar (2.5 oz.) Green Giant® sliced mushrooms, well drained	1/2	teaspoon salt
		1/8	teaspoon pepper
1	cup shredded Swiss cheese (4 oz.)	1/8	teaspoon ground nutmeg

1 Heat oven to 350°F. Place pie crust in 9-inch glass pie pan as directed on box for one-crust filled pie. Place asparagus and mushrooms in crust.

2 In large bowl, toss cheese with flour. Stir in eggs, half-and-half, salt, pepper and nutmeg. Pour over asparagus and mushrooms.

3 Bake 55 to 60 minutes or until knife inserted in center comes out clean. Let stand 5 minutes before serving.

HIGH ALTITUDE (3500-6500 FT): Cover crust edge with strips of foil after first 20 minutes of baking to prevent excessive browning.

NUTRITION INFORMATION PER SERVING: Calories 310 • Total Fat 20g • Saturated Fat 9g • Cholesterol 135mg • Sodium 620mg • Total Carbohydrate 23g • Dietary Fiber 1g • Protein 11g. DIETARY EXCHANGES: 1-1/2 Starch • 1 Medium-Fat Meat • 3 Fat • 1-1/2 Carb Choices.

LISA KRAMER
Madison, Indiana
Bake-Off® Contest 43, 2008

kitchen tip

When cutting dried fruit, to

prevent the fruit from sticking

to the knife blade, sprinkle

some powdered sugar over the

fruit and on the blade.

cranberry-pecan crescent sausage wraps

PREP TIME: 35 Minutes ✱ **READY IN:** 1 Hour 20 Minutes ✱ **SERVINGS:** 32

1/2 cup sweetened dried cranberries, coarsely chopped	32 cocktail-size smoked link sausages (from 16-oz. pkg.)
1 cup orange juice	1/2 cup packed Domino® or C&H® light brown sugar
1 can (8 oz.) Pillsbury® refrigerated crescent dinner rolls (8 rolls)	2/3 cup Fisher® Chef's Naturals® chopped pecans

1 Heat oven to 400°F. In small bowl, mix cranberries and orange juice. Let stand 15 minutes. Meanwhile, separate dough into rectangles; press each into 8x4-inch rectangle. Cut each rectangle into 8 (about 2-inch) squares.

2 Place 1 sausage on each square; wrap dough around sausage. Pinch edges to seal. Place sausage rolls seam side down in 13x9-inch (3-quart) glass baking dish. Bake 10 to 15 minutes or until light golden brown.

3 Meanwhile, drain orange juice from cranberries into 2-quart saucepan; reserve cranberries. Stir brown sugar into orange juice. Cook over medium heat 2 to 3 minutes, stirring occasionally, until sugar is dissolved.

4 Remove sausage rolls from oven. Pour orange juice mixture evenly over sausage rolls. Sprinkle with cranberries and pecans. Bake 10 to 13 minutes longer or until golden brown and bubbly. Serve warm.

HIGH ALTITUDE (3500-6500 FT): In Step 2, bake 15 to 18 minutes.

NUTRITION INFORMATION PER SERVING: Calories 120 • Total Fat 8g • Saturated Fat 2.5g • Cholesterol 10mg • Sodium 210mg • Total Carbohydrate 9g • Dietary Fiber 0g • Protein 3g. DIETARY EXCHANGES: 1/2 Other Carbohydrate • 1/2 High-Fat Meat • 1 Fat • 1/2 Carb Choice.

broccoli, potato and bacon quiche

PREP TIME: 20 Minutes ✻ **READY IN:** 1 Hour ✻ **SERVINGS:** 8

1 bag (19 oz.) Green Giant® frozen roasted potatoes with broccoli & cheese sauce

1 Pillsbury® refrigerated pie crust, softened as directed on box

4 Eggland's Best® eggs

2/3 cup whipping cream

7 slices bacon, cooked, crumbled (about 1/3 cup)

1 cup finely shredded Parmesan cheese (4 oz.)

1 cup finely shredded Cheddar cheese (4 oz.)

1/2 teaspoon dried basil leaves

1/2 teaspoon pepper

1/4 teaspoon parsley flakes

1/8 teaspoon salt, if desired

1 teaspoon finely chopped fresh chives

1 Heat oven to 350°F. Cook frozen potatoes with broccoli and cheese sauce in microwave as directed on bag. Meanwhile, place pie crust in 9-inch glass pie plate as directed on box for one-crust filled pie.

2 In large bowl, beat eggs and whipping cream with wire whisk until well blended. Stir in cooked potato mixture and remaining ingredients except chives. Pour filling into crust-lined plate; spread evenly. Sprinkle chives over filling.

3 Bake 30 to 40 minutes or until edge of filling is light golden brown and knife inserted in center comes out clean. Let stand 5 minutes before serving.

HIGH ALTITUDE (3500-6500 FT): Heat oven to 375°F. Bake 33 to 43 minutes.

NUTRITION INFORMATION PER SERVING: Calories 410 • Total Fat 29g • Saturated Fat 14g • Cholesterol 165mg • Sodium 880mg • Total Carbohydrate 21g • Dietary Fiber 1g • Protein 17g. DIETARY EXCHANGES: 1-1/2 Starch • 1-1/2 Medium-Fat Meat • 4 Fat • 1-1/2 Carb Choices.

TONYA NICOLE MARGALA
Newport Beach, California
Bake-Off® Contest 42, 2006

cook's notes

Perfect for brunch or supper, this hearty quiche can be made in just minutes with frozen vegetables and refrigerated pie crusts.

blueberry-oat pancakes

READY IN: 30 Minutes ✳ SERVINGS: 6 (2 pancakes each)

1 cup Cheerios® cereal	2 tablespoons canola oil
3/4 cup Gold Medal® whole wheat flour	1 egg
1/2 cup Gold Medal® all-purpose flour	1 cup fresh or frozen blueberries (do not thaw)
2 teaspoons baking powder	Additional Yoplait® Original 99% fat free lemon burst or French vanilla yogurt, if desired
1/2 teaspoon baking soda	
1 container (6 oz.) Yoplait® Original 99% fat free lemon burst or French vanilla yogurt	Additional fresh blueberries, if desired
3/4 cup fat-free (skim) milk	

1 Place cereal in food-storage plastic bag; seal bag and slightly crush with rolling pin. In medium bowl, mix cereal, flours, baking powder and baking soda. In small bowl, beat 1 container yogurt, the milk, oil and egg with wire whisk until well blended. Stir yogurt mixture into flour mixture with wire whisk until blended. Stir in 1 cup blueberries.

2 Brush griddle or 10-inch skillet with canola oil. Heat griddle to 375°F or heat skillet over medium heat. For each pancake, pour slightly less than 1/4 cup batter onto hot griddle.

3 Cook about 2 minutes or until puffed and dry around edges. Turn; cook other sides 1 to 2 minutes or until golden brown. Top individual servings with additional yogurt and blueberries.

HIGH ALTITUDE (3500-6500 FT): Increase skim milk to 1-1/4 cups.

NUTRITION INFORMATION PER SERVING: Calories 220 • Total Fat 7g • Saturated Fat 1g • Cholesterol 40mg • Sodium 340mg • Total Carbohydrate 34g • Dietary Fiber 3g • Protein 7g. DIETARY EXCHANGES: 2 Starch • 1/2 Other Carbohydrate • 1 Fat • 2 Carb Choices.

crunchy apple yogurt sundaes

READY IN: 10 Minutes ✳ SERVINGS: 3

2 cups Yoplait® 99% fat free creamy strawberry yogurt (from 2-lb. container)	1 small apple, unpeeled, cut into chunks
12 medium fresh whole strawberries	1 cup Cinnamon Toast Crunch® cereal

1 Set aside 3 strawberries. Remove stems from remaining 9 strawberries; cut each into 4 slices. Into each of 3 parfait glasses or clear drinking glasses, spoon 1 tablespoon yogurt. Place 6 strawberry slices and 2 apple chunks over yogurt in each glass. Sprinkle each with 1/4 cup cereal. Spoon about 1/3 cup yogurt over cereal.

2 Repeat layers with remaining sliced strawberries, apple chunks, cereal and yogurt. Garnish each sundae with reserved whole strawberry. Serve immediately.

NUTRITION INFORMATION PER SERVING: Calories 260 • Total Fat 3g • Saturated Fat 1g • Cholesterol 10mg • Sodium 190mg • Total Carbohydrate 52g • Dietary Fiber 2g • Protein 7g. DIETARY EXCHANGES: 1/2 Starch • 1/2 Fruit • 1-1/2 Other Carbohydrate • 1 Skim Milk • 3-1/2 Carb Choices.

blueberry-oat pancakes

wake-up espresso cereal bars

PREP TIME: 20 Minutes ✳ READY IN: 2 Hours 20 Minutes ✳ SERVINGS: 12

1/2 cup corn syrup	2 teaspoons boiling water
1/3 cup packed brown sugar	1/2 cup creamy peanut butter
2 teaspoons instant espresso coffee granules or instant coffee granules	2 cups Basic 4® cereal
	1 cup broken pretzel sticks

1 Butter bottom and sides of 8-inch square pan. In 3-quart saucepan, heat corn syrup and brown sugar to boiling over medium-high heat, stirring constantly. Remove from heat. In small bowl, stir coffee granules into boiling water until dissolved; stir into corn syrup mixture along with peanut butter until smooth. Add cereal and pretzels, stirring until evenly coated.

2 Press evenly in pan. Let stand about 2 hours or until set. For bars, cut into 4 rows by 3 rows. Store covered.

NUTRITION INFORMATION PER SERVING: Calories 190 • Total Fat 6g • Saturated Fat 1g • Cholesterol 0mg • Sodium 160mg • Total Carbohydrate 29g • Dietary Fiber 1g • Protein 4g. DIETARY EXCHANGES: 1 Starch • 1 Other Carbohydrate • 1 Fat • 2 Carb Choices.

cook's notes

Serve this energizing fruit shake as a quick breakfast or as an after-school snack.

peach-berry smoothies

READY IN: 10 Minutes ✳ SERVINGS: 4

2 cups Yoplait® Original 99% fat free strawberry yogurt	1 cup sliced fresh strawberries
1 cup sliced fresh or frozen peaches or nectarines	1 cup crushed ice

1 In blender or food processor, place all ingredients. Cover; blend on high speed 30 to 60 seconds or until smooth. Pour into 4 glasses. Serve immediately.

NUTRITION INFORMATION PER SERVING: Calories 130 • Total Fat 0g • Saturated Fat 0g • Cholesterol 0mg • Sodium 60mg • Total Carbohydrate 26g • Dietary Fiber 3g • Protein 5g. DIETARY EXCHANGES: 1-1/2 Other Carbohydrate • 1/2 Skim Milk • 2 Carb Choices.

sunny-side up waffles

READY IN: 15 Minutes ✳ SERVINGS: 4

4 frozen buttermilk waffles	4 canned apricot halves, drained
2 containers (6 oz. each) Yoplait® thick & creamy vanilla yogurt	

1 Heat waffles as directed on box. Place 1 waffle on each of 4 plates. Spoon about half of each container of yogurt onto each waffle. Smooth the yogurt around with the back of the spoon until it almost covers the top of each waffle. Top each waffle with an apricot half, rounded side up. Serve immediately.

NUTRITION INFORMATION PER SERVING: Calories 210 • Total Fat 5g • Saturated Fat 1.5g • Cholesterol 15mg • Sodium 290mg • Total Carbohydrate 35g • Dietary Fiber 1g • Protein 7g. DIETARY EXCHANGES: 2 Starch • 2 Carb Choices.

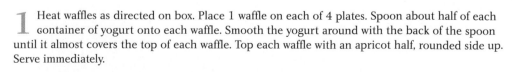

shrimp and spinach strata

PREP TIME: 25 Minutes ✳ READY IN: 9 Hours 40 Minutes ✳ SERVINGS: 8

- 10 to 12 slices French bread (1/2 inch thick)
- 1/2 cup purchased pesto
- 2 cups shredded Gouda cheese (8 oz.)
- 1 lb. shelled deveined uncooked medium shrimp, tails removed
- 1 bag (1 lb.) frozen cut leaf spinach, thawed, squeezed to drain well

- 1 bag (1 lb.) frozen bell pepper and onion stir-fry, thawed, drained
- 8 eggs
- 2 cups milk
- 1/2 teaspoon seasoned salt

1 Spray 13x9-inch (3-quart) glass baking dish with nonstick cooking spray. Arrange bread slices in bottom of sprayed baking dish. Cut cubes from bread to fill in empty spaces.

2 Spread pesto over bread. Sprinkle with 1 cup of the cheese. Layer shrimp, spinach, bell pepper and onion stir-fry, and remaining 1 cup cheese over bread.

3 In large bowl, beat eggs, milk and seasoned salt until well blended. Pour over mixture in baking dish. Cover with foil; refrigerate at least 8 hours or overnight.

4 Heat oven to 350°F. Uncover baking dish; bake 40 to 50 minutes or until set and knife inserted in center comes out clean. Let stand 15 minutes before serving.

NUTRITION INFORMATION PER SERVING: Calories 420 • Total Fat 24g • Saturated Fat 9g • Cholesterol 330mg • Sodium 790mg • Total Carbohydrate 22g • Dietary Fiber 2g • Protein 29g. DIETARY EXCHANGES: 1 Starch • 2 Vegetable • 3 Lean Meat • 3 Fat • 1-1/2 Carb Choices.

cook's note

Squeeze the spinach and bell pepper mixture completely dry between paper towels to keep any additional moisture out of the strata.

deviled ham and eggs

PREP TIME: 15 Minutes ✻ READY IN: 45 Minutes ✻ SERVINGS: 12

6 eggs	2 teaspoons yellow mustard
1 cup finely chopped cooked ham	1 teaspoon vinegar
1/4 cup fat-free mayonnaise or salad dressing	1 tablespoon chopped fresh chives
2 teaspoons sweet pickle relish	

1 In 3-quart saucepan, place eggs in single layer. Add enough cold water to cover eggs by 1 inch. Heat to boiling. Immediately remove from heat; cover and let stand 15 minutes. Drain; rinse with cold water. Let stand in ice water 10 minutes.

2 Peel eggs; cut in half lengthwise. Into medium bowl, slip out yolks; mash with fork. Stir in all remaining ingredients except chives. Spoon yolk mixture into egg white halves. Sprinkle with chives.

NUTRITION INFORMATION PER SERVING: Calories 70 • Total Fat 4g • Saturated Fat 1.5g • Cholesterol 115mg • Sodium 95mg • Total Carbohydrate 1g • Dietary Fiber 0g • Protein 6g. DIETARY EXCHANGE: 1 Medium-Fat Meat.

ham and broccoli quiche

PREP TIME: 15 Minutes ✹ READY IN: 1 Hour 5 Minutes ✹ SERVINGS: 6

1 Pillsbury® refrigerated pie crust, softened as directed on box	4 eggs
1-1/2 cups cubed cooked ham	1 cup milk
1-1/2 cups shredded Swiss cheese (6 oz.)	1/2 teaspoon salt
1 cup Green Giant Select® frozen broccoli florets (from 14-oz. box), thawed, well drained	1/2 teaspoon dry ground mustard
	1/2 teaspoon pepper

1 Heat oven to 375°F. Make pie crust as directed on box for one crust filled pie using 9-inch glass pie pan.

2 Layer ham, cheese and thawed broccoli in pie crust-lined pan. In medium bowl, beat all remaining ingredients until well blended. Pour over broccoli.

3 Bake 35 to 45 minutes or until knife inserted in center comes out clean. Let stand 5 minutes before serving. Cut into wedges.

HIGH ALTITUDE **(3500-6500 FT):** Bake at 375°F 45 to 55 minutes; during last 15 minutes of baking, cover edge of crust with strips of foil to prevent excessive browning.

NUTRITION INFORMATION PER SERVING: Calories 560 • Total Fat 34g • Saturated Fat 16g • Cholesterol 205mg • Sodium 1130mg • Total Carbohydrate 39g • Dietary Fiber 0g • Protein 24g. DIETARY EXCHANGES: 2-1/2 Starch • 2-1/2 High-Fat Meat • 2-1/2 Fat • 2-1/2 Carb Choices.

cook's notes

Cut up the ham, thaw the broccoli (cutting large pieces into smaller ones), shred the cheese and combine the egg mixture the night before you serve the quiche. Cover and refrigerate all ingredients separately. In the morning, combine all ingredients just before baking.

A frittata is nothing more than an Italian-style omelet that has the ingredients mixed with the eggs rather than folded inside. Frittatas are cooked slowly over low heat and typically cut into wedges to serve.

potato and asparagus frittata

READY IN: 40 Minutes ✷ **SERVINGS:** 4

2 tablespoons olive or vegetable oil	6 eggs
6 small red potatoes (12 oz.), each cut into 8 pieces	1/3 cup milk
2 cups (8 oz.) cut-up asparagus spears	1/2 teaspoon salt
2 tablespoons sliced green onions	1/8 teaspoon pepper
1 garlic clove, minced	1/2 cup crumbled feta cheese (2 oz.)
	1 tablespoon chopped fresh basil

1 Heat oil in large nonstick skillet over medium heat until hot. Add potatoes; cover and cook 10 to 12 minutes or until almost tender, stirring occasionally. Add asparagus, onions and garlic; cook 4 to 5 minutes or until asparagus is almost tender, stirring occasionally.

2 Meanwhile, beat eggs in medium bowl. Add milk, salt and pepper; beat well. Pour egg mixture over vegetables in skillet. Sprinkle with cheese and basil. Reduce heat to medium-low; cover and cook 12 to 14 minutes or until eggs are set. To serve, cut into wedges.

NUTRITION INFORMATION PER SERVING: Calories 330 • Total Fat 18g • Saturated Fat 6g • Cholesterol 335mg • Sodium 540mg • Total Carbohydrate 27g • Dietary Fiber 3g • Protein 15g. DIETARY EXCHANGES: 1-1/2 Starch • 1-1/2 Other Carbohydrate • 1 Vegetable • 1 Medium-Fat Meat • 2-1/2 Fat.

strawberry-topped french toast bake

PREP TIME: 30 Minutes ✳ READY IN: 9 Hours ✳ SERVINGS: 6

FRENCH TOAST BAKE

- 1 loaf (16 oz.) French bread (about 18 inches long), cut into 24 (3/4-inch-thick) slices
- 1 container (8 oz.) pineapple cream cheese spread
- 4 eggs
- 1 cup milk
- 1/4 cup sugar
- 1/4 teaspoon salt
- 1/4 teaspoon ground cinnamon
- 2 tablespoons butter, melted

TOPPING

- 1 quart (4 cups) fresh strawberries
- 1/2 cup sugar
- 2 tablespoons amaretto, if desired

1 Spray 13x9-inch (3-quart) glass baking dish with cooking spray. Spread about 1 tablespoon cream cheese on 12 bread slices. Top with remaining bread slices to form 12 sandwiches. Place sandwiches in baking dish to cover bottom of dish.

2 In medium bowl, beat eggs. Beat in milk, 1/4 cup sugar, the salt and cinnamon until well blended. Pour over bread in baking dish. Let stand at room temperature 5 minutes. Turn bread slices over. Cover; refrigerate 8 hours or overnight.

3 Chop 1 cup of the strawberries. (Refrigerate remaining berries.) In nonmetal bowl, gently stir chopped strawberries, 1/2 cup sugar and the amaretto until mixed. Cover; refrigerate 8 hours or overnight.

4 When ready to bake, heat oven to 400°F. Uncover baking dish; drizzle bread slices with melted butter. Bake 25 to 30 minutes or until golden brown.

5 Meanwhile, slice remaining strawberries and add to chilled strawberry mixture; mix lightly. Serve French toast with strawberry topping.

NUTRITION INFORMATION PER SERVING: Calories 600 • Total Fat 24g • Saturated Fat 13g • Cholesterol 195mg • Sodium 760mg • Total Carbohydrate 77g • Dietary Fiber 5g • Protein 16g. DIETARY EXCHANGES: 3 Starch • 2 Fruit • 5 Other Carbohydrate • 1 Medium-Fat Meat • 3-1/2 Fat.

cook's notes

Use a serrated bread knife to easily cut through the bread slices. Slice off the loaf ends so each slice will readily soak up the egg mixture.

country blueberry coffee cake

PREP TIME: 15 Minutes ✳ READY IN: 1 Hour 10 Minutes ✳ SERVINGS: 9

- 1/2 cup firmly packed brown sugar
- 1/2 teaspoon cinnamon
- 1 can (12 oz.) Pillsbury® Big Country® refrigerated buttermilk biscuits
- 1/4 cup butter or margarine, melted
- 1 cup quick-cooking rolled oats
- 1-1/2 cups fresh or frozen blueberries
- 1/4 cup sugar
- 2 tablespoons butter or margarine, cut into small pieces

1 Heat oven to 375°F. Generously grease 8- or 9-inch square (2-quart) baking dish. In small bowl, combine brown sugar and cinnamon; mix well with fork.

2 Separate dough into 10 biscuits. Cut each biscuit into quarters. Dip each piece in melted butter; coat with brown sugar mixture. Arrange in single layer in greased baking dish. Sprinkle with 1/2 cup of the oats.

3 In medium bowl, combine blueberries and sugar; toss to coat. Spoon over oats and biscuits; sprinkle with remaining 1/2 cup oats. Top with butter pieces.

4 Bake at 375°F for 30 to 35 minutes or until coffee cake is golden brown and center is done. Cool 20 minutes. Serve warm.

NUTRITION INFORMATION PER SERVING: Calories 300 • Total Fat 13g • Saturated Fat 6g • Cholesterol 20mg • Sodium 420mg • Total Carbohydrate 42g • Dietary Fiber 2g • Protein 4g. DIETARY EXCHANGES: 1-1/2 Starch • 1-1/2 Fruit • 3 Other Carbohydrate • 2 Fat.

Pillsbury Bake-Off®

WENDY HART
Ray City, Georgia
Bake-Off® Contest 38, 1998
Prize Winner

strawberry smoothies

strawberry smoothies

READY IN: 5 Minutes ✳ **SERVINGS:** 8

4 cups milk	2 cups vanilla or strawberry yogurt
1 package (10 oz.) frozen strawberries in syrup, partially thawed	1/2 cup strawberry-flavored syrup
	Fresh strawberries for garnish

1 In blender container, combine 2 cups of the milk and the strawberries; blend until smooth and thick.

2 Add yogurt and syrup; blend at low speed until mixed. Pour into pitcher or container. Stir in remaining 2 cups milk; mix well. Garnish with fresh strawberries, if desired.

NUTRITION INFORMATION PER SERVING: Calories 210 • Total Fat 3g • Saturated Fat 2g • Cholesterol 15mg • Sodium 115mg • Total Carbohydrate 39g • Dietary Fiber 0g • Protein 7g. DIETARY EXCHANGES: 2 Other Carbohydrate • 1 Skim Milk • 2-1/2 Carb Choices.

cook's notes

Thaw the strawberries only enough to slightly break them up. Almost-frozen berries make the beverage nice and thick.

turkey and egg brunch bake

PREP TIME: 40 Minutes ✳ **READY IN:** 10 Hours ✳ **SERVINGS:** 12

EGG BAKE

1-1/4 lb. bulk Italian-seasoned lean ground turkey	8 eggs
5 cups frozen country-style shredded hash-brown potatoes (from 30-oz. bag)	1-1/2 cups fat-free (skim) milk
	1/2 teaspoon salt
1/2 cup sliced green onions (8 medium)	**TOPPING**
2 jars (4.5 oz. each) Green Giant® sliced mushrooms, drained	1 clove garlic, minced
	6 medium Italian plum tomatoes, chopped (about 2 cups)
1 can (2-1/4 oz.) sliced ripe olives, drained	1/4 teaspoon salt
1 tablespoon chopped fresh or 1 teaspoon dried basil leaves	2 tablespoons chopped fresh or 2 teaspoons dried basil leaves
3 cups shredded reduced-fat Cheddar cheese (12 oz.)	

1 Spray 13x9-inch (3-quart) glass baking dish and 10-inch nonstick skillet with cooking spray. In skillet, cook ground turkey over medium-high heat, stirring frequently, until no longer pink. Remove turkey from skillet; drain on paper towels.

2 In large bowl, mix potatoes, onions, mushrooms, olives, 1 tablespoon basil and 2 cups of the cheese. Stir in turkey; spoon evenly into baking dish. Sprinkle with remaining 1 cup cheese.

3 In large bowl, beat eggs. Stir in milk and 1/2 teaspoon salt; pour over potato mixture in baking dish. Cut sheet of foil large enough to cover baking dish; spray with cooking spray. Cover baking dish with foil, sprayed side down. Refrigerate at least 8 hours or overnight.

4 When ready to bake, heat oven to 350°F. Bake covered 45 minutes. Uncover; bake 20 to 25 minutes longer or until center is set. Let stand 10 minutes before serving.

5 Meanwhile, spray 8-inch nonstick skillet with cooking spray. Add garlic; cook and stir over medium heat 1 minute. Stir in tomatoes and 1/4 teaspoon salt; cook about 5 minutes, stirring occasionally, until tomatoes are tender. Stir in 2 tablespoons basil. To serve, cut egg bake into squares; serve with warm topping.

HIGH ALTITUDE (3500-6500 FT): Bake covered at 350°F 45 minutes. Uncover; bake 25 to 30 minutes longer. Continue as directed above.

NUTRITION INFORMATION PER SERVING: Calories 280 • Total Fat 10g • Saturated Fat 3g • Cholesterol 180mg • Sodium 840mg • Total Carbohydrate 22g • Dietary Fiber 2g • Protein 25g. DIETARY EXCHANGES: 1 Starch • 3 Lean Meat • 1-1/2 Carb Choices.

cook's notes

Using bulk seasoned lean ground turkey for bulk pork sausage, reduced-fat Cheddar in place of regular cheese and skim milk instead of whole, you save 15 grams of fat and 80 calories per serving.

RENEE HEIMERL
Oakfield, Wisconsin
Bake-Off® Contest 43, 2008

cook's notes

Blueberry preserves can be substituted for the spreadable fruit.

quick and fruity crescent waffles

PREP TIME: 25 Minutes ❋ **READY IN:** 25 Minutes ❋ **SERVINGS:** 4

1/4 cup Fisher® Chef's Naturals® pecan pieces	1 firm ripe banana, cut into 1/4-inch slices
1 can (8 oz.) Pillsbury® refrigerated crescent dinner rolls (8 rolls)	1/2 cup whipped cream from aerosol can
1/2 cup Smucker's® Simply Fruit® blueberry spreadable fruit	1/4 teaspoon ground cinnamon
1 container (6 oz.) Yoplait® Original 99% fat free mountain blueberry yogurt	Fresh blueberries, if desired

1　Heat oven to 200°F. Heat square or rectangular waffle maker. Spray with Crisco® original no-stick cooking spray.

2　Meanwhile, in 8-inch nonstick skillet, toast pecans over medium heat 5 to 7 minutes, stirring frequently, until lightly browned. Remove from skillet; set aside.

3　Separate crescent dough into 8 triangles. Place 2 or 3 triangles at a time on waffle maker, leaving at least 1/2 inch of space around each triangle. Close lid of waffle maker; cook 1 to 2 minutes or until golden brown. Place cooked waffles on cookie sheet in oven to keep warm.

4　In 1-quart saucepan, heat spreadable fruit and yogurt over medium heat 2 to 3 minutes, stirring occasionally, until hot.

5　To serve, stack 2 crescent waffles, slightly overlapping, on each of 4 serving plates. Spoon 1/4 of the fruit sauce over each serving; top each serving with 1/4 of the banana slices and 1 tablespoon of the pecans. Top with whipped cream; sprinkle lightly with cinnamon. Garnish with blueberries.

NUTRITION INFORMATION PER SERVING: Calories 450 • Total Fat 19g • Saturated Fat 6g • Cholesterol 10mg • Sodium 470mg • Total Carbohydrate 63g • Dietary Fiber 5g • Protein 7g. DIETARY EXCHANGES: 2-1/2 Starch • 1-1/2 Other Carbohydrate • 3-1/2 Fat • 4 Carb Choices.

crunchy oven french toast

PREP TIME: 20 Minutes ✳ READY IN: 2 Hours 40 Minutes ✳ SERVINGS: 4

3 eggs
1 cup half-and-half
2 tablespoons sugar
1 teaspoon vanilla
1/4 teaspoon salt
3 cups corn flakes cereal, crushed to 1 cup

8 (3/4-inch-thick) diagonally cut slices French bread
Strawberry syrup
Fresh strawberries, raspberries and/or blueberries
Whipped topping

1 Grease 15x10x1-inch baking pan. In shallow bowl, combine eggs, half-and-half, sugar, vanilla and salt; beat well. Place crushed cereal in another shallow bowl. Dip each bread slice in egg mixture, making sure all egg mixture is absorbed. Coat each slice with crumbs. Place in greased pan; cover. Freeze 1 to 2 hours or until firm.

2 Heat oven to 425°F. Bake bread slices 15 to 20 minutes or until golden brown, turning once. Serve with syrup and strawberries. If desired, garnish with whipped topping.

NUTRITION INFORMATION PER SERVING: Calories 390 • Total Fat 13g • Saturated Fat 6g • Cholesterol 180mg • Sodium 690mg • Total Carbohydrate 55g • Dietary Fiber 2g • Protein 13g. DIETARY EXCHANGES: 2 Starch • 1-1/2 Other Carbohydrate • 1 Medium-Fat Meat • 1-1/2 Fat • 3-1/2 Carb Choices.

cook's notes

Start Sunday morning off with a bang with this easy baked version of French toast that is given an appealing crunch with corn flakes.

french toast with raspberry-cranberry syrup

PREP TIME: 10 Minutes ✳ READY IN: 30 Minutes ✳ SERVINGS: 4

FRENCH TOAST

2 whole eggs plus 1 egg white, lightly beaten, or 1/2 cup fat-free egg product

1 cup fat-free (skim) milk

2 teaspoons rum extract

1/4 teaspoon ground nutmeg

8 slices (1 inch thick) French bread

SYRUP

1/2 cup frozen (thawed) raspberry blend juice concentrate

1/2 cup jellied cranberry sauce

1 tablespoon powdered sugar

1 Heat oven to 425°F. In medium bowl, mix beaten eggs and egg white, the milk, rum extract and nutmeg until well blended.

2 Dip bread slices into egg mixture, coating both sides well. Place in ungreased 11x7-inch (2-quart) glass baking dish, place bread slices. Pour remaining egg mixture over bread slices. Let stand at room temperature 10 minutes.

3 Spray cookie sheet with cooking spray. Remove bread slices from dish; place on cookie sheet. Bake 12 to 15 minutes or until golden brown, turning slices once halfway through baking.

4 Meanwhile, in 1-quart saucepan, mix syrup ingredients; cook over medium-low heat, stirring occasionally, until cranberry sauce and sugar have melted. Serve French toast with syrup.

NUTRITION INFORMATION PER SERVING: Calories 300 • Total Fat 4.5g • Saturated Fat 1.5g • Cholesterol 105mg • Sodium 340mg • Total Carbohydrate 55g • Dietary Fiber 2g • Protein 10g. DIETARY EXCHANGES: 1-1/2 Starch • 2 Other Carbohydrate • 1 Medium-Fat Meat • 3-1/2 Carb Choices.

ham and eggs frittata biscuits

PREP TIME: 15 Minutes ✳ READY IN: 35 Minutes ✳ SERVINGS: 8

1 can (16.3 oz.) Pillsbury® Grands!® refrigerated buttermilk or Southern-style biscuits

3 Eggland's Best® eggs

1-1/4 to 1-1/2 teaspoons Italian seasoning

1/2 cup diced cooked ham

1 cup shredded Italian cheese blend (4 oz.)

1/4 cup roasted red bell peppers (from a jar), drained, chopped

1/2 cup diced seeded plum (Roma) tomatoes

2 tablespoons thinly sliced fresh basil leaves

Fresh basil sprigs

Cherry tomatoes

SANDY BRADLEY
Bolingbrook, Illinois
Bake-Off® Contest 40, 2002

1 Heat oven to 375°F. Spray large cookie sheet with Crisco® original no-stick cooking spray. Separate dough into 8 biscuits; place 3 inches apart on cookie sheet. Press out each biscuit to form 4-inch round with 1/4-inch-high rim around outside edge.

2 In small bowl, beat 1 of the eggs. Brush over tops and sides of biscuits. Sprinkle with 1 teaspoon of the Italian seasoning.

3 In another small bowl, beat remaining 2 eggs and remaining 1/4 to 1/2 teaspoon Italian seasoning. Spoon egg mixture evenly into indentations in each biscuit. Top with ham, 1/2 cup of the cheese, the roasted peppers, tomatoes, sliced basil and remaining 1/2 cup cheese.

4 Bake 15 to 20 minutes or until biscuits are golden brown and eggs are set. Garnish with basil sprigs and cherry tomatoes.

NUTRITION INFORMATION PER SERVING: Calories 290 • Total Fat 16g • Saturated Fat 6g • Cholesterol 100mg • Sodium 840mg • Total Carbohydrate 25g • Dietary Fiber 0g • Protein 12g. DIETARY EXCHANGES: 1-1/2 Starch • 1 High-Fat Meat • 1-1/2 Fat • 1-1/2 Carb Choices.

Gifts from the Kitchen

Sweets and candies made from scratch make wonderful gifts with a personal touch. These goodies are sure to put smiles on the lucky ones who receive them.

p. 207

p. 199

p. 215

p. 218

p. 211

chocolate chip and peppermint cookie bark p. 214

fancy dipped strawberries

PREP TIME: 45 Minutes ✳ SERVINGS: 40

TOPPINGS
Miniature semisweet chocolate chips

Chopped nuts

Colored sugars and candy sprinkles

Grated chocolate

Shredded coconut

DIPPED BERRIES
1 quart fresh whole strawberries with stems (4 cups)

1 cup vanilla creamy ready-to-spread frosting

1 Tear off 1 piece of waxed paper. Put it on the large cookie sheet. Decide what toppings you want to put on your strawberries. Put some of each of the toppings you pick in a different custard cup.

2 Put the colander in the sink. Put the strawberries in the colander. Rinse them with cold water. Put the washed strawberries on paper towels. Pat them dry.

3 Measure out the frosting. Use the rubber spatula to scrape all of it out of the measuring cup and into the bowl. Microwave the frosting on High 15 to 20 seconds, until it is melted. Stir the frosting once with the spoon.

4 Dip the bottom of the each strawberry halfway into the melted frosting. Right away, dip the strawberry into 1 of the toppings you picked. Put the strawberries on the waxed paper-lined cookie sheets. Put the cookie sheets in the refrigerator for 5 minutes or until the frosting on the strawberries is hard.

NUTRITION INFORMATION PER SERVING: Calories 50 • Total Fat 2g • Saturated Fat 1.5g • Cholesterol 0mg • Sodium 0mg • Total Carbohydrate 8g • Dietary Fiber 0g • Protein 0g. DIETARY EXCHANGES: 1/2 Fruit • 1/2 Fat • 1/2 Carb Choice.

cook's notes

Try dipping these scrumptious strawberries in chocolate frosting instead of vanilla.

crunchy cinnamon snack mix

PREP TIME: 10 Minutes ✳ **READY IN:** 30 Minutes ✳ **SERVINGS:** 30

5 cups Cinnamon Toast Crunch® cereal

3 cup Cheerios® cereal

1 bag (6.6 oz.) original-flavored tiny fish-shaped crackers

1 bag (7 oz.) pretzel sticks

1/2 cup butter or margarine, melted

1 Heat oven to 300 F. In large bowl, mix all ingredients except butter. Pour melted butter over mixture; toss until evenly coated. Spread in ungreased 13x9-inch pan. Bake 25 minutes, stirring occasionally.

NUTRITION INFORMATION PER SERVING: Calories 120 • Total Fat 6g • Saturated Fat 2.5g • Cholesterol 10mg • Sodium 220mg • Total Carbohydrate 17g • Dietary Fiber 1g • Protein 1g. DIETARY EXCHANGES: 1 Starch • 1 Fat • 1 Carb Choice.

cook's notes

Use your imagination—try fish-shaped pretzels, pretzel twists or Cheddar crackers in this flavorful snack mix.

orange-cranberry pound cake

PREP TIME: 20 Minutes ✳ READY IN: 3 Hours ✳ SERVINGS: 16

3/4 cup butter, softened	1 teaspoon baking powder
3/4 cup granulated sugar	1/4 teaspoon salt
3 eggs	3/4 cup sweetened dried cranberries
2 tablespoons orange juice	1 tablespoon grated orange peel
1 teaspoon vanilla	2 tablespoons coarse or granulated sugar
1-1/2 cups all-purpose flour	

1 Heat oven to 350°F. Grease and flour 9x5-inch loaf pan. In large bowl, beat butter and 3/4 cup granulated sugar with electric mixer on medium speed 3 minutes until light and fluffy. Add eggs, one at a time, beating well after each addition. Add orange juice and vanilla; beat 30 seconds or until well blended.

2 Add flour, baking powder and salt; beat on low speed 30 seconds or just until blended. With spoon, fold in cranberries and orange peel. Spoon batter into pan. Sprinkle with coarse sugar.

3 Bake 50 to 55 minutes or until toothpick inserted in center comes out clean. Cool 15 minutes. Remove from pan to cooling rack. Cool completely, about 1 hour 30 minutes.

NUTRITION INFORMATION PER SERVING: Calories 200 • Total Fat 10g • Saturated Fat 6g • Cholesterol 65mg • Sodium 140mg • Total Carbohydrate 25g • Dietary Fiber 0g • Protein 3g. DIETARY EXCHANGES: 1 Starch • 1/2 Other Carbohydrate • 2 Fat • 1-1/2 Carb Choices.

cathedral window fudge

PREP TIME: 15 Minutes ✳ READY IN: 2 Hours 15 Minutes ✳ SERVINGS: 36

1 package (12 oz.) semisweet chocolate chips (2 cups)	1 can (16 oz.) chocolate frosting
	2 cups multicolored miniature marshmallows

1 Melt chocolate chips in large saucepan over low heat, stirring constantly until smooth. Remove from heat. Stir in frosting. Fold in marshmallows. Let stand 15 minutes or until mixture is cool enough to handle.

2 Divide mixture in half. Pour mixture onto sheet of plastic wrap, scraping mixture from saucepan. Shape each half into 9x2-inch log.

3 Wrap tightly in waxed paper; refrigerate 2 hours or until firm. With thin sharp knife, cut each log into 1/2-inch-thick slices.

NUTRITION INFORMATION PER SERVING: Calories 110 • Total Fat 5g • Saturated Fat 2g • Cholesterol 0mg • Sodium 30mg • Total Carbohydrate 16g • Dietary Fiber 1g • Protein 1g. DIETARY EXCHANGES: 1 Fruit • 1 Other Carbohydrate • 1 Fat.

orange-cranberry pound cake

cook's notes

Be sure to use a large saucepan when preparing the caramel, because the baking soda will cause the mixture to foam up.

caramel corn

PREP TIME: 55 Minutes ✳ READY IN: 1 Hour 25 Minutes ✳ SERVINGS: 6

6	cups popped popcorn	2	tablespoons water
1/2	cup toasted slivered almonds, if desired	2	tablespoons light corn syrup
3/4	cup firmly packed brown sugar	1/8	teaspoon salt
1/2	cup butter	1/4	teaspoon baking soda

1 Heat oven to 250°F. Spread popcorn in ungreased 15x10x1-inch baking pan. Sprinkle almonds over popcorn.

2 In large saucepan, combine brown sugar, butter, water, corn syrup and salt; mix well. Bring to a boil over medium heat. Boil 2 minutes, stirring constantly.

3 Remove saucepan from heat. Stir in baking soda until well mixed. Immediately pour mixture over popcorn and almonds; toss until coated.

4 Bake at 250°F for 15 minutes. Stir; bake an additional 15 minutes. Stir; bake 5 minutes. Immediately spread on foil or waxed paper. Cool 30 minutes before serving.

NUTRITION INFORMATION PER SERVING: Calories 380 • Total Fat 23g • Saturated Fat 11g • Cholesterol 40mg • Sodium 530mg • Total Carbohydrate 40g • Dietary Fiber 2g • Protein 3g. DIETARY EXCHANGES: 1 Starch • 1-1/2 Fruit • 2-1/2 Other Carbohydrate • 4-1/2 Fat.

pistachio brittle

PREP TIME: 45 Minutes ✳ READY IN: 1 Hour 45 Minutes ✳ SERVINGS: 64

2 cups sugar
1 cup light corn syrup
1/2 cup water

1 cup butter
2 cups salted shelled pistachios
1 teaspoon baking soda

1 Heat oven to 200°F. Grease 2 cookie sheets. In heavy 5- to 6-quart saucepan, place sugar, corn syrup and water. Heat to boiling over medium heat, stirring frequently. Stir in butter.

2 Cook over medium heat, stirring occasionally for about 10 minutes until candy thermometer reaches 240°F. Meanwhile, place cookie sheets in oven. (Warm cookie sheets allow the candy to spread easily before it sets up.)

3 Stir pistachios into sugar mixture; continue cooking, stirring frequently, until candy thermometer reaches 300°F. Remove from heat; stir in baking soda (mixture will be light and foamy).

4 Remove cookie sheets from oven; pour candy onto cookie sheets. With buttered spatula, spread until candy is about 1/4 inch thick. Cool completely, about 1 hour. Break into pieces. Store in tightly covered container.

HIGH ALTITUDE (3500-6500 FT): In Step 3, cook until thermometer reaches 290°F.

NUTRITION INFORMATION PER SERVING: Calories 90 • Total Fat 4.5g • Saturated Fat 2g • Cholesterol 10mg • Sodium 45mg • Total Carbohydrate 11g • Dietary Fiber 0g • Protein 0g. DIETARY EXCHANGES: 1/2 Other Carbohydrate • 1 Fat • 1 Carb Choice.

cook's notes

You can use any kind of combination of salted nuts; cashews, pecans or almonds are crunchy and delicious in this brittle.

taco snack mix

PREP TIME: 15 Minutes ✳ READY IN: 1 Hour 40 Minutes ✳ SERVINGS: 10

3 cups Corn Chex® cereal

2 cups mini cheese-filled buttery cracker sandwiches (from 9-1/2-oz. box)

1-3/4 cups tiny fish-shaped pretzels (from 8.7-oz. pkg.)

1 cup salted peanuts

2 tablespoons vegetable oil

2 tablespoons Old El Paso® taco seasoning mix (from 1-oz. pkg.)

1 Heat oven to 250°F. In 4-quart bowl, mix cereal, cracker sandwiches, pretzels and peanuts. In small bowl, mix oil and taco seasoning mix. Pour over cereal mixture; toss to coat. Pour into ungreased 13x9-inch pan. Bake 1 hour, stirring every 15 minutes. Cool completely, about 25 minutes.

NUTRITION INFORMATION PER SERVING: Calories 270 • Total Fat 16g • Saturated Fat 3.5g • Cholesterol 0mg • Sodium 560mg • Total Carbohydrate 25g • Dietary Fiber 2g • Protein 7g. DIETARY EXCHANGES: 1-1/2 Starch • 1/2 High-Fat Meat • 2 Fat • 1-1/2 Carb Choices.

rocky road pretzels

READY IN: 20 Minutes ✳ SERVINGS: 24

6 oz. milk chocolate, chopped

2 oz. bittersweet baking chocolate or mildly sweet dark chocolate, chopped

1/3 cup coarsely chopped cashews

1/3 cup miniature marshmallows

24 lattice pretzels or small pretzel twists

1 Line large cookie sheet with waxed paper or cooking parchment paper. In medium microwavable bowl, microwave chocolates uncovered on High about 1 minute or until chocolates can be stirred smooth. Fold in cashews and marshmallows.

2 Arrange pretzels on cookie sheet 2 inches apart. Spoon heaping teaspoon chocolate onto each pretzel. Let stand in cool place until set, about 15 minutes (do not refrigerate).

NUTRITION INFORMATION PER SERVING: Calories 70 • Total Fat 4g • Saturated Fat 2g • Cholesterol 0mg • Sodium 25mg • Total Carbohydrate 7g • Dietary Fiber 0g • Protein 1g. DIETARY EXCHANGES: 1/2 Other Carbohydrate • 1 Fat • 1/2 Carb Choice.

cook's notes

Refrigerating these pretzels will cause the chocolate to lose some of its shine.

raisin-peanut treats

PREP TIME: 10 Minutes ✳ READY IN: 1 Hour 10 Minutes ✳ SERVINGS: 24

3 tablespoons butter or margarine

1 bag (10-1/2 oz.) miniature marshmallows (6 cups)

5 cups Cheerios® cereal

1 cup raisins

1/2 cup dry-roasted peanuts

1 Butter 13x9-inch pan. In large microwavable bowl, microwave butter and marshmallows uncovered on High about 2 minutes, stirring after every minute, until smooth.

2 Immediately stir in cereal, raisins and peanuts until coated. Press in pan, using buttered back of spoon. Cool about 1 hour or until firm. For bars, cut into 6 rows by 4 rows. Store loosely covered.

STOVETOP DIRECTIONS: Butter 13x9-inch pan. In 3-quart saucepan, heat butter and marshmallows over low heat, stirring frequently, until melted. Remove from heat. Immediately stir in cereal, raisins and peanuts until coated. Press in pan, using buttered back of spoon. Cool about 1 hour or until firm. For bars, cut into 6 rows by 4 rows. Store loosely covered.

NUTRITION INFORMATION PER SERVING: Calories 120 • Total Fat 3.5g • Saturated Fat 1g • Cholesterol 0mg • Sodium 90mg • Total Carbohydrate 20g • Dietary Fiber 1g • Protein 2g. DIETARY EXCHANGES: 1/2 Starch • 1 Other Carbohydrate • 1/2 Fat • 1 Carb Choice.

cook's notes

Try dried cranberries instead of raisins and chopped walnuts instead of peanuts.

trail mix-peanut butter bark

PREP TIME: 25 Minutes ✳ READY IN: 55 Minutes ✳ SERVINGS: 12

2 cups small pretzel twists (from 15-oz. bag)	1/2 cup cashew halves
1 cup Cheerios® cereal	10 oz. vanilla-flavored candy coating (almond bark), cut into small pieces
2/3 cup sweetened dried cranberries	1/3 cup creamy peanut butter

1 Cut 24x12-inch sheet of waxed paper. In large bowl, mix pretzels, cereal, cranberries and cashews.

2 In small microwavable bowl, microwave candy coating and peanut butter on High 1 minute. Stir well; microwave 15 to 30 seconds longer or until melted and mixture can be stirred smooth.

3 Gradually pour melted candy coating mixture over pretzel mixture, stirring to coat all pieces. Quickly spread mixture onto waxed paper into 12x8-inch rectangle, about 1/2 inch thick. Let stand 30 minutes or until set. Break into 2x2-inch pieces.

NUTRITION INFORMATION PER SERVING: Calories 270 • Total Fat 14g • Saturated Fat 6g • Cholesterol 0mg • Sodium 190mg • Total Carbohydrate 30g • Dietary Fiber 1g • Protein 5g. DIETARY EXCHANGES: 1/2 Starch • 1-1/2 Other Carbohydrate • 1/2 High-Fat Meat • 2 Fat • 2 Carb Choices.

hazelnut and candied cherry bark

PREP TIME: 30 Minutes ✻ **READY IN:** 50 Minutes ✻ **SERVINGS:** 32

3/4 cup hazelnuts (filberts)

1-1/2 lb. vanilla-flavored candy coating or almond bark, cut into pieces

1/2 cup coarsely chopped candied red cherries

1/2 cup coarsely chopped candied green cherries

1 Heat oven to 350°F. Place hazelnuts on ungreased cookie sheet. Bake at 350°F for 5 to 8 minutes or until lightly browned and skins have loosened. Turn hazelnuts onto clean, cloth towel; rub nuts between towel to remove skins. Cool 10 minutes. Coarsely chop nuts.

2 Meanwhile, line cookie sheet or 15x10x1-inch baking pan with waxed paper. Place candy coating in microwaveable bowl. Microwave on High for 1 minute. Stir; continue to microwave in 15-second increments until coating can be stirred smooth.

3 Stir in hazelnuts and cherries. Spread mixture on paper-lined cookie sheet. Cool 20 minutes or until completely cooled. Break into pieces.

NUTRITION INFORMATION PER SERVING: Calories 160 • Total Fat 9g • Saturated Fat 4g • Cholesterol 4mg • Sodium 35mg • Total Carbohydrate 19g • Dietary Fiber 0g • Protein 2g. DIETARY EXCHANGES: 1/2 Starch • 1/2 Fruit • 1 Other Carbohydrate • 2 Fat.

cook's notes

For a variation, prepare recipe as directed at left. Spread the mixture on a paper-lined cookie sheet. Immediately sprinkle with 1/2 cup semi-sweet chocolate chips; press into mixture. Cool as directed.

MRS. JOHN HAMLON
Fergus Falls, Minnesota
Bake-Off® Contest 04, 1952
Prize Winner

peanut brittle cookies

PREP TIME: 25 Minutes ✹ READY IN: 50 Minutes ✹ SERVINGS: 24

1/2 cup packed brown sugar	1/4 teaspoon baking soda
1/2 cup butter or margarine, softened	1/2 teaspoon ground cinnamon
1 egg, beaten, 1 tablespoon reserved	1/2 cup salted peanuts, finely chopped
1 teaspoon vanilla	Reserved 1 tablespoon beaten egg
1 cup all-purpose flour	1/2 cup salted peanuts or nuts

1 Heat oven to 325°F. Grease large cookie sheet with shortening or cooking spray. In large bowl, beat brown sugar and butter with electric mixer on medium speed, scraping bowl occasionally, until well blended. Beat in 2 tablespoons beaten egg and the vanilla. On low speed, beat in flour, baking soda and cinnamon until dough forms. Stir in 1/2 cup finely chopped peanuts. Refrigerate dough 30 minutes.

2 Crumble chilled dough onto cookie sheet. With floured hands, press dough into 14x10-inch rectangle. Brush with reserved 1 tablespoon egg. Sprinkle with 1/2 cup peanuts; press into dough.

3 Bake 20 to 25 minutes or until dark golden brown. Cool 5 minutes; while warm, cut or break into 24 pieces.

HIGH ALTITUDE (3500-6500 FT): Bake 20 to 23 minutes.

NUTRITION INFORMATION PER SERVING: Calories 110 • Total Fat 7g • Saturated Fat 3g • Cholesterol 20mg • Sodium 65mg • Total Carbohydrate 9g • Dietary Fiber 0g • Protein 3g. DIETARY EXCHANGES: 1/2 Other Carbohydrate • 1/2 High-Fat Meat • 1/2 Fat • 1/2 Carb Choice.

cook's notes

Out of waxed paper? Just grease the cookie sheet.

banana split bark

PREP TIME: 40 Minutes ✹ READY IN: 1 Hour 10 Minutes ✹ SERVINGS: 40

16 oz. chocolate-flavored candy coating, chopped	1/2 cup chopped pecans, toasted
2 dried pineapple rings, coarsely chopped (1/2 cup)	1/3 cup dried cherries
	1/2 cup white vanilla baking chips
3/4 cup dried sweetened banana chips, broken into large pieces	

1 Line large cookie sheet with waxed paper. In 2-quart saucepan, melt candy coating over low heat, stirring constantly.

2 In medium bowl, mix pineapple, banana chips, pecans and cherries; reserve 1/2 cup. Add remaining fruit mixture to melted candy coating; toss to coat. Cool 5 minutes at room temperature. Gently fold in baking chips. Spread mixture evenly into 12x9-inch rectangle on waxed paper-lined cookie sheet; sprinkle with reserved fruit mixture. Cool until set, about 30 minutes. Break into 1-1/2x1-1/2-inch pieces. Store in airtight container.

NUTRITION INFORMATION PER SERVING: Calories 100 • Total Fat 6g • Saturated Fat 3.5g • Cholesterol 0mg • Sodium 15mg • Total Carbohydrate 11g • Dietary Fiber 0g • Protein 1g. DIETARY EXCHANGES: 1 Other Carbohydrate • 1 Fat • 1 Carb Choice.

peanut brittle cookies

peppermint frosted cookie pops

PREP TIME: 45 Minutes ✳ **READY IN:** 1 Hour 45 Minutes ✳ **SERVINGS:** 24

1 roll (16.5 oz.) Pillsbury® refrigerated sugar cookies

24 flat wooden sticks with rounded ends (6 inch)

1/2 teaspoon peppermint extract

1 container (12 oz.) fluffy white whipped ready-to-spread frosting

2 tablespoons edible glitter or colored sugar

1 Heat oven to 350°F. Work with half of cookie dough at a time; refrigerate remaining dough until needed.

2 Cut dough into 12 equal pieces. Roll each piece into ball; flatten each until 1/2 inch thick. Place each flattened ball on one end of 1 wooden stick, covering 1 inch of stick. Place stick side down 3 inches apart on ungreased large cookie sheets, overlapping sticks as needed. Repeat with remaining dough and sticks.

3 Bake 10 to 13 minutes or until edges are light golden brown. Cool 1 minute; remove from cookie sheets. Cool completely, about 15 minutes. Do not pick up cookie pops using sticks until completely cooled.

4 Stir peppermint extract into frosting until well blended. Frost cookies. Sprinkle with edible glitter. Let stand until frosting is set, about 1 hour. Store between sheets of waxed paper in tightly covered container.

NUTRITION INFORMATION PER SERVING: Calories 150 • Total Fat 6g • Saturated Fat 3g • Cholesterol 5mg • Sodium 60mg • Total Carbohydrate 24g • Dietary Fiber 0g • Protein 0g. DIETARY EXCHANGES: 1-1/2 Other Carbohydrate • 1 Fat • 1-1/2 Carb Choices.

double-layer mint fudge

PREP TIME: 30 Minutes ✳ READY IN: 1 Hour 30 Minutes ✳ SERVINGS: 117

FUDGE LAYER
1 bag (12 oz.) semisweet chocolate chips (2 cups)

1 can (16 oz.) creamy chocolate ready-to-spread frosting

PEPPERMINT LAYER
1 bag (12 oz.) white vanilla baking chips (2 cups)

1 can (1 lb.) vanilla creamy ready-to-spread frosting

2 drops red food color

1/2 cup finely crushed peppermint candy

2 milk chocolate candy bars (1.55 oz. each), chopped

1 Line 13x9-inch pan with foil so foil extends over sides of pan; lightly butter foil. In 3-quart saucepan, melt chocolate chips over low heat, stirring constantly, until smooth. Remove from heat. Stir in chocolate frosting. Spread in pan. Refrigerate 20 minutes.

2 Meanwhile, in 3-quart saucepan, melt vanilla baking chips over low heat, stirring constantly, until smooth. Remove from heat. Stir in vanilla frosting and food color until well blended. Fold in crushed peppermint candy.

3 Spread carefully over chilled chocolate layer. Sprinkle chopped candy bars over top; press in lightly. Refrigerate just until set, about 1 hour.

4 As soon as fudge is set, use foil to lift fudge from pan; remove foil. Cut into 13 rows by 9 rows. Store at room temperature.

NUTRITION INFORMATION PER SERVING: Calories 70 • Total Fat 3.5g • Saturated Fat 2.5g • Cholesterol 0mg • Sodium 0mg • Total Carbohydrate 10g • Dietary Fiber 0g • Protein 0g. DIETARY EXCHANGES: 1/2 Other Carbohydrate • 1 Fat • 1/2 Carb Choice.

sugar and spice nuts

sugar and spice nuts

PREP TIME: 15 Minutes ✳ READY IN: 1 Hour 30 Minutes ✳ SERVINGS: 21

3/4 cup sugar

1 teaspoon salt

2 tablespoons ground cinnamon

1 teaspoon ground ginger

1/2 teaspoon ground cloves

1/2 teaspoon ground nutmeg

1 tablespoon water

1 egg white

1 cup pecan halves

1 cup whole cashews

1 cup walnut halves

1 cup red and green candy-coated chocolate candies

1 Heat oven to 300°F. Spray 15x10x1-inch pan with cooking spray. In large bowl, beat sugar, salt, cinnamon, ginger, cloves, nutmeg, water and egg white with electric mixer on high speed 1 to 2 minutes or until mixture is frothy. With rubber spatula, fold in nuts until evenly coated. Spread mixture evenly in pan.

2 Bake 45 to 50 minutes, stirring occasionally, until nuts are fragrant and toasted. Cool completely in pan, about 30 minutes. Stir in chocolate candies. Store in tightly covered container.

NUTRITION INFORMATION PER SERVING: Calories 190 • Total Fat 12g • Saturated Fat 2.5g • Cholesterol 0mg • Sodium 120mg • Total Carbohydrate 18g • Dietary Fiber 2g • Protein 3g. DIETARY EXCHANGES: 1 Other Carbohydrate • 1/2 High-Fat Meat • 1-1/2 Fat • 1 Carb Choice.

special touch

To make paper cones, cut food-safe paper into 6-inch squares. Roll into cone-shape and tape to secure.

buttered rum fudge

PREP TIME: 10 Minutes ✳ READY IN: 1 Hour 10 Minutes ✳ SERVINGS: 64

1 package (11 oz.) butterscotch chips

1 container (1 lb.) vanilla creamy ready-to-spread frosting

1/2 teaspoon rum extract

1/4 teaspoon nutmeg

3/4 cup chopped pecans

1 Line 8-inch square pan with foil. Spray foil with nonstick cooking spray. Melt butterscotch chips in medium saucepan over low heat, stirring constantly. Remove from heat. Stir in all remaining ingredients until well mixed. Spread fudge in foil-lined pan. Refrigerate 1 hour or until firm. Use foil to lift candy from pan. Remove foil; cut into 1-inch squares. Store at room temperature.

NUTRITION INFORMATION PER SERVING: Calories 70 • Total Fat 4g • Saturated Fat 2g • Cholesterol 0mg • Sodium 20mg • Total Carbohydrate 8g • Dietary Fiber 0g • Protein 0g. DIETARY EXCHANGES: 1/2 Fruit • 1/2 Other Carbohydrate • 1 Fat.

special touch

Cut this bark into diamond-shaped bars instead of breaking it into pieces, if desired.

chocolate chip and peppermint cookie bark

PREP TIME: 40 Minutes ✳ READY IN: 50 Minutes ✳ SERVINGS: 36

12 round starlight mints
1 roll (16.5 oz.) Pillsbury® refrigerated chocolate chip cookies

3/4 cup white vanilla baking chips
2 teaspoons vegetable oil

1 Heat oven to 350°F. In resealable food-storage plastic bag, place mints. With rolling pin or flat side of meat mallet, coarsely crush mints.

2 In ungreased 15x10x1-inch pan, break up cookie dough. In fine strainer and over dough, pour crushed mints; shake lightly so tiny pieces fall onto dough (reserve larger pieces of mints for garnish). With hands, knead tiny pieces of mints into dough; press dough in bottom of pan. Bake 14 to 16 minutes or until golden brown. Cool completely, about 10 minutes.

3 In small microwavable bowl, microwave vanilla baking chips and oil on High 30 to 60 seconds, stirring every 15 seconds, until melted and smooth.

4 With fork, drizzle half of melted chip mixture over cooled bars. Sprinkle with reserved crushed mints. Drizzle with remaining melted chip mixture (if mixture begins to firm up, microwave 10 to 15 seconds). Let stand until set, about 10 minutes. Break into irregular 2- to 3-inch pieces. Store between sheets of waxed paper in a tightly covered container.

NUTRITION INFORMATION PER SERVING: Calories 110 • Total Fat 6g • Saturated Fat 2g • Cholesterol 0mg • Sodium 50mg • Total Carbohydrate 13g • Dietary Fiber 0g • Protein 0g. DIETARY EXCHANGES: 1/2 Starch • 1/2 Other Carbohydrate • 1 Fat • 1 Carb Choice.

crème de menthe truffles

PREP TIME: 2 Hours 15 Minutes ✳ **READY IN:** 3 Hours 55 Minutes ✳ **SERVINGS:** 24

1/2 cup whipping cream
1 bag (10 oz.) crème de menthe baking chips
1 cup semisweet chocolate chips (6 oz.)

10 oz. vanilla-flavored candy coating (almond bark)
2 drops green food color
Mini foil candy cups (1-1/2 inch), if desired

1 In 2-quart saucepan, heat whipping cream over low heat 2 to 3 minutes or until cream is warm. Remove from heat. Add baking chips and chocolate chips; stir until melted and smooth. Cover; refrigerate 1 hour or until firm.

2 Line cookie sheets with waxed paper. Shape mixture into 1-inch balls, dusting hands with powdered sugar or cocoa, if necessary; place 2 inches apart on cookie sheets. Refrigerate 30 minutes.

3 Meanwhile, in deep 1-quart saucepan, melt candy coating over low heat, stirring frequently, until smooth. Remove for heat; cool 10 minutes. In small resealable freezer plastic bag, place 1/4 cup melted coating and the green food color; seal bag. Squeeze bag to mix until uniform color; set aside.

4 Using fork, dip 1 truffle at a time into white candy coating to coat. Return to waxed paper-lined cookie sheets. Cut off tiny corner of bag containing green coating. Squeeze bag to drizzle coating over each truffle (if necessary, reheat green coating in microwave on High a few seconds to make coating drizzle). Let truffles stand until coating is set, about 10 minutes, before placing in foil candy cups. Store in refrigerator.

NUTRITION INFORMATION PER SERVING: Calories 120 • Total Fat 7g • Saturated Fat 4.5g • Cholesterol 0mg • Sodium 10mg • Total Carbohydrate 13g • Dietary Fiber 0g • Protein 1g. DIETARY EXCHANGES: 1 Other Carbohydrate • 1-1/2 Fat • 1 Carb Choice.

cook's notes

Place truffles in a covered container and store in the refrigerator up to 2 weeks.

cranberry-white chip-oatmeal cookie mix

READY IN: 5 Minutes ✳ SERVINGS: 1 Jar

1-1/2 cups all-purpose flour
1 teaspoon baking powder
1/4 teaspoon salt
1/2 cup crisp rice cereal
1/2 cup white vanilla chips

1/2 cup sweetened dried cranberries
1/2 cup rolled oats
1/2 cup firmly packed brown sugar
1/2 cup sugar

1 In medium bowl, combine flour, baking powder and salt. Spoon into 1-quart wide mouth canning jar.

2 Add layers of cereal, chips, cranberries, oats, brown sugar and sugar, pressing each layer firmly in place before adding next ingredient. Seal jar.

cranberry-white chip-oatmeal cookies

READY IN: 35 Minutes ✳ SERVINGS: 24

3/4 cup margarine or butter, softened
1 teaspoon vanilla

1 egg
Contents of jar of Cranberry-White Chip-Oatmeal Cookie Mix (recipe above)

1 Heat oven to 350°F. Spray cookie sheets with nonstick cooking spray. In large bowl, combine margarine, vanilla and egg; beat well. Add contents of jar; mix until well blended. Drop dough by rounded tablespoonfuls onto sprayed cookie sheets.

2 Bake at 350°F for 9 to 12 minutes or until edges are golden brown. Cool 1 minute. Remove from cookie sheets.

HIGH ALTITUDE (3500-6500 FT): Add 3 tablespoons of flour to contents of jar. Bake as directed above.

NUTRITION INFORMATION PER SERVING: Calories 160 • Total Fat 7g • Saturated Fat 2g • Cholesterol 10mg • Sodium 125mg • Total Carbohydrate 21g • Dietary Fiber 1g • Protein 2g. DIETARY EXCHANGES: 1/2 Starch • 1 Fruit • 1-1/2 Other Carbohydrate • 1-1/2 Fat.

spunky monkey snack mix

READY IN: 5 Minutes ✳ SERVINGS: 14

3 cups Golden Grahams® cereal
1 bag (7 oz.) malted milk balls (2 cups)

1 cup dried banana chips
1 cup honey-roasted peanuts

1 In covered container or large resealable food-storage plastic bag, gently toss all ingredients. Tightly cover container or seal bag.

NUTRITION INFORMATION PER SERVING: Calories 190 • Total Fat 8g • Saturated Fat 3.5g • Cholesterol 0mg • Sodium 150mg • Total Carbohydrate 27g • Dietary Fiber 2g • Protein 4g. DIETARY EXCHANGES: 1 Starch • 1 Other Carbohydrate • 1-1/2 Fat • 2 Carb Choices.

cranberry-white chip-oatmeal cookie mix
cranberry-white chip-oatmeal cookies

cinnamon-popcorn snack

PREP TIME: 10 Minutes ✳ READY IN: 30 Minutes ✳ SERVINGS: 24

8 cups popped microwave popcorn (from 3-oz. bag)

5 cups Cheerios® cereal

1 cup honey-roasted peanuts

1 cup raisins

1/2 cup light corn syrup

1/3 cup honey

2 tablespoons butter or margarine

1/4 teaspoon ground cinnamon

1/2 teaspoon vanilla

1 Heat oven to 350°F. Remove and discard unpopped kernels from popped popcorn. In large bowl, mix popcorn, cereal, peanuts and raisins; set aside.

2 In 1-quart saucepan, heat corn syrup, honey, butter and cinnamon to boiling. Remove from heat; stir in vanilla. Pour over cereal mixture; toss until evenly coated. Spread in ungreased 15x10x1-inch pan.

3 Bake 15 minutes, stirring occasionally. Cool pan on cooling rack, stirring occasionally. Store loosely covered.

HIGH ALTITUDE (3500-6500 FT): Heat oven to 375°F.

NUTRITION INFORMATION PER SERVING: Calories 150 • Total Fat 6g • Saturated Fat 1.5g • Cholesterol 0mg • Sodium 110mg • Total Carbohydrate 22g • Dietary Fiber 2g • Protein 3g. DIETARY EXCHANGES: 1/2 Starch • 1 Other Carbohydrate • 1 Fat • 1-1/2 Carb Choices.

chai crunch

PREP TIME: 10 Minutes ✱ **READY IN:** 1 Hour 25 Minutes ✱ **SERVINGS:** 22

1/2 cup butter or margarine

1/2 cup honey

1 teaspoon instant nonfat dry milk or non-dairy original-flavor creamer, if desired

1/2 teaspoon ground cardamom

1/2 teaspoon ground ginger

1/2 teaspoon ground cinnamon

1/2 teaspoon ground nutmeg

1/2 teaspoon ground cloves

1/2 teaspoon dried orange peel

1 teaspoon vanilla

3 cups Corn Chex® cereal

3 cups Wheat Chex® cereal

3 cups Honey Nut Cheerios® cereal

1 cup dried banana chips

1-1/2 cups sliced almonds

1 Heat oven to 300°F. In 1-quart saucepan, melt butter over medium heat. Remove from heat. Stir in honey, dry milk, cardamom, ginger, cinnamon, nutmeg, cloves, orange peel and vanilla until well mixed.

2 In 15x11-inch roasting pan, mix all remaining ingredients. Pour butter mixture over cereal mixture; toss until evenly coated.

3 Bake at 300°F for 45 to 60 minutes or until golden brown, stirring every 15 minutes. Pour mixture onto waxed paper or paper towels. Cool 15 minutes before serving. Store in tightly covered container.

NUTRITION INFORMATION PER SERVING: Calories 160 • Total Fat 8g • Saturated Fat 2.5g • Cholesterol 10mg • Sodium 170mg • Total Carbohydrate 20g • Dietary Fiber 2g • Protein 3g. DIETARY EXCHANGES: 1 Starch • 1/2 Other Carbohydrate • 1-1/2 Fat • 1 Carb Choice.

Pillsbury
Bake-Off®

CAROL THORESON
Rockford, Illinois
Bake-Off® Contest 41, 2004

cook's notes

For spicy flavor, omit dried milk or creamer. If dried milk is used, flavor will be less spicy and a little sweeter.

party snack mix

party snack mix

PREP TIME: 10 Minutes ✳ **READY IN:** 1 Hour 20 Minutes ✳ **SERVINGS:** 24

4 cups Corn Chex® cereal	1 tablespoon Worcestershire sauce
2 cups Wheat Chex® cereal	1/8 teaspoon hot pepper sauce
2 cups small pretzel sticks	1 teaspoon salt
2 cups Spanish peanuts or mixed nuts	1/4 teaspoon garlic powder
1/2 cup butter or margarine, melted	

1 Heat oven to 325°F. In large bowl, mix cereals, pretzel sticks and peanuts. In small bowl, mix butter, Worcestershire sauce, hot pepper sauce, salt and garlic powder. Pour over cereal mixture; toss to coat. Spread in ungreased 15x10x1-inch pan.

2 Bake 25 to 30 minutes or until lightly toasted, stirring occasionally. Cool 30 minutes. Store in tightly covered container.

HIGH ALTITUDE (3500-6500 FT): Decrease melted butter to 1/3 cup.

NUTRITION INFORMATION PER SERVING: Calories 160 • Total Fat 10g • Saturated Fat 3.5g • Cholesterol 10mg • Sodium 320mg • Total Carbohydrate 12g • Dietary Fiber 2g • Protein 5g. DIETARY EXCHANGES: 1 Starch • 2 Fat • 1 Carb Choice.

special touch

For variety, make this mix with fun-shaped pretzels instead of the pretzel sticks.

chex® caramel corn

PREP TIME: 10 Minutes ✳ **READY IN:** 55 Minutes ✳ **SERVINGS:** 19

4-1/2 cups Chex® cereal (corn, rice or combination)	1/4 cup butter or margarine
4 cups popped popcorn	6 tablespoons packed brown sugar
1/2 cup cashew halves or honey-roasted peanuts, if desired	2 tablespoons light corn syrup
	1/4 teaspoon vanilla

1 Heat oven to 250°F. In large ungreased roasting pan, mix cereal, popcorn and cashews; set cereal mixture aside.

2 In 2-qt. saucepan, heat butter, brown sugar, corn syrup and vanilla to boiling over medium heat, stirring frequently. Pour over cereal mixture; stir until evenly coated.

3 Bake uncovered 45 minutes, stirring every 15 minutes. Spread on waxed paper to cool, stirring occasionally to break up. Store in airtight container.

MICROWAVE DIRECTIONS: In large microwavable bowl, mix cereal, popcorn and cashews; set aside. In another large microwavable bowl, microwave butter, brown sugar, corn syrup and vanilla uncovered on High about 2 minutes, stirring after 1 minute, until mixture is boiling. Pour over cereal mixture; stir until evenly coated. Microwave 5-6 minutes, stirring and scraping bowl after every minute. Spread on waxed paper to cool, stirring occasionally to break up. Store in airtight container.

NUTRITION INFORMATION PER SERVING: Calories 90 • Total Fat 4g • Saturated Fat 1g • Cholesterol 0mg • Sodium 110mg • Total Carbohydrate 14g • Dietary Fiber 1g • Protein 1g. DIETARY EXCHANGE: 1 Starch.

cook's notes

Do not use spread or tub products in place of the butter or margarine.

Winter Wonderland Sweets

Homemade goodies come from the heart and make impressive, edible Christmas presents. This collection of creative bites will warm hearts all season long.

p. 235

p. 233

p. 243

p. 233

p. 234

hanukkah rugelach p. 238

cook's notes

Instead of using cherries for the nose, candy-coated chocolate candies or gumdrops may be used instead.

reindeer cookies

PREP TIME: 40 Minutes ✳ READY IN: 55 Minutes ✳ SERVINGS: 32

1 roll (16.5 oz.) Pillsbury® refrigerated gingerbread or peanut butter cookies

64 small pretzel twists

64 semisweet chocolate chips (about 1/4 cup)

16 candied cherries, cut in half, if desired

1 Heat oven to 350°F. With hands, shape roll of cookie dough into triangle-shaped log. (If dough is too soft to cut, place in freezer 30 minutes.)

2 With thin sharp knife, cut dough into 32 (1/4-inch-thick) triangular slices; on ungreased cookie sheets, place 2 inches apart. Place 2 pretzel twists on each triangle near corners for antlers.

3 Bake 7 to 11 minutes or until set. While warm, lightly press 2 chocolate chips into each cookie for eyes and 1 cherry half for nose. Remove from cookie sheets. Let stand until chocolate chips are set, about 15 minutes. Store between sheets of waxed paper in a tightly covered container.

NUTRITION INFORMATION PER SERVING: Calories 90 • Total Fat 4g • Saturated Fat 1g • Trans Fat 0g • Cholesterol 10mg • Sodium 95mg • Total Carbohydrate 13g • Dietary Fiber 0g • Protein 1g. DIETARY EXCHANGES: 1 Other Carbohydrate • 1 Fat • 1 Carb Choice.

eggnog logs

PREP TIME: 45 Minutes ✳ **READY IN:** 1 Hour 15 Minutes ✳ **SERVINGS:** 4 Dozen

COOKIES

1	roll (18 oz.) Pillsbury® refrigerated sugar cookies
3	tablespoons all-purpose flour
1/4	cup finely chopped pecans
1/2	teaspoon ground nutmeg
1	teaspoon rum extract

FROSTING

1	to 2 tablespoons milk
1	tablespoon butter, softened
1-1/4	cups powdered sugar
1/4	teaspoon ground nutmeg
1/4	teaspoon rum extract
1/4	cup finely chopped pecans

1 Heat oven to 350°F. In large bowl, break up cookie dough. Stir or knead in remaining cookie ingredients until well blended. Shape dough into 8 (2-inch) balls, using about 1/4 cup dough per ball. Work with 1 ball of dough at a time; refrigerate remaining balls of dough until needed.

2 On lightly floured surface, roll dough into 12-inch rope; cut into 2-inch pieces. Place 2 inches apart on ungreased cookie sheets. Repeat with remaining dough; refrigerate until ready to bake.

3 Bake 7 to 11 minutes or until cookies are set and edges just begin to brown. Cool 1 minute; remove from cookie sheets. Cool completely, about 15 minutes.

4 Meanwhile, in small bowl, mix 1 tablespoon milk, the butter, powdered sugar, 1/4 teaspoon nutmeg and 1/4 teaspoon rum extract with spoon until creamy, adding enough milk for desired spreading consistency.

5 Frost cooled cookies. Sprinkle with 1/4 cup pecans; press in lightly. Let stand until frosting is set, about 15 minutes. Store between sheets of waxed paper in tightly covered container.

NUTRITION INFORMATION PER SERVING: Calories 70 • Total Fat 3g • Saturated Fat 0.5g • Cholesterol 0mg • Sodium 30mg • Total Carbohydrate 10g • Dietary Fiber 0g • Protein 0g. DIETARY EXCHANGES: 1/2 Other Carbohydrate • 1 Fat • 1/2 Carb Choice.

cook's notes

Do not be tempted to use real rum in the cookie dough instead of rum extract. The alcohol in the rum makes the finished cookies dry and a bit crumbly.

north star cookies

PREP TIME: 45 Minutes ✷ READY IN: 1 Hour ✷ SERVINGS: 12 Large and 6 Small Sandwich Cookies

1 roll (18 oz.) Pillsbury® refrigerated sugar cookies	1/3 cup seedless raspberry jam
	1 tablespoon powdered sugar

1 Heat oven to 350°F. Work with half of cookie dough at a time; refrigerate remaining dough until needed.

2 On floured surface with rolling pin, roll dough to 1/4-inch thickness (about 9-inch round). Cut with floured 3-inch star-shaped cookie cutter. With 1-inch star-shaped cutter, cut out small star from center of half of the cookies. Place large stars 1 inch apart on ungreased cookie sheets. Place small stars 1 inch apart on another ungreased cookie sheet; refrigerate while baking large stars. Repeat with remaining dough.

3 For large stars, bake 7 to 10 minutes or until edges just begin to brown. Cool 1 minute; remove from cookie sheets. For small stars, bake 4 to 6 minutes or until edges just begin to brown. Cool 1 minute; remove from cookie sheet. Cool all cookies completely, about 15 minutes.

4 Spread each large whole cookie with 1 teaspoon jam. Sprinkle large cutout cookies with powdered sugar; place over jam-topped cookies, pressing lightly. Spread half of small cookies with about 1/4 teaspoon jam. Sprinkle remaining half of small cookies with powdered sugar; place over jam-topped cookies, pressing lightly. Store between sheets of waxed paper in tightly covered container.

HIGH ALTITUDE (**3500-6500** FT): In Step 1, in large bowl, break up cookie dough; stir or knead in 1/4 cup all-purpose flour. Work with half of cookie dough at a time; refrigerate remaining dough until needed. Bake large stars 8 to 11 minutes.

NUTRITION INFORMATION PER SERVING: Calories 150 • Total Fat 6g • Saturated Fat 1.5g • Cholesterol 10mg • Sodium 80mg • Total Carbohydrate 23g • Dietary Fiber 0g • Protein 0g. DIETARY EXCHANGES: 1/2 Starch • 1 Other Carbohydrate • 1 Fat • 1-1/2 Carb Choices.

red and green holiday pinwheels

PREP TIME: 20 Minutes ✷ READY IN: 1 Hour 10 Minutes ✷ SERVINGS: 32

1 roll (16.5 oz.) Pillsbury® refrigerated sugar cookies	2 tablespoons red sugar
1/4 cup all-purpose flour	2 tablespoons green sugar

1 In large bowl, break up cookie dough. Stir or knead in flour until well blended. Divide dough in half. On lightly floured surface, roll out each half of dough to 11x7-inch rectangle. Sprinkle red sugar evenly over 1 rectangle; sprinkle green sugar evenly over second rectangle.

2 Starting with shortest side, roll up each rectangle jelly-roll fashion. Wrap rolls in plastic wrap; freeze 30 minutes for easier handling.

3 Heat oven to 350°F. Cut each roll into 16 slices. On ungreased cookie sheets, place slices 1 inch apart.

4 Bake 8 to 11 minutes or until edges are light golden brown. Cool 1 minute; remove from cookie sheets to cooling racks.

HIGH ALTITUDE (**3500-6500** FT): Bake 12 to 14 minutes.

NUTRITION INFORMATION PER SERVING: Calories 70 • Total Fat 3g • Saturated Fat 1g • Cholesterol 5mg • Sodium 40mg • Total Carbohydrate 11g • Dietary Fiber 0g • Protein 0g. DIETARY EXCHANGES: 1 Other Carbohydrate • 1/2 Fat • 1 Carb Choice.

north star cookies

swedish kringla

PREP TIME: 1 Hour 15 Minutes ✳ **READY IN:** 5 Hours 15 Minutes ✳ **SERVINGS:** 3-1/2 Dozen

1-1/2 cups sugar	4 egg yolks
1/2 cup butter, softened	5-1/3 cups all-purpose flour
1 cup buttermilk	4 teaspoons baking powder
1 container (8 oz.) sour cream	1-1/2 teaspoons baking soda
1 teaspoon almond extract	3/4 teaspoon salt
1 teaspoon vanilla	

1 In large bowl, combine sugar and butter; beat until light and fluffy. Add buttermilk, sour cream, almond extract, vanilla and egg yolks; beat well.

2 Lightly spoon flour into measuring cup; level off. Add 4 cups flour and all remaining ingredients; mix well. With wooden spoon, stir in remaining 1-1/3 cups flour. Cover dough with plastic wrap; refrigerate at least 4 hours or overnight for easier handling.

3 Heat oven to 425°F. Lightly grease cookie sheets or spray with nonstick cooking spray. Shape dough into 1-1/2-inch balls. On floured surface, roll each ball into 10-inch-long rope; shape into figure eight (8) or pretzel shape. Place on greased cookie sheets.

4 Bake at 425°F for 6 to 9 minutes or until edges are light golden brown. Immediately transfer from cookie sheets to cooling racks.

HIGH ALTITUDE (3500-6500 FT): Increase flour to 5-2/3 cups. Bake as directed above.

NUTRITION INFORMATION PER SERVING: Calories 130 • Total Fat 4g • Saturated Fat 2g • Cholesterol 30mg • Sodium 160mg • Total Carbohydrate 21g • Dietary Fiber 0g • Protein 2g. DIETARY EXCHANGES: 1 Starch • 1/2 Fruit • 1-1/2 Other Carbohydrate • 1/2 Fat.

candy cane chocolate chip cookies

PREP TIME: 50 Minutes ✱ **READY IN:** 1 Hour 10 Minutes ✱ **SERVINGS:** 1-1/2 Dozen

1 roll (18 oz.) Pillsbury® refrigerated chocolate chip cookies	1/3 cup red cinnamon candies
White decorating icing (from 6.4-oz. aerosol can)	

1 Heat oven to 350°F. Drop cookie dough by rounded teaspoonfuls 2 inches apart onto ungreased cookie sheets.

2 Bake 10 to 14 minutes or until golden brown. Cool 1 minute; remove from cookie sheets. Cool completely, about 10 minutes.

3 With can of decorating icing fitted with ribbon tip, pipe candy cane shape on each cookie. Arrange cinnamon candies, spacing evenly, on white cane shape to form stripes. Let stand until frosting is set, about 20 minutes. Store between sheets of waxed paper in tightly covered container.

NUTRITION INFORMATION PER SERVING: Calories 190 • Total Fat 9g • Saturated Fat 3.5g • Cholesterol 0mg • Sodium 90mg • Total Carbohydrate 28g • Dietary Fiber 0g • Protein 1g. DIETARY EXCHANGES: 1/2 Starch • 1-1/2 Other Carbohydrate • 1-1/2 Fat • 2 Carb Choices.

cook's notes

Candy-coated baking bits can be substituted for the red cinnamon candies.

santa cookies

READY IN: 1 Hour 45 Minutes ✱ **SERVINGS:** 2-1/2 Dozen

1/2 cup sugar	1/4 cup semisweet chocolate chips
1/2 cup butter or margarine, softened	1 tablespoon red cinnamon candies
1/2 teaspoon vanilla	1/2 cup fluffy white whipped ready-to-spread frosting (from 12-oz. container)
1 egg	
1-1/2 cups all-purpose flour	1/4 cup flaked coconut or edible glitter
1/4 teaspoon baking soda	1 roll (0.75 oz.) chewy fruit snack in 3-foot rolls (any red flavor)
1/4 teaspoon salt	

cook's notes

Let the kids decorate the cookies using an assortment of decorating candies and sprinkles.

1 Heat oven to 350°F. In large bowl, beat sugar and butter with electric mixer on medium speed until blended. Beat in vanilla and egg. On low speed, beat in flour, baking soda and salt.

2 Shape dough into 1-inch balls. For each cookie, flatten ball into about 1-1/2-inch round with fingers; place 2 inches apart on ungreased cookie sheets. Lightly press 2 chocolate chips into upper third of each dough round for eyes.

3 Bake 9 to 11 minutes or until edges are light golden brown. Immediately press 1 cinnamon candy onto each cookie for nose. Remove from cookie sheets to cooling racks. Cool 15 minutes.

4 Place frosting in small resealable food-storage plastic bag. Seal bag; cut off small corner of bag. Squeeze bag to pipe frosting along bottom edge of cookie and above cinnamon candy for beard. Lightly sprinkle coconut over frosting; gently press into frosting.

5 Cut fruit snack into 2-inch-long pieces. Cut each piece diagonally in half to make 2 triangles. With small amount of frosting, attach fruit snack triangle on each cookie for hat. Fold top corner of each triangle over; pipe frosting "tassle" on pointed end of each "hat."

NUTRITION INFORMATION PER SERVING: Calories 90 • Total Fat 4.5g • Saturated Fat 2.5g • Cholesterol 15mg • Sodium 60mg • Total Carbohydrate 12g • Dietary Fiber 0g • Protein 0g. DIETARY EXCHANGES: 1 Other Carbohydrate • 1 Fat • 1 Carb Choice.

cook's notes

Place decorating gel in the refrigerator about 5 minutes if it is too soft to form bows.

merry berry wreath cookies

READY IN: 1 Hour 15 Minutes ✳ SERVINGS: 24

1 roll (16.5 oz.) Pillsbury® refrigerated sugar cookies

1 container (1 lb.) vanilla creamy ready-to-spread frosting

4 or 5 drops green food color

2 tubes (0.68 oz. each) red decorating gel

About 2 tablespoons holiday red and green candy decors

1 Heat oven to 350°F. Remove half of cookie dough from wrapper; refrigerate remaining dough until needed. Cut dough into 12 slices, 1/4 inch thick. On floured work surface, roll each into 6-inch long rope. On ungreased cookie sheet, form into wreath shapes 2 inches apart; pinch ends of each wreath together.

2 Bake 9 to 12 minutes or until edges are light golden brown. Cool 1 minute. Remove from cookie sheet to cooling rack. Cool completely, about 15 minutes. Repeat with remaining half of cookie dough.

3 In medium bowl, mix frosting and food color until well blended. Frost tops of cookies. With decorating gel, form bow at top of each wreath. Sprinkle with candy decors.

HIGH ALTITUDE (3500-6500 FT): In Step 1, crumble half of dough into medium bowl. Knead 2 tablespoons all-purpose flour into dough and divide into 12 pieces. Repeat with remaining half of cookie dough.

NUTRITION INFORMATION PER SERVING: Calories 200 • Total Fat 8g • Saturated Fat 2.5g • Cholesterol 5mg • Sodium 105mg • Total Carbohydrate 31g • Dietary Fiber 0g • Protein 0g. DIETARY EXCHANGES: 1/2 Starch • 1-1/2 Other Carbohydrate • 1-1/2 Fat • 2 Carb Choices.

rudolph brownie cupcakes

PREP TIME: 30 Minutes ✳ READY IN: 1 Hour 45 Minutes ✳ SERVINGS: 12

1 box (19.8 oz.) fudge brownie mix	24 holiday-shaped pretzels or small pretzel twists
1/2 cup vegetable oil	12 red spiced gumdrops
1/4 cup water	24 miniature candy-coated chocolate baking bits
3 eggs	
1-1/2 cups chocolate creamy ready-to-spread frosting (from 1-lb. container)	

1 Heat oven to 350°F. Line 12 regular-size muffin cups with paper baking cups. In large bowl, stir brownie mix, oil, water and eggs with spoon until well blended. Spoon about 1/4 cup batter into each muffin cup.

2 Bake 32 to 36 minutes or until toothpick inserted in center of muffin comes out clean. Cool in pan 10 minutes. Remove from pan; cool completely, about 30 minutes.

3 Spread cupcakes with frosting. Decorate each with 2 pretzels for antlers, 1 red candy for nose and 2 baking bits for eyes.

HIGH ALTITUDE (3500-6500 FT): Makes 18 cupcakes.

NUTRITION INFORMATION PER SERVING: Calories 480 • Total Fat 21g • Saturated Fat 9g • Cholesterol 55mg • Sodium 240mg • Total Carbohydrate 67g • Dietary Fiber 2g • Protein 4g. DIETARY EXCHANGES: 1 Starch • 3-1/2 Other Carbohydrate • 4 Fat • 4-1/2 Carb Choices.

almond tree cookies

almond tree cookies

READY IN: 2 Hours ✳ SERVINGS: 4 Dozen

COOKIES

- 1 cup butter or margarine, softened
- 1/2 cup granulated sugar
- 1/2 teaspoon almond extract
- 2 cups all-purpose flour

FROSTING

- 1 cup powdered sugar
- 2 tablespoons butter or margarine, softened
- 1 to 2 tablespoons milk
- 8 or 10 drops green food color

1 Heat oven to 350°F. In medium bowl, beat 1 cup butter, the granulated sugar and almond extract with electric mixer on medium speed until smooth. On low speed, beat in flour. Shape dough into 1-inch balls; place 2 inches apart on ungreased cookie sheets.

2 Bake 12 to 15 minutes or until firm to the touch. Cool 1 minute; remove from cookie sheets to cooling racks. Cool completely, about 30 minutes.

3 In small bowl, beat powdered sugar, 2 tablespoons butter and the milk on medium speed until smooth and spreadable. Stir in green food color until uniform color.

4 Spoon frosting into resealable food-storage plastic bag. Seal bag; cut off tiny corner of bag. Squeeze bag to make tree shape in a zigzag pattern on each cookie with frosting.

NUTRITION INFORMATION PER SERVING: Calories 80 • Total Fat 4.5g • Saturated Fat 3g • Trans Fat 0g • Cholesterol 10mg • Sodium 30mg • Total Carbohydrate 9g • Dietary Fiber 0g • Protein 0g. DIETARY EXCHANGES: 1/2 Other Carbohydrate • 1 Fat • 1/2 Carb Choice.

meringue candy canes

READY IN: 1 Hour 20 Minutes ✳ SERVINGS: 3-1/2 Dozen

- 3 egg whites
- 1/2 teaspoon cream of tartar
- 3/4 cup sugar

- 1/4 teaspoon peppermint extract
- Red or pink food color

1 Heat oven to 200°F. Line 2 cookie sheets with cooking parchment paper or foil. In large bowl, beat egg whites and cream of tartar with electric mixer on high speed until foamy. Gradually add sugar, 1 tablespoon at a time, beating until meringue is stiff and glossy. Beat in peppermint extract.

2 Fit large decorating bag with 1/4-inch star tip. With small brush, paint 3 to 4 evenly spaced stripes of food color on inside of decorating bag, from tip to upper edge. Carefully spoon meringue into bag. Pipe 2-1/2-inch candy canes onto paper-lined cookie sheets. Bake about 1 hour or until dry but not brown.

NUTRITION INFORMATION PER SERVING: Calories 15 • Total Fat 0g • Saturated Fat 0g • Cholesterol 0mg • Sodium 0mg • Total Carbohydrate 4g • Dietary Fiber 0g • Protein 0g. DIETARY EXCHANGE: Free.

snow fun snowmen

PREP TIME: 25 Minutes ✲ READY IN: 55 Minutes ✲ SERVINGS: 6

1 container (1 lb.) creamy vanilla ready-to-spread frosting

6 plain mini cake doughnuts

12 plain cake doughnut holes

2 tablespoons coarse white sugar

6 thin pretzel sticks, broken in half

2 chewy fruit snacks in three-foot rolls (any flavor from 4.5-oz. box), cut into six 7- or 8-inch pieces

1 tube black decorating gel (or other colors)

6 orange candy sprinkles

12 candy-coated chocolate or fruit-flavored candies (about 1 tablespoon)

1 Place 12x12-inch sheet of waxed paper on work surface. In small microwavable bowl, microwave frosting on High 10 to 20 seconds or until soft.

2 For each snowman, dip 1 doughnut into frosting to cover; place on waxed paper. Dip 1 doughnut hole into frosting to cover; press on doughnut for snowman body. Dip second doughnut hole into frosting to cover; press on top of first doughnut hole for head. Sprinkle with about 1 teaspoon coarse sugar. If frosting becomes too thick for dipping, microwave on High 5 to 10 seconds to soften.

3 Gently push 2 pretzel stick pieces into opposite sides near top of each snowman body for arms. Peel off paper from fruit snack roll pieces; fold each in half lengthwise to make scarf. Wrap scarf around neck of each snowman. With scissors, make several thin cuts on each end of each scarf for fringe. With decorating gel, draw dots on heads for eyes; insert orange candy sprinkles for noses.

4 Gently press 1 candy-coated chocolate candy into frosting on each side of each snowman head. Draw line of decorating gel over top of each head to connect 2 candies and form earmuffs. For easier eating, let stand until frosting is set, about 30 minutes. To serve, place on serving tray or platter.

NUTRITION INFORMATION PER SERVING: Calories 540 • Total Fat 21 g • Saturated Fat 12g • Cholesterol 20mg • Sodium 130mg • Total Carbohydrate 85g • Dietary Fiber 0g • Protein 3g. DIETARY EXCHANGES: 1 Starch • 4-1/2 Other Carbohydrate • 4 Fat • 5-1/2 Carb Choices.

eggnog cutout cookies

PREP TIME: 1 Hour 50 Minutes ✳ **READY IN:** 2 Hours 20 Minutes ✳ **SERVINGS:** 8 Dozen

COOKIES
- 2 cups sugar
- 1 cup butter, softened
- 2 eggs
- 1/3 cup eggnog
- 1 teaspoon vanilla
- 4 cups all purpose flour
- 1 teaspoon nutmeg
- 2 teaspoons baking powder

EGG YOLK PAINT
- 2 egg yolks
- 1/2 teaspoon water
- Assorted colors of liquid food color

1 In large bowl, combine sugar, butter and eggs; beat until light and fluffy. Stir in eggnog and vanilla. Lightly spoon flour into measuring cup; level off. In medium bowl, combine flour, nutmeg and baking powder. Add flour mixture to butter mixture; blend well. Cover with plastic wrap; refrigerate 30 minutes for easier handling.

2 Meanwhile, in small bowl, combine egg yolks and water; blend well. Divide mixture into several small cups; tint with food color. If paint thickens, add a few drops water.

3 Heat oven to 350°F. Divide dough in half. On lightly floured surface, roll half of dough to 1/8-inch thickness. Cut with assorted cutters. Place 2 inches apart on ungreased cookie sheets. Using small paint brush, paint designs on cookies with egg yolk paint.

4 Bake at 350°F for 7 to 10 minutes or until cookies are light golden brown. Remove from cookie sheets.

HIGH ALTITUDE (3500-6500 FT): Increase flour to 4-1/4 cups. Bake as directed above.

NUTRITION INFORMATION PER SERVING: Calories 50 • Total Fat 2g • Saturated Fat 1g • Cholesterol 15mg • Sodium 30mg • Total Carbohydrate 8g • Dietary Fiber 0g • Protein 1g. DIETARY EXCHANGES: 1/2 Starch • 1/2 Other Carbohydrate • 1/2 Fat.

poinsettia cookies

PREP TIME: 40 Minutes ✻ **READY IN:** 50 Minutes ✻ **SERVINGS:** 2 Dozen

- 1 roll (16.5 oz.) Pillsbury® refrigerated sugar cookies
- 1/4 cup all-purpose flour
- 1/4 teaspoon red food color
- 1/3 cup red sugar
- 24 yellow gumdrops (1/2 to 1 inch)

1 Heat oven to 350°F. In large bowl, break up cookie dough. Stir or knead in flour and food color until blended and color is even. Remove half the dough, and refrigerate remaining dough until needed.

2 Shape dough into 12 (1-1/4-inch) balls; roll in red sugar and place 2 inches apart on ungreased cookie sheets. With thin sharp knife dipped into flour, cut each ball into 6 wedges, cutting 3/4 of the way down into ball but not through bottom. Spread wedges apart very slightly to form flower petals (cookies will separate and flatten as they bake). Repeat with remaining dough and red sugar.

3 Bake 10 to 12 minutes or until set and edges just begin to brown. Immediately press 1 gumdrop in center of each cookie. Cool 1 minute; carefully remove from cookie sheets to cooling racks. Cool completely, about 10 minutes. Store in tightly covered container.

HIGH ALTITUDE (3500-6500 FT): Bake 11 to 13 minutes.

NUTRITION INFORMATION PER SERVING: Calories 120 • Total Fat 4g • Saturated Fat 1g • Cholesterol 5mg • Sodium 60mg • Total Carbohydrate 20g • Dietary Fiber 0g • Protein 0g. DIETARY EXCHANGES: 1-1/2 Other Carbohydrate • 1 Fat • 1 Carb Choice.

holiday sandwich cookies

READY IN: 1 Hour ✻ **SERVINGS:** 30

- 1 roll (16.5 oz.) Pillsbury® refrigerated sugar cookies
- 1/2 cup miniature candy-coated semisweet chocolate baking bits
- 3/4 cup white vanilla baking chips
- 3/4 cup vanilla ready-to-spread frosting (from 16-oz. container)

1 Heat oven to 350°F. In large bowl, break up cookie dough. Stir in chocolate baking bits. Shape dough into 3/4-inch balls; place 2 inches apart on ungreased cookie sheets. With glass dipped in sugar, flatten each ball slightly.

2 Bake 8 to 10 minutes or until edges are golden brown. Immediately remove from cookie sheets; place on cooling racks. Cool completely, about 15 minutes.

3 In medium microwavable bowl, microwave vanilla baking chips on High 20 to 30 seconds or until melted, stirring every 15 seconds. Stir in frosting until smooth. For each sandwich cookie, spread 1 to 2 teaspoons frosting mixture on bottom of 1 cookie. Top with second cookie, bottom side down; press gently.

NUTRITION INFORMATION PER SERVING: Calories 150 • Total Fat 7g • Saturated Fat 3.5g • Cholesterol 5mg • Sodium 65mg • Total Carbohydrate 21g • Dietary Fiber 0g • Protein 1g. DIETARY EXCHANGES: 1-1/2 Other Carbohydrate • 1-1/2 Fat • 1-1/2 Carb Choices.

whole wheat gingerbread cutouts

READY IN: 1 Hour 40 Minutes ✳ **SERVINGS:** 8 Dozen

COOKIES

1-1/2 cups granulated sugar
1 cup butter or margarine, softened
1/3 cup molasses
1 egg
2-1/4 cups all-purpose flour
1 cup whole wheat flour
2 teaspoons baking soda
2 teaspoons ground ginger

2 teaspoons ground cinnamon
1/2 teaspoon salt

FROSTING

1/4 cup butter, softened
2 tablespoons shortening
1/2 teaspoon vanilla
Dash salt
2 cups powdered sugar
1 to 2 tablespoons milk

special touch

For a children's party or family get-together with dozens of cousins, make a gingerbread cookie to represent each child. Decorate accordingly, and pipe the name or initials of each child onto the cookie. Or let children create gingerbread "families."

1 In large bowl, beat granulated sugar and 1 cup butter with electric mixer on medium speed until light and fluffy. Beat in molasses and egg until well blended. On low speed, beat in remaining cookie ingredients until well mixed. If necessary, cover with plastic wrap; refrigerate 1 hour for easier handling.

2 Heat oven to 350°F. On lightly floured surface, roll out 1/4 of dough at a time to 1/8-inch thickness. (Keep remaining dough refrigerated.) Cut with floured 2-1/2-inch round or desired shape cookie cutters. On ungreased cookie sheets, place 1 inch apart.

3 Bake 6 to 9 minutes or until set. Cool 1 minute; remove from cookie sheets to cooling racks. Cool completely, about 15 minutes.

4 In small bowl, beat 1/4 cup butter and the shortening on medium speed until light and fluffy. Beat in vanilla and dash salt. On low speed, gradually beat in powdered sugar until smooth. On high speed, beat in 1 tablespoon milk until light and fluffy. Add enough additional milk until frosting can be spread or piped. Frost or decorate cookies as desired. Let stand until frosting is set, about 30 minutes. Store in loosely covered container.

HIGH ALTITUDE (3500-6500 FT): Decrease sugar to 1 cup; increase all-purpose flour to 2-3/4 cups.

NUTRITION INFORMATION PER SERVING: Calories 70 • Total Fat 3g • Saturated Fat 1.5g • Cholesterol 10mg • Sodium 60mg • Total Carbohydrate 10g • Dietary Fiber 0g • Protein 0g. DIETARY EXCHANGES: 1/2 Other Carbohydrate • 1/2 Fat • 1/2 Carb Choice.

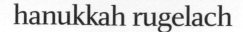

hanukkah rugelach

PREP TIME: 1 Hour 25 Minutes ✻ READY IN: 2 Hours 55 Minutes ✻ SERVINGS: 64

1 cup butter, softened	1/2 cup finely chopped shelled pistachios
2 tablespoons sugar	1/3 cup sugar
1 package (8 oz.) cream cheese, softened	2 teaspoons cinnamon
2 cups all-purpose flour	1/4 cup butter, softened
1/2 cup finely chopped dates	1 tablespoon powdered sugar

1 In large bowl, combine 1 cup butter, 2 tablespoons sugar and cream cheese; beat until light and fluffy.

2 Lightly spoon flour into measuring cup; level off. Add flour to butter mixture; blend well. Shape dough into ball; divide into 4 pieces. Shape each piece into ball; flatten into 1/2-inch-thick disk. Wrap each in plastic wrap; refrigerate 1 hour for easier handling.

3 Heat oven to 375°F. Grease 2 cookie sheets or spray with nonstick cooking spray. In small bowl, combine dates, pistachios, 1/3 cup sugar, cinnamon and 1/4 cup butter; blend well.

4 On floured surface with floured rolling pin, roll out 1 disk of dough at a time to 1/8-inch thickness, forming 12-inch round. (Keep remaining disks of dough refrigerated.) Sprinkle 1/4 of date-nut mixture onto round; press into dough slightly. Cut round into 16 wedges. Roll up each wedge from curved edge to point. Place on greased cookie sheets.

5 Bake at 375°F for 13 to 18 minutes or until light golden brown. Immediately remove from cookie sheets; place on wire racks. Cool 30 minutes or until completely cooled. Sprinkle with powdered sugar.

NUTRITION INFORMATION PER SERVING: Calories 70 • Total Fat 5g • Saturated Fat 3g • Cholesterol 15mg • Sodium 45mg • Total Carbohydrate 6g • Dietary Fiber 0g • Protein 1g. DIETARY EXCHANGES: 1/2 Fruit • 1/2 Other Carbohydrate • 1 Fat.

chocolate chip tree cookies

PREP TIME: 1 Hour 5 Minutes ✻ READY IN: 1 Hour 15 Minutes ✻ SERVINGS: 20

1 roll (16.5 oz.) Pillsbury® refrigerated chocolate chip cookies	1/2 cup semisweet chocolate chips, melted
	Miniature candy-coated chocolate baking bits

1 Heat oven to 350°F. In large bowl, break up cookie dough. Shape half of dough into 1-inch balls. With floured fingers, roll each ball into 10-inch rope, about 1/4 inch wide. Break off small piece from each rope for tree trunk. Carefully place ropes on ungreased cookie sheet.

2 With each rope, starting at top, twist rope back and forth into tree shape, gradually making larger at bottom (rows of dough should touch). If rope breaks, press dough together. Place small piece at bottom of each tree for trunk. Repeat with remaining half of dough.

3 Bake 9 to 11 minutes or until edges are light golden brown. Cool 1 minute; remove from cookie sheet to cooling rack. Cool completely, about 15 minutes.

4 Drizzle each cookie with melted chocolate chips; place baking bits on top of drizzled chocolate to look like ornaments or lights.

HIGH ALTITUDE (3500-6500 FT): Bake 12 to 14 minutes.

NUTRITION INFORMATION PER SERVING: Calories 100 • Total Fat 4g • Saturated Fat 1g • Cholesterol 0mg • Sodium 70mg • Total Carbohydrate 14g • Dietary Fiber 0g • Protein 0g. DIETARY EXCHANGES: 1 Other Carbohydrate • 1 Fat • 1 Carb Choice.

hanukkah rugelach

cook's notes

No round cookie cutters on hand? Try using a small, clean empty can.

snowman cookies

PREP TIME: 1 Hour ✳ READY IN: 1 Hour 15 Minutes ✳ SERVINGS: 12

1   roll (16.5 oz.) Pillsbury® refrigerated sugar cookies

1/4   cup all-purpose flour

1   cup fluffy white frosting

Decorating icing (from 6.4-oz. aerosol can) or decorating gel (from 0.68-oz. tube)

Assorted small candies or decorating decors

1   Heat oven to 350°F. Remove cookie dough from wrapper. On lightly floured surface, knead flour into dough. Roll dough to 1/4-inch thickness. Using cookie cutters or biscuit cutters, cut 12 (1-1/4-inch), 12 (1-1/2-inch) and 12 (2-inch) circles. To form each snowman, place 1 circle of each size, slightly overlapping, on ungreased cookie sheet.

2   Bake 7 to 9 minutes or until edges are light golden brown. Cool 1 minute; remove from cookie sheet to cooling rack. Cool completely, about 15 minutes. Frost cookies with frosting; decorate with icing and candies.

NUTRITION INFORMATION PER SERVING: Calories 250 • Total Fat 11 g • Saturated Fat 3g • Cholesterol 15mg • Sodium 125mg • Total Carbohydrate 36g • Dietary Fiber 0g • Protein 2g. DIETARY EXCHANGES: 1/2 Starch • 2 Other Carbohydrate • 2 Fat • 2-1/2 Carb Choices.

red-nosed reindeer cookies

READY IN: 15 Minutes ✳ **SERVINGS:** 12

12 white fudge coated creme-filled chocolate sandwich cookies

24 miniature pretzel twists

1 can (6.4 oz.) white decorating icing

1 tube (0.68 oz.) black decorating gel

12 small round chewy red candies (from 9.2-oz. box)

1 Place cookies on tray or flat surface. Break pretzel twists in half to form antlers. Place small amount of white decorating icing on bottom edge of each pretzel; attach 2 pieces at top of each cookie to form reindeer antlers.

2 Using black decorating gel, make 2 small dots to form eyes on each cookie. Cut off top 1/3 of each red candy; attach with small amount of icing to form nose on each cookie.

NUTRITION INFORMATION PER SERVING: Calories 160 • Total Fat 7g • Saturated Fat 5g • Cholesterol 0mg • Sodium 100mg • Total Carbohydrate 25g • Dietary Fiber 0g • Protein 0g. DIETARY EXCHANGES: 1-1/2 Other Carbohydrate • 1-1/2 Fat • 1-1/2 Carb Choices.

cook's notes

If you prefer, you can dip chocolate sandwich cookies into melted white chocolate. Attach the antlers and nose before chocolate hardens; then there is no need to use decorating icing.

santa cupcakes

PREP TIME: 40 Minutes ✳ READY IN: 1 Hour 30 Minutes ✳ SERVINGS: 24

1 box cake mix with pudding in the mix (any flavor)

Water

Oil

Eggs

1 container (1 lb.) vanilla creamy ready-to-spread frosting

2 tablespoons red decorator sugar

48 chocolate chips

24 red cinnamon candies

144 miniature marshmallows (1-1/2 cups)

1 Heat oven to 350°F. Line 24 muffin cups with paper baking cups. Prepare and bake cake mix according to package directions for cupcakes. Cool completely.

2 Spread frosting over cupcakes. Sprinkle top 1/3 of each cupcake with about 1/8 teaspoon red sugar to form Santa's hat.

3 To make each Santa's face, place chocolate chips for eyes and cinnamon candy for nose. Cut 2 marshmallows in half lengthwise; arrange to form rim of hat. Cut 4 marshmallows in half crosswise; cover lower part of cupcake to form beard.

NUTRITION INFORMATION PER SERVING: Calories 250 • Total Fat 11g • Saturated Fat 3g • Cholesterol 25mg • Sodium 210mg • Total Carbohydrate 35g • Dietary Fiber 1g • Protein 2g. DIETARY EXCHANGES: 1 Starch • 1-1/2 Fruit • 2-1/2 Other Carbohydrate • 2 Fat.

no-roll sugar cookies

PREP TIME: 1 Hour 20 Minutes ✳ READY IN: 3 Hours 20 Minutes ✳ SERVINGS: 10 Dozen

1 cup granulated sugar	4-1/4 cups all-purpose flour
1 cup powdered sugar	1 teaspoon baking soda
1 cup butter or margarine, softened	1 teaspoon cream of tartar
1 cup vegetable oil	1 teaspoon salt
1 teaspoon vanilla	Colored sugar
2 eggs	

1 In large bowl with electric mixer, beat granulated sugar, powdered sugar and butter on medium speed until light and fluffy. Beat in oil, vanilla and eggs until well blended.

2 On low speed, beat in flour, baking soda, cream of tartar and salt until a dough forms. Cover with plastic wrap; refrigerate at least 2 hours or overnight for easier handling.

3 Heat oven to 375°F. Shape dough into 1-inch balls; place 2 inches apart on ungreased cookie sheets. Flatten each with bottom of glass dipped in colored sugar. Bake 5 to 8 minutes or until set but not brown. Immediately remove from cookie sheets.

HIGH ALTITUDE (3500-6500 FT): Bake 6 to 7 minutes.

NUTRITION INFORMATION PER SERVING: Calories 60 • Total Fat 3.5g • Saturated Fat 1g • Cholesterol 10mg • Sodium 40mg • Total Carbohydrate 6g • Dietary Fiber 0g • Protein 0g. DIETARY EXCHANGES: 1/2 Other Carbohydrate • 1/2 Fat • 1/2 Carb Choice.

special touch

For the prettiest cookies, look for a "cut-glass" tumbler with a pretty design on the bottom.

snow-covered christmas trees

PREP TIME: 1 Hour 10 Minutes ✳ READY IN: 1 Hour 25 Minutes ✳ SERVINGS: 4 Dozen

1 roll (18 oz.) Pillsbury® refrigerated sugar cookies	2 cups powdered sugar
3 tablespoons all-purpose flour	2 to 3 tablespoons fresh orange juice
1 tablespoon grated orange peel	3 to 4 drops green food color
	3 tablespoons white nonpareils

1 Heat oven to 350°F. In large bowl, break up cookie dough. Stir or knead in flour and orange peel until well blended. Work with half of dough at a time; refrigerate remaining dough until needed.

2 On floured surface with rolling pin, roll dough to 1/8-inch thickness (about 11-inch round). Cut with floured 3- to 3-1/2-inch tree-shaped cookie cutter; place 1 inch apart on ungreased cookie sheets. Repeat with remaining dough.

3 Bake 6 to 9 minutes or until cookies are set and edges just begin to brown. Cool 1 minute; remove from cookie sheets. Cool completely, about 10 minutes.

4 In small bowl, mix powdered sugar and enough orange juice until smooth and desired spreading consistency. Stir in green food color until well blended. Frost cooled cookies; sprinkle with nonpareils. Let stand until icing is set, about 15 minutes. Store between sheets of waxed paper in tightly covered container.

NUTRITION INFORMATION PER SERVING: Calories 70 • Total Fat 2g • Saturated Fat 0.5g • Cholesterol 0mg • Sodium 30mg • Total Carbohydrate 13g • Dietary Fiber 0g • Protein 0g. DIETARY EXCHANGES: 1 Other Carbohydrate • 1/2 Fat • 1 Carb Choice.

cook's notes

The icing on these cookies sets up quickly, so frost a few at a time, then sprinkle with the nonpareils so they'll stick and not roll off.

Joyous Cookies & Bars

This classic collection of treats is perfect for filling up holiday gift tins and cookie trays. Enjoy a few over coffee or share with friends at your next get-together.

p. 268

p. 257

p. 274

p. 258

p. 247

rich espresso bars with buttercream frosting p. 249

ginger macaroons

PREP TIME: 1 Hour ✳ READY IN: 1 Hour 25 Minutes ✳ SERVINGS: 2-1/2 Dozen

3 egg whites	1/4 teaspoon salt
2/3 cup sugar	1/4 cup finely chopped candied ginger
3 tablespoons all-purpose flour	2 cups flaked coconut
1 teaspoon pumpkin pie spice	1/3 cup semisweet chocolate chips
1/8 to 1/4 teaspoon ground ginger	1 teaspoon shortening

1 Heat oven to 325°F. Spray cookie sheets with baking spray with flour. In large bowl, beat egg whites with electric mixer on high speed until frothy. Gradually beat in sugar until stiff. In small bowl, stir together flour, pumpkin pie spice, ground ginger and salt; fold into beaten egg whites. Fold in candied ginger and coconut.

2 Drop by tablespoonfuls 2 inches apart onto cookie sheets. Bake 15 to 20 minutes or until macaroons feel firm and are very lightly browned. Cool 10 minutes; remove from cookie sheets to cooling rack. Cool completely, about 15 minutes.

3 In small microwavable bowl, place chocolate chips and shortening. Microwave uncovered on High 30 seconds; stir until melted and smooth. Drizzle over cookies.

NUTRITION INFORMATION PER SERVING: Calories 50 • Total Fat 2g • Saturated Fat 1.5g • Cholesterol 0mg • Sodium 40mg • Total Carbohydrate 8g • Dietary Fiber 0g • Protein 0g. DIETARY EXCHANGES: 1/2 Other Carbohydrate • 1/2 Fat • 1/2 Carb Choice.

linzer sandwich cookies

PREP TIME: 1 Hour ✳ READY IN: 4 Hours ✳ SERVINGS: 26

3/4 cup hazelnuts (filberts)	1/4 teaspoon ground cinnamon
1/2 cup packed light brown sugar	1 cup butter, softened
2-1/2 cups all-purpose flour	1 egg
2 teaspoons cream of tartar	1 teaspoon vanilla
1 teaspoon baking soda	Powdered sugar, if desired
1/2 teaspoon salt	1/2 cup seedless raspberry jam

1 Heat oven to 350°F. Spread hazelnuts in ungreased shallow baking pan. Bake uncovered about 6 minutes, stirring occasionally. Rub nuts in a kitchen towel to remove loose skins (some skins may not come off); cool 5 to 10 minutes. Turn off oven.

2 In food processor bowl with metal blade, place nuts and 1/4 cup of the brown sugar. Cover; process with about 10 on-and-off pulses, 2 to 3 seconds each, until the nuts are finely ground but not oily.

3 In small bowl, mix flour, cream of tartar, baking soda, salt and cinnamon; set aside. In large bowl, beat butter and remaining 1/4 cup brown sugar with electric mixer on medium speed about 3 minutes or until smooth. Add nut mixture; beat about 1 minute or until mixed. Beat in egg and vanilla. With spoon, stir in flour mixture about 1 minute or just until blended. Shape the dough into 2 balls; flatten each ball into a disk. Wrap separately in plastic wrap; refrigerate at least 2 hours until firm.

4 Heat oven to 425°F. Remove 1 dough disk from refrigerator. On well floured surface, roll dough with floured rolling pin until about 1/8 inch thick. Cut with 2-1/2-inch cookie cutter in desired shape. On ungreased cookie sheets, place cutouts about 1 inch apart.

5 Roll and cut other half of dough. Using a 1-inch square or round cutter, cut out the center of half of the cookies. Reroll dough centers and cut out more cookies.

6 Bake 4 to 5 minutes or until edges are light golden brown. Remove from cookie sheets to cooling rack. Cool about 10 minutes.

7 Lightly sprinkle powdered sugar over cookies with center cutouts. Or drizzle with powdered sugar icing, and sprinkle with colored sugars or decors. Spread about 1 teaspoon raspberry jam over bottom side of each whole cookie. Top with a cutout cookie. Cool completely, about 1 hour.

NUTRITION INFORMATION PER SERVING: Calories 170 • Total Fat 9g • Saturated Fat 4.5g • Cholesterol 25mg • Sodium 150mg •
Total Carbohydrate 18g • Dietary Fiber 0g • Protein 2g. DIETARY EXCHANGES: 1/2 Starch • 1/2 Other Carbohydrate • 2 Fat • 1 Carb Choice.

special touch

With lovely raspberry filling, these stunning linzer cookies add festive flair to Christmas dessert buffets.

sandwiched sugar cookies

PREP TIME: 1 Hour 15 Minutes ✳ **READY IN:** 3 Hours 15 Minutes
SERVINGS: 48 Sandwich Cookies and 48 Small Cookies

1 cup sugar	1/2 teaspoon vanilla
1 cup butter, softened	1 egg yolk
1 package (3 oz.) cream cheese, softened	2 cups all-purpose flour
1 teaspoon grated lemon peel	1-1/4 cups any flavor preserves
1/2 teaspoon salt	1/4 cup powdered sugar
1/2 teaspoon almond extract	

1 In large bowl, combine sugar, butter, cream cheese, lemon peel, salt, almond extract, vanilla and egg yolk; blend well. Lightly spoon flour into measuring cup; level off. Add flour; mix well. Cover with plastic wrap; refrigerate 2 hours for easier handling.

2 Heat oven to 375°F. On lightly floured surface, roll out 1/3 of dough at a time to 1/8-inch thickness. (Keep remaining dough refrigerated.) Cut with floured 2-1/2-inch fluted round cookie cutter. Place half of cookies 1 inch apart on ungreased cookie sheets. Cut 1-inch shapes from centers of remaining cookies. Place cookies and small cutouts 1 inch apart on separate ungreased cookie sheets.

3 Bake at 375°F. For small cookies, bake 6 minutes; for large cookies, bake 7 to 10 minutes or until light golden brown. Immediately remove from cookie sheets. Cool cookies 5 minutes or until completely cooled.

4 Spread bottom of each whole cookie with about 1 teaspoon preserves. Sprinkle powdered sugar over cookies with cutout centers. To make each sandwich cookie, place one powdered sugar cookie over preserves on whole cookie.

HIGH ALTITUDE (3500-6500 FT): Increase flour to 2-1/4 cups. Bake as directed above.

NUTRITION INFORMATION PER SERVING: Calories 90 • Total Fat 4g • Saturated Fat 2g • Cholesterol 15mg • Sodium 55mg • Total Carbohydrate 13g • Dietary Fiber 0g • Protein 1g. DIETARY EXCHANGES: 1/2 Starch • 1/2 Fruit • 1 Other Carbohydrate • 1/2 Fat.

rich espresso bars with buttercream frosting

PREP TIME: 25 Minutes ✳ **READY IN:** 3 Hours 50 Minutes ✳ **SERVINGS:** 32

Bars

1/2	cup butter
1	cup packed light brown sugar
1	teaspoon vanilla
2	eggs
3/4	cup all-purpose flour
2	tablespoons plus 2 teaspoons instant espresso coffee powder
1/4	teaspoon baking powder
1/4	teaspoon salt
3/4	cup finely chopped pecans or walnuts, if desired

Espresso Buttercream Frosting

1/3	cup whipping cream
1/4	cup butter
1	cup white vanilla baking chips
1	tablespoon instant espresso coffee powder
1/2	teaspoon vanilla
1/2	cup powdered sugar

Garnish

32	chocolate-covered espresso coffee beans

cook's notes

These bars can be made ahead, wrapped airtight and frozen. Take them out of the freezer at least 1 hour before serving.

1 Heat oven to 350°F. Lightly grease bottom and sides of 13x9-inch pan with shortening, or spray with cooking spray.

2 In 2-quart saucepan, heat 1/2 cup butter and the brown sugar over medium heat, stirring frequently, until butter is melted and sugar is moistened. Remove from heat. Add 1 teaspoon vanilla and the eggs; beat with spoon until smooth.

3 In small bowl, stir together flour, 2 tablespoons plus 2 teaspoons espresso powder, the baking powder and salt. Add to egg mixture. Beat with spoon until well blended. Stir in pecans. Spread evenly in pan.

4 Bake 15 to 20 minutes or until toothpick inserted in center comes out clean. Cool in pan on cooling rack about 30 minutes.

5 In 2-quart saucepan, heat whipping cream, 1/4 cup butter and the baking chips over medium heat, stirring frequently, until chips and butter are melted. Remove from heat. Stir in 1 tablespoon espresso powder, 1/2 teaspoon vanilla and the powdered sugar; beat well with spoon (mixture will be lumpy). Refrigerate until chilled, about 30 minutes.

6 Beat chilled mixture with electric mixer on high speed 2 to 3 minutes or until light and fluffy. Spread evenly over bars. Refrigerate at least 2 hours. For bars, cut into 8 rows by 4 rows. Top each bar with 1 coffee bean. Cover and refrigerate any remaining bars.

NUTRITION INFORMATION PER SERVING: Calories 140 • Total Fat 8g • Saturated Fat 5g • Cholesterol 30mg • Sodium 75mg • Total Carbohydrate 17g • Dietary Fiber 0g • Protein 1g. DIETARY EXCHANGES: 1/2 Starch • 1/2 Other Carbohydrate • 1-1/2 Fat • 1 Carb Choice.

porcelain cookies

PREP TIME: 1 Hour 30 Minutes ✳ **READY IN:** 3 Hours 30 Minutes ✳ **SERVINGS:** 32

COOKIES
- 3/4 cup butter, softened
- 3/4 cup granulated sugar
- 1 egg
- 1 tablespoon finely grated lemon peel
- 2 tablespoons lemon juice
- 2-1/2 cups all-purpose flour
- 1 teaspoon baking soda
- 1/4 teaspoon salt

ROYAL ICING
- 3 cups powdered sugar
- 2 tablespoons meringue powder
- 5 teaspoons lemon juice
- 4 to 5 tablespoons water

DECORATIONS
- Colored sugars
- Colored candy sprinkles

1 In large bowl, beat butter and granulated sugar with electric mixer on medium speed until creamy. On low speed, beat in egg, lemon peel and 2 tablespoons lemon juice. Stir in flour, baking soda and salt until well blended.

2 Divide dough into 4 parts; flatten each part into 1/2-inch-thick round. Wrap each in waxed paper or plastic wrap; refrigerate 30 minutes.

3 Heat oven to 350°F. Remove 1 round of dough at a time from refrigerator. Between sheets of floured waxed paper or plastic wrap, roll dough until 1/4 to 3/8 inch thick. Cut with 3-inch cookie cutters in various shapes. On ungreased cookie sheets, place cutouts 1 inch apart.

4 Bake 10 to 12 minutes or just until edges are golden. Cool on cookie sheets about 1 minute before removing to cooling rack.

5 To make cookies for hanging, using a toothpick or end of plastic straw, carefully poke a hole in the top of each cookie while cookies are still hot. Cool 10 to 15 minutes before frosting.

6 In medium bowl, stir together powdered sugar and meringue powder. Stir in 5 teaspoons lemon juice and enough of the 4 to 5 tablespoons water to make a thin icing. Transfer 1/2 cup of the icing into small bowl; set aside. Using a flexible pastry brush, paint cookies to the edges with icing. Place on cooling rack to dry completely, about 30 minutes.

7 Beat reserved icing with electric mixer on high speed 5 to 7 minutes or until peaks form. Place in small resealable food-storage plastic bag; cut a very small hole in the bottom of the bag with plain white icing. Squeeze icing onto glazed cookies. Before icing dries, sprinkle with decorations, and tap off excess. Dry thoroughly on cooling rack. Thread cookies with narrow ribbon for hanging.

NUTRITION INFORMATION PER SERVING: Calories 150 • Total Fat 4.5g • Saturated Fat 3g • Cholesterol 20mg • Sodium 100mg • Total Carbohydrate 25g • Dietary Fiber 0g • Protein 2g. DIETARY EXCHANGES: 1/2 Starch • 1 Other Carbohydrate • 1 Fat • 1-1/2 Carb Choices.

porcelain cookies

cook's notes

Cherry-flavored dried and sweetened cranberries can be used instead of dried cherries.

triple-layered brownies

PREP TIME: 35 Minutes ✳ READY IN: 2 Hours 35 Minutes ✳ SERVINGS: 48

BROWNIES
1/2	cup butter
2	oz. unsweetened baking chocolate
2	eggs
1	cup packed light brown sugar
1/2	cup all-purpose flour
1	teaspoon vanilla

FILLING
1/2	cup whipping cream
1	bag (12 oz.) white vanilla baking chips (2 cups)
1	cup dried cherries, chopped

GLAZE
1/2	cup semisweet chocolate chips
2	tablespoons butter

1 Heat oven to 350°F. Grease bottom and sides of 9-inch square pan with shortening and lightly flour, or spray with baking spray with flour.

2 In 2-quart saucepan, melt 1/2 cup butter and the unsweetened chocolate over medium heat, stirring constantly. Remove from heat; cool 5 minutes. Stir in eggs, brown sugar, flour and vanilla until smooth. Spread evenly in pan.

3 Bake 25 to 30 minutes or until toothpick inserted in center comes out clean. Cool in pan on cooling rack about 30 minutes.

4 Meanwhile, in 1-quart saucepan, heat whipping cream and white baking chips just to boiling over medium heat, stirring frequently. Remove from heat. Stir in cherries. Spread filling over brownies. Refrigerate about 30 minutes or until set.

5 In small microwavable bowl, place chocolate chips and 2 tablespoons butter. Microwave uncovered on High 30 seconds; stir. Microwave 15 seconds longer; stir until melted and smooth. Spread glaze evenly over filling. Refrigerate at least 30 minutes. For brownies, cut into 8 rows by 6 rows. Cover and refrigerate any remaining brownies.

NUTRITION INFORMATION PER SERVING: Calories 120 • Total Fat 6g • Saturated Fat 4g • Cholesterol 20mg • Sodium 40mg • Total Carbohydrate 13g • Dietary Fiber 0g • Protein 1g. DIETARY EXCHANGES: 1 Starch • 1 Fat • 1 Carb Choice.

ginger shortbread cookies

PREP TIME: 25 Minutes ✶ **READY IN:** 2 Hours ✶ **SERVINGS:** 4 Dozen

1 cup butter, softened (do not use margarine)	1/2 teaspoon ground nutmeg
1/2 cup packed brown sugar	1/3 cup finely chopped crystallized ginger
2-1/4 cups all-purpose flour	4 oz. bittersweet baking chocolate, chopped
1 teaspoon ground ginger	

1 Heat oven to 350°F. Line bottom and sides of 13x9-inch pan with foil, extending foil 2 inches on 2 opposite sides of pan.

2 In large bowl, beat butter and brown sugar with electric mixer on medium speed, scraping bowl occasionally, until fluffy. On low speed, beat in flour, ground ginger and nutmeg until crumbly. Stir in crystallized ginger. Press dough firmly in pan. Prick surface generously with fork.

3 Bake 18 to 22 minutes or until light golden brown and set. Cool 10 minutes. Remove from pan by lifting foil. To make 24 squares, cut into 6 rows by 4 rows by pressing down with a long knife (do not use sawing motion). Cut each square diagonally in half to make triangles. Cool completely, about 1 hour.

4 In small microwavable bowl, microwave chocolate uncovered on High 1 minute. Stir; microwave 30 seconds longer, stirring every 15 seconds, until completely melted. Dip one short, flat edge of each triangular cookie in chocolate; if necessary, shake off any excess chocolate. Place on waxed paper; let stand until chocolate is set before storing between layers of waxed paper in loosely covered container.

NUTRITION INFORMATION PER SERVING: Calories 80 • Total Fat 5g • Saturated Fat 3g • Cholesterol 10mg • Sodium 30mg • Total Carbohydrate 8g • Dietary Fiber 0g • Protein 1g. DIETARY EXCHANGES: 1/2 Starch • 1 Fat • 1/2 Carb Choice.

cook's notes

To quickly set the chocolate, place the dipped cookies in the refrigerator for a few minutes. You can use semisweet baking chocolate instead of bittersweet chocolate. Melt as directed in Step 4.

my chai cookies

my chai cookies

PREP TIME: 45 Minutes ✹ READY IN: 1 Hour ✹ SERVINGS: 3 Dozen

1 roll (16.5 oz.) Pillsbury® refrigerated sugar cookies	1 package (1 oz.) vanilla or original chai tea latte mix
1/4 cup all-purpose flour	3/4 cup powdered sugar
1/4 cup finely chopped pecans	

1 Heat oven to 350°F. In large bowl, break up cookie dough. Stir or knead in flour, pecans and 2 teaspoons of the chai tea mix until well blended. Shape dough into 36 (1-inch) balls; place 1 inch apart on ungreased cookie sheets.

2 Bake 11 to 15 minutes or until tops appear dry and edges just begin to brown. Cool 1 minute; remove from cookie sheets.

3 In shallow dish, mix remaining chai tea mix and the powdered sugar. Roll warm cookies in sugar mixture. Cool completely, about 15 minutes. Reroll cookies in powdered sugar mixture. Store in tightly covered container.

NUTRITION INFORMATION PER SERVING: Calories 80 • Total Fat 3.5g • Saturated Fat 0.5g • Cholesterol 0mg • Sodium 45mg • Total Carbohydrate 12g • Dietary Fiber 0g • Protein 0g. DIETARY EXCHANGES: 1/2 Other Carbohydrate • 1 Fat • 1 Carb Choice.

cook's notes

The chai tea latte mix contains black tea, honey, spices and dried milk. Look for it near the other packages of tea.

choco-caramel turtles

PREP TIME: 1 Hour 10 Minutes ✹ READY IN: 1 Hour 30 Minutes ✹ SERVINGS: 24

6 oz. (1-1/2 cups) pecan halves (about 120 pieces)	1 roll (16.5 oz.) Pillsbury® refrigerated chocolate chip cookies
8 caramels, unwrapped	3/4 cup chocolate creamy ready-to-spread frosting (from 1-lb. container)

1 Heat oven to 350°F. Arrange pecans in groups of 5 on ungreased cookie sheets to resemble head and legs of turtle.

2 Cut each caramel into 3 equal pieces. Wrap 1 tablespoon cookie dough around each piece of caramel. Press dough lightly onto pecans, covering half of each. (Tips of pecans should show after baking.)

3 Bake 10 to 14 minutes or until golden brown. Immediately remove from cookie sheets to cooling racks. Cool completely, about 20 minutes. Spread about 1 rounded teaspoon frosting on each cooled cookie.

NUTRITION INFORMATION PER SERVING: Calories 180 • Total Fat 11g • Saturated Fat 3.5g • Cholesterol 0mg • Sodium 65mg • Total Carbohydrate 18g • Dietary Fiber 1g • Protein 1g. DIETARY EXCHANGES: 1/2 Starch • 1/2 Other Carbohydrate • 2 Fat • 1 Carb Choice.

cook's notes

You could use sugar cookie dough instead of the chocolate chip dough if you like.

chocolate-filled meringue snowballs

PREP TIME: 40 Minutes ✳ READY IN: 1 Hour 10 Minutes ✳ SERVINGS: 4 Dozen

1/2 cup powdered sugar

1/2 cup chocolate creme-filled cookie crumbs

1/2 cup finely chopped pecans

1/4 cup miniature semisweet chocolate chips

2 tablespoons bourbon or water

1 teaspoon light corn syrup

2 egg whites

2/3 cup sugar

1/2 teaspoon vanilla

1 Heat oven to 250°F. Generously grease cookie sheets with shortening. In medium bowl, stir powdered sugar, cookie crumbs, pecans, chocolate chips, bourbon and corn syrup until well mixed. Shape 1/2 teaspoonfuls into balls; place on sheet of waxed paper. (If necessary, flour hands to shape balls.)

2 In small bowl, beat egg whites with electric mixer on high speed until soft peaks form. Gradually add sugar, beating until stiff peaks form. Stir in vanilla.

3 Drop balls 1 at a time into meringue. With spoon, coat well to form 1-inch balls; place on cookie sheets. Swirl top of meringue with spoon. Bake 30 minutes or until meringue snowballs are crisp. Immediately remove from cookie sheets.

NUTRITION INFORMATION PER SERVING: Calories 40 • Total Fat 1.5g • Saturated Fat 0.5g • Cholesterol 0mg • Sodium 5mg • Total Carbohydrate 6g • Dietary Fiber 0g • Protein 0g. DIETARY EXCHANGES: 1/2 Other Carbohydrate • 1/2 Fat • 1/2 Carb Choice.

cook's notes

Twenty crushed chocolate wafer cookies can be used in place of the chocolate cookie crumbs. To crush the wafers, place them in a plastic bag or between two pieces of waxed paper and simply roll with a rolling pin. Measure 1/2 cup of the crushed wafers to use in the recipe.

mocha pecan balls

PREP TIME: 55 Minutes ✳ READY IN: 1 Hour 10 Minutes ✳ SERVINGS: 4 Dozen

1 roll (16.5 oz.) Pillsbury® refrigerated sugar cookies

1/4 cup unsweetened baking cocoa

1 tablespoon instant espresso coffee granules

1 cup finely chopped pecans

48 milk chocolate candy drops or pieces, unwrapped

3/4 cup powdered sugar

1 Heat oven to 375°F. In large bowl, break up cookie dough. Stir or knead in cocoa, espresso granules and pecans until well blended.

2 Shape dough into 48 (1-inch) balls; wrap each around 1 milk chocolate candy. On ungreased cookie sheet, place 2 inches apart.

3 Bake 8 to 10 minutes or until set. Immediately remove from cookie sheets to cooling racks. Cool slightly, about 5 minutes.

4 Roll cookies in powdered sugar. Cool completely, about 15 minutes. Reroll cookies in powdered sugar. Store in tightly covered container.

HIGH ALTITUDE (3500-6500 FT): Heat oven to 350°F.

NUTRITION INFORMATION PER SERVING: Calories 90 • Total Fat 5g • Saturated Fat 1.5g • Cholesterol 0mg • Sodium 30mg • Total Carbohydrate 11g • Dietary Fiber 0g • Protein 0g. DIETARY EXCHANGES: 1/2 Starch • 1 Fat • 1 Carb Choice.

gourmet mint brownies

PREP TIME: 30 Minutes ✳ **READY IN:** 2 Hours 15 Minutes ✳ **SERVINGS:** 36

BROWNIES

1	package (8 oz.) cream cheese, softened
1/4	cup sugar
1	egg
1	teaspoon mint extract
4	drops green food color
1	cup butter or margarine
4	oz. unsweetened baking chocolate, cut into pieces
2	cups sugar
2	teaspoons vanilla

4	eggs
1	cup all-purpose or unbleached flour

FROSTING

2	tablespoons butter or margarine
2	tablespoons corn syrup
2	tablespoons water
2	oz. unsweetened baking chocolate, cut into pieces
1	teaspoon vanilla
1	cup powdered sugar

1 Heat oven to 350°F. Grease and flour 13x9-inch pan. In small bowl, beat cream cheese and 1/4 cup sugar until smooth. Add egg, mint extract and food color; mix well. Set aside.

2 In 3- to 4-quart saucepan, melt 1 cup butter and 4 oz. chocolate over very low heat, stirring constantly. Remove from heat; cool slightly. Stir in 2 cups sugar and 2 teaspoons vanilla. Add eggs 1 at a time, beating well after each addition.

3 Stir in flour; mix well. Spread in pan. Carefully spoon cheese filling over brownie mixture. Gently cut through layers with knife to marble. Bake 45 to 50 minutes or until set. Cool completely.

4 In heavy saucepan, heat 2 tablespoons butter, corn syrup and water to a rolling boil. Remove from heat. Add 2 oz. chocolate; stir until melted.

5 Stir in 1 teaspoon vanilla and powdered sugar; beat until smooth. Frost cooled brownies. Cut into 9 rows by 4 rows. Cover and refrigerate any remaining brownies.

HIGH ALTITUDE (3500-6500 FT): Bake 48 to 53 minutes.

NUTRITION INFORMATION PER SERVING: Calories 200 • Total Fat 11 g • Saturated Fat 7g • Cholesterol 50mg • Sodium 70mg • Total Carbohydrate 21g • Dietary Fiber 0g • Protein 2g. DIETARY EXCHANGES: 1 Starch • 1/2 Other Carbohydrate • 2 Fat • 1-1/2 Carb Choices.

special touch

Garnish each brownie square with a fresh mint leaf and a raspberry or small strawberry dipped in chocolate.

SISTER MARIA JOSE CANNON
Honolulu, Hawaii
Bake-Off® Contest 5, 1953

kitchen tip

Baking soda will keep in your

cupboard for up to 6 months.

To test if it's still active, stir 1/4

teaspoon into 2 teaspoons of

vinegar. If it bubbles rapidly,

it's fine to use.

coconut islands

READY IN: 1 Hour 20 Minutes ✳ **SERVINGS:** 3-1/2 Dozen

COOKIES

3	oz. unsweetened baking chocolate, chopped
1/4	cup hot brewed coffee
2	cups all-purpose flour
1/2	teaspoon salt
1/2	teaspoon baking soda
1/2	cup shortening
1	cup packed brown sugar
1	egg
2/3	cup sour cream
1/3	cup flaked coconut

FROSTING

1-1/2	oz. unsweetened baking chocolate, chopped
1/4	cup sour cream
1	tablespoon butter or margarine
1-1/2 to 2	cups powdered sugar
1 to 2	teaspoons cold brewed coffee

GARNISH

1	cup flaked coconut

1 Heat oven to 375°F. Grease large cookie sheets with shortening or cooking spray. In 1-quart saucepan, melt 3 oz. chocolate in hot coffee over low heat, stirring frequently; cool. Meanwhile, in small bowl, stir together flour, salt, and baking soda; set aside.

2 In large bowl, beat shortening and brown sugar with electric mixer on medium speed, scraping bowl occasionally, until well blended. Beat in egg and chocolate mixture. Beat in 2/3 cup sour cream alternately with the flour mixture until well blended. Stir in 1/3 cup coconut.

3 Onto cookie sheets, drop dough by heaping teaspoonfuls about 2 inches apart. Bake 10 to 12 minutes or until set. Meanwhile, in 1-1/2-quart heavy saucepan, heat 1-1/2 oz. chocolate, 1/4 cup sour cream and the butter, stirring constantly, until chocolate is melted. Immediately remove from heat. Gradually stir in enough powdered sugar until frosting is spreadable. If necessary, thin with coffee or water, a few drops at a time.

4 Remove cookies from cookie sheets to cooling racks; cool about 2 minutes. Spread cookies with frosting. Sprinkle tops with 1 cup coconut. Store in tightly covered container.

HIGH ALTITUDE (3500-6500 FT): Bake 9 to 11 minutes.

NUTRITION INFORMATION PER SERVING: Calories 130 • Total Fat 6g • Saturated Fat 3g • Cholesterol 10mg • Sodium 60mg • Total Carbohydrate 16g • Dietary Fiber 0g • Protein 1g. DIETARY EXCHANGES: 1/2 Starch • 1/2 Other Carbohydrate • 1 Fat • 1 Carb Choice.

midnight espresso crinkles

READY IN: 1 Hour 40 Minutes ✻ **SERVINGS:** 3 Dozen

6 oz. unsweetened baking chocolate, cut into small pieces

3/4 cup butter or margarine, softened

1/4 cup vegetable oil

1 cup granulated sugar

1 cup packed brown sugar

2 eggs

2 tablespoons instant coffee or espresso coffee granules

2 tablespoons water

1 teaspoon vanilla

2 cups all-purpose flour

2 teaspoons baking powder

1/2 teaspoon salt

1/2 cup dark chocolate chips (from 12-oz. bag)

1/4 cup decorator sugar crystals

cook's notes

These cookies are like fudgy brownies—slightly soft when done. They won't feel set if you gently tap them, but the tops will look dry.

1 In small microwavable bowl, microwave baking chocolate uncovered on High 1 minute. Stir; microwave 1 minute longer, stirring every 15 seconds, until melted and smooth.

2 In large bowl, beat butter, oil, granulated sugar and brown sugar with electric mixer on medium speed, scraping bowl occasionally, until light and fluffy. Beat in melted chocolate and eggs until well blended.

3 In small bowl, dissolve coffee granules in water. Add coffee mixture and vanilla to batter; beat until well blended. On low speed, beat in flour, baking powder and salt. Stir in chocolate chips. Cover with plastic wrap; refrigerate 30 minutes for easier handling.

4 Heat oven to 350°F. Place sugar crystals in small bowl. Shape dough by rounded tablespoonfuls into 1-1/2-inch balls; dip tops of balls in sugar. On ungreased cookie sheets, place balls, sugar sides up, 3 inches apart.

5 Bake 11 to 13 minutes or until tops look dry (do not overbake). Cool 5 minutes; remove from cookie sheets to cooling racks.

NUTRITION INFORMATION PER SERVING: Calories 170 • Total Fat 9g • Saturated Fat 4.5g • Cholesterol 20mg • Sodium 95mg • Total Carbohydrate 21g • Dietary Fiber 1g • Protein 2g. DIETARY EXCHANGES: 1/2 Starch • 1 Other Carbohydrate • 1-1/2 Fat • 1-1/2 Carb Choices.

Mrs. F. H. Speers
Midland, Texas
Bake-Off® Contest 04, 1952

cook's notes

To prevent Brazil nuts from

becoming rancid, store them

in the fridge. If you do not want

to use Brazil nuts, try almonds,

pecans or macadamia nuts.

brazilian jubilee cookies

READY IN: 1 Hour 15 Minutes ✳ SERVINGS: 3 Dozen

3/4 cup granulated sugar	1 teaspoon baking powder
1/4 cup packed brown sugar	1/2 teaspoon salt
1/2 cup shortening	1/2 teaspoon ground cinnamon
2 teaspoons vanilla	1 cup chopped Brazil nuts
1 egg	36 milk chocolate stars (from 14-oz. bag)
1-1/2 cups all-purpose flour	Additional chopped Brazil nuts, if desired
1 to 2 tablespoons instant coffee granules or crystals	

1 Heat oven to 350°F. Grease cookie sheets with shortening or cooking spray. In large bowl, beat sugars and shortening with electric mixer on medium speed, scraping bowl occasionally, until well blended. Beat in vanilla and egg. On low speed, beat in flour, instant coffee, baking powder, salt, cinnamon and 1 cup nuts until dough forms.

2 Shape dough by tablespoonfuls into balls. Place 2 inches apart on cookie sheets. Bake 12 to 15 minutes or until golden brown.

3 Immediately top each cookie with 1 chocolate star. Remove from cookie sheets to cooling rack; cool 5 minutes (chocolate will soften). Spread chocolate over cookies to frost. Sprinkle with additional chopped nuts.

NUTRITION INFORMATION PER SERVING: Calories 120 • Total Fat 7g • Saturated Fat 2g • Cholesterol 5mg • Sodium 50mg • Total Carbohydrate 13g • Dietary Fiber 0g • Protein 2g. DIETARY EXCHANGES: 1 Other Carbohydrate • 1-1/2 Fat • 1 Carb Choice.

kitchen tip

After squeezing lemons for

fresh lemon juice, if you have

any left over, pour into ice cube

trays and freeze to use later.

lemon-cranberry bars

PREP TIME: 35 Minutes ✳ READY IN: 1 Hour 35 Minutes ✳ SERVINGS: 16

1/2 roll (16.5 oz.) Pillsbury® refrigerated sugar cookies	1 teaspoon cornstarch
1 egg yolk	2 tablespoons grated lemon peel
1 egg	3 tablespoons fresh lemon juice
1/2 cup sugar	3 tablespoons butter
	32 sweetened dried cranberries

1 Heat oven to 350°F. Break up cookie dough into ungreased 8-inch square pan. Press dough in bottom of pan to form crust.

2 Bake at 350°F for 12 to 17 minutes or until edges are golden brown. Meanwhile, in medium bowl, combine egg yolk and egg; beat well. Set aside.

3 In medium saucepan, combine sugar, cornstarch, lemon peel, lemon juice and butter. Bring to a boil, stirring frequently until butter is melted. Remove from heat. Gradually add mixture to eggs, beating constantly with wire whisk. Return mixture to saucepan. Cook over medium-low heat until mixture thickens, stirring constantly.

4 Remove crust from oven. Pour lemon mixture over partially baked crust; spread to within 1/4 inch of edges.

5 Return to oven; bake an additional 10 minutes. Cool 1 hour or until completely cooled. Cut into bars. Garnish each bar with 2 cranberries.

NUTRITION INFORMATION PER SERVING: Calories 130 • Total Fat 6g • Saturated Fat 2g • Cholesterol 35mg • Sodium 85mg • Total Carbohydrate 17g • Dietary Fiber 0g • Protein 1g. DIETARY EXCHANGES: 1 Fruit • 1 Other Carbohydrate • 1-1/2 Fat.

brazilian jubilee cookies

double-chocolate cranberry cookies

PREP TIME: 40 Minutes ✳ **READY IN:** 1 Hour 20 Minutes ✳ **SERVINGS:** 2 Dozen

1   roll (16.5 oz.) Pillsbury® refrigerated chocolate chip cookies

1/2 cup sweetened dried cranberries

1/4 cup chopped pecans

1/2 cup white chocolate chunks or white vanilla baking chips

1   teaspoon vegetable oil

1 Heat oven to 350°F. In large bowl, break up cookie dough. Stir or knead in cranberries and pecans. Work with half of dough at a time; refrigerate remaining dough until needed.

2 Drop dough by well-rounded tablespoonfuls 2 inches apart onto ungreased cookie sheets. Repeat with remaining dough.

3 Bake 9 to 13 minutes or until light golden brown. Cool 1 minute; remove from cookie sheets. Cool completely, about 15 minutes.

4 In small microwavable bowl, microwave white chocolate chunks and oil on High 30 seconds. Stir; if necessary, microwave 10 to 15 seconds longer until smooth. Place melted chocolate in small resealable food-storage plastic bag; seal bag. Cut 1/8-inch hole in bottom corner of bag.

5 Squeeze bag gently to drizzle white chocolate over cookies. Let stand until white chocolate is set, about 40 minutes. Store between sheets of waxed paper in tightly covered container.

HIGH ALTITUDE (3500-6500 FT): Bake 10 to 13 minutes.

NUTRITION INFORMATION PER SERVING: Calories 130 • Total Fat 6g • Saturated Fat 2g • Cholesterol 5mg • Sodium 75mg • Total Carbohydrate 17g • Dietary Fiber 0g • Protein 1g. DIETARY EXCHANGES: 1 Other Carbohydrate • 1-1/2 Fat • 1 Carb Choice.

jelly-filled thumbprints

READY IN: 1 Hour ✳ SERVINGS: 3 Dozen

1 roll (16.5 oz.) Pillsbury® refrigerated sugar cookies

1 cup coconut

1/2 cup seedless raspberry jam or red currant jelly

1/3 cup white vanilla chips

1 Heat oven to 350°F. Break up cookie dough into large bowl. Add coconut; mix well. Shape dough into 1-inch balls; place 2 inches apart on ungreased cookie sheets. With thumb or handle of wooden spoon, make indentation in center of each cookie. Spoon about 1/2 teaspoon jam into each indentation.

2 Bake at 350°F for 10 to 13 minutes or until edges are light golden brown. Immediately remove from cookie sheets; place on wire racks. Cool 5 minutes.

3 Place white vanilla chips into small resealable food storage plastic bag; partially seal bag. Microwave on High for 45 to 60 seconds. Squeeze bag until chips are smooth. If necessary, microwave an additional 10 seconds. Cut small hole in bottom corner of bag. Squeeze bag gently to drizzle melted chips over cookies.

NUTRITION INFORMATION PER SERVING: Calories 90 • Total Fat 3g • Saturated Fat 2g • Cholesterol 0mg • Sodium 55mg • Total Carbohydrate 15g • Dietary Fiber 0g • Protein 1g. DIETARY EXCHANGES: 1 Other Carbohydrate • 1/2 Fat • 1 Carb Choice.

JANICE OEFFLER
Danbury, Wisconsin
Bake-Off® Contest 39, 2000

pecan toffee squares

PREP TIME: 20 Minutes ✳ READY IN: 1 Hour 50 Minutes ✳ SERVINGS: 36

BASE

1 package (18.25 oz.) yellow cake mix with pudding in the mix

1/2 cup margarine or butter, softened

1 egg

FILLING

1 can (14 oz.) sweetened condensed milk (not evaporated)

1 teaspoon vanilla

1 egg

1 package (6 oz.) chocolate-coated toffee bits

1 cup chopped pecans

1 Heat oven to 350°F. Grease 13x9-inch pan. In large bowl, combine cake mix, margarine and 1 egg; mix well with pastry blender or fork. Press mixture in bottom of greased pan. Bake at 350°F for 7 minutes.

2 Meanwhile, in medium bowl, combine condensed milk, vanilla and 1 egg; mix well. Stir in toffee bits and pecans.

3 Remove pan from oven. Pour filling evenly over warm base. Return to oven; bake an additional 22 to 30 minutes or until filling is set. Cool 1 hour or until completely cooled. Cut into bars. Store in refrigerator.

NUTRITION INFORMATION PER SERVING: Calories 170 • Total Fat 9g • Saturated Fat 3g • Cholesterol 20mg • Sodium 170mg • Total Carbohydrate 21g • Dietary Fiber 0g • Protein 2g. DIETARY EXCHANGES: 1/2 Starch • 1 Fruit • 1-1/2 Other Carbohydrate • 1-1/2 Fat.

cook's notes

If you can't find chocolate-coated toffee bits, coarsely chop four 1.4-oz. chocolate-covered toffee bars. Chop them by hand or place the bars in the food processor and pulse until they are coarsely chopped.

choco-cherry cheesecake bars

PREP TIME: 35 Minutes ✹ **READY IN:** 2 Hours 10 Minutes ✹ **SERVINGS:** 48

1	roll (16.5 oz.) Pillsbury® refrigerated sugar cookies
1	egg, separated
1	package (8 oz.) cream cheese, softened
2	eggs
1	can (14 oz.) sweetened condensed milk (not evaporated)
1/4	teaspoon almond extract

3	drops red food color
1	jar (10 oz.) maraschino cherries, finely chopped, drained on paper towels
1	bag (12 oz.) semisweet chocolate chips (2 cups)
1/2	cup butter or margarine
1/2	cup whipping cream

1 Heat oven to 350°F. In ungreased 13x9-inch pan, break up cookie dough. With floured fingers, press dough evenly in bottom of pan to form crust. Bake 10 to 15 minutes or until light golden brown. Meanwhile, beat 1 egg white in small bowl until frothy.

2 Remove partially baked crust from oven. Brush egg white over crust. Return to oven; bake 3 minutes longer or until egg white is set.

3 Meanwhile, in large bowl, beat cream cheese with electric mixer on medium speed until smooth. Add egg yolk, 2 eggs, sweetened condensed milk, almond extract and food color; beat until well blended. Stir in chopped cherries.

4 Remove partially baked crust from oven. Pour cherry mixture evenly over crust. Return to oven; bake 16 to 20 minutes longer or until set. Cool completely, about 45 minutes.

5 Meanwhile, in medium saucepan, place chocolate chips and butter. Cook over low heat until melted and smooth, stirring frequently. Remove from heat. Cool 20 minutes.

6 Stir whipping cream into chocolate mixture until well blended. Spread over cooled bars. Refrigerate until chocolate is set, about 30 minutes. For bars, cut into 8 rows by 6 rows. Store bars in refrigerator.

HIGH ALTITUDE (3500-6500 FT): Bake crust 13 to 18 minutes.

NUTRITION INFORMATION PER SERVING: Calories 160 • Total Fat 9g • Saturated Fat 5g • Cholesterol 30mg • Sodium 70mg • Total Carbohydrate 17g • Dietary Fiber 0g • Protein 2g. DIETARY EXCHANGES: 1/2 Starch • 1/2 Other Carbohydrate • 2 Fat • 1 Carb Choice.

chocolate-caramel layer bars

PREP TIME: 30 Minutes ❋ **READY IN:** 2 Hours 25 Minutes ❋ **SERVINGS:** 32

1 box (18.25 oz.) chocolate fudge cake mix with pudding in the mix	35 vanilla caramels, unwrapped
1/2 cup butter or margarine, melted	1 cup miniature candy-coated semisweet chocolate baking bits
1 cup evaporated milk	

1 Heat oven to 350°F. Grease 13x9-inch pan with shortening. In large bowl, mix cake mix, butter and 2/3 cup of the milk with spoon until well blended. Spread half of mixture (about 2 cups) in pan. Bake 15 minutes.

2 Meanwhile, in 1-quart saucepan, heat caramels with remaining 1/3 cup milk over low heat, stirring occasionally, until melted.

3 Remove partially baked crust from oven. Sprinkle 1/2 cup of the baking bits evenly over crust. Drizzle with caramel mixture. Drop remaining batter by heaping teaspoonfuls over caramel mixture. Sprinkle with remaining 1/2 cup baking bits; press in lightly.

4 Return to oven; bake 20 to 24 minutes longer or until center is set. Cool completely, about 1-1/2 hours. Cut into 8 rows by 4 rows.

HIGH ALTITUDE (3500-6500 FT): Add 1/4 cup flour to dry cake mix. Bake as directed above.

NUTRITION INFORMATION PER SERVING: Calories 170 • Total Fat 7g • Saturated Fat 4g • Cholesterol 10mg • Sodium 180mg • Total Carbohydrate 26g • Dietary Fiber 0g • Protein 2g. DIETARY EXCHANGES: 1/2 Starch • 1 Other Carbohydrate • 1-1/2 Fat • 2 Carb Choices.

cook's notes

Drizzle the caramel mixture to within 1/4 inch of the sides of the pan. The bars are easier to remove when the caramel doesn't touch the sides.

pecan-rum bars

pecan-rum bars

PREP TIME: 40 Minutes ✳ READY IN: 2 Hours 15 Minutes ✳ SERVINGS: 32

CRUST
1 cup butter, softened
1 cup packed brown sugar
2 cups all-purpose flour

FILLING
2 eggs
1/2 cup packed brown sugar

1/2 cup dark corn syrup
1 tablespoon rum or 1 teaspoon rum extract
2 cups pecan halves

ICING
1/2 cup powdered sugar
1 tablespoon butter, softened
2 teaspoons rum or 1/2 teaspoon rum extract plus 2 teaspoons water

1 Heat oven to 375°F. Grease bottom and sides of 13x9-inch pan with shortening or cooking spray (do not use dark pan).

2 In medium bowl, beat 1 cup butter and 1 cup brown sugar with electric mixer on low speed until creamy. Stir in flour. Press evenly in pan.

3 Bake 12 to 14 minutes or until edges are golden brown and center springs back when touched lightly.

4 Meanwhile, in medium bowl, mix all filling ingredients except pecans. Stir in pecans. Pour over crust, spreading pecans evenly. Bake 12 to 15 minutes or until filling is set. Cool completely, about 1 hour.

5 In small bowl, mix icing ingredients (add additional rum or water, 1/2 teaspoon at a time, if icing is too thick to drizzle). Drizzle icing over bars. For bars, cut into 8 rows by 4 rows.

NUTRITION INFORMATION PER SERVING: Calories 200 • Total Fat 11 g • Saturated Fat 4.5g • Cholesterol 30mg • Sodium 55mg • Total Carbohydrate 23g • Dietary Fiber 0g • Protein 2g. DIETARY EXCHANGES: 1 Starch • 1/2 Other Carbohydrate • 2 Fat • 1 Carb Choice.

cook's notes

Create triangles by cutting each bar diagonally in half. To keep bars longer, wrap tightly, label and freeze for up to 6 months.

raspberry meringues

PREP TIME: 20 Minutes ✳ READY IN: 2 Hours 50 Minutes ✳ SERVINGS: 3 Dozen

3 egg whites, room temperature
1/4 teaspoon cream of tartar
Dash salt

3/4 cup sugar
1/4 cup seedless raspberry jam
1/4 teaspoon red paste food color

1 Heat oven to 225°F. Line cookie sheets with parchment paper. In small bowl, combine egg whites, cream of tartar and salt; beat until soft peaks form. Gradually add sugar, beating until very stiff peaks form, about 10 minutes.

2 Add jam and food color; beat 1 minute at high speed. Pipe or spoon 1-inch mounds onto paper-lined cookie sheets.

3 Bake at 225°F for 2 hours or until crisp and dry. Cool 30 minutes or until completely cooled. Remove cookies from paper.

NUTRITION INFORMATION PER SERVING: Calories 25 • Total Fat 0g • Saturated Fat 0g • Cholesterol 0mg • Sodium 9mg • Total Carbohydrate 6g • Dietary Fiber 0g • Protein 0g. DIETARY EXCHANGES: 1/2 Fruit • 1/2 Other Carbohydrate.

peanut butter cup cookies

READY IN: 40 Minutes ✳ SERVINGS: 24

- 1 roll (16.5 oz.) Pillsbury® refrigerated peanut butter cookies
- 1 cup miniature candy-coated chocolate baking bits, fall colored (yellow, orange, brown, green, red)
- 1/2 cup salted peanuts
- 24 miniature chocolate-covered peanut butter cup candies, unwrapped

1 Heat oven to 350°F. In large bowl, break up cookie dough. Stir or knead in baking bits and peanuts until well blended.

2 Onto ungreased cookie sheets, drop dough by 24 heaping tablespoonfuls 2 inches apart; flatten each slightly with fingers.

3 Bake 10 to 14 minutes or until light golden brown. Immediately top each cookie with 1 peanut butter cup; press lightly into dough. Cool 2 minutes; remove from cookie sheets. Let cookies stand until peanut butter cups are set before storing, about 3 hours.

NUTRITION INFORMATION PER SERVING: Calories 180 • Total Fat 9g • Saturated Fat 3g • Cholesterol 0mg • Sodium 120mg • Total Carbohydrate 20g • Dietary Fiber 0g • Protein 3g. DIETARY EXCHANGES: 1-1/2 Other Carbohydrate • 1/2 High-Fat Meat • 1 Fat • 1 Carb Choice.

praline sugar cookies

READY IN: 1 Hour 10 Minutes ✳ SERVINGS: 3 Dozen

- 1/2 cup granulated sugar
- 1/4 cup pecan halves
- 1 roll (16.5 oz.) Pillsbury® refrigerated sugar cookies
- 1/4 cup packed brown sugar
- 1 teaspoon vanilla

1 In 8-inch heavy skillet, melt 1/4 cup of the granulated sugar over medium-low heat about 3 minutes, without stirring, until golden brown. Watch carefully to avoid scorching. Remove from heat. Stir in pecan halves until coated. Pour mixture onto sheet of foil. Cool until hard, about 15 minutes. Finely chop pecan-sugar candy.

2 Heat oven to 325°F. In large bowl, break up cookie dough. Stir in brown sugar and vanilla until well blended. Stir in chopped pecan-sugar candy.

3 Using about 1 measuring teaspoon dough for each, shape dough into balls and roll in remaining 1/4 cup granulated sugar; place 2 inches apart on ungreased cookie sheets.

4 Bake 11 to 16 minutes or until edges are light golden brown. Cool 2 minutes; remove from cookie sheets.

HIGH ALTITUDE (3500-6500 FT): In 8-inch heavy skillet, melt 1/4 cup of the granulated sugar over medium heat 10 to 12 minutes, without stirring, until golden brown. Watch carefully to avoid scorching.

NUTRITION INFORMATION PER SERVING: Calories 80 • Total Fat 3g • Saturated Fat 0.5g • Cholesterol 0mg • Sodium 45mg • Total Carbohydrate 12g • Dietary Fiber 0g • Protein 0g. DIETARY EXCHANGES: 1 Other Carbohydrate • 1/2 Fat • 1 Carb Choice.

dulce de leche bars

PREP TIME: 30 Minutes ✳ READY IN: 2 Hours 55 Minutes ✳ SERVINGS: 48

2 rolls (16.5 oz. each) Pillsbury® refrigerated sugar cookies

1-3/4 cups quick-cooking or old-fashioned oats

2/3 cup packed brown sugar

2 teaspoons vanilla

1 bag (14 oz.) caramels, unwrapped, or 1 bag (11 oz.) caramel bits

1/2 cup butter or margarine

1 can (14 oz.) sweetened condensed milk (not evaporated)

3 tablespoons caramel topping

1 Heat oven to 350°F. In large bowl, break up 1 roll of cookie dough. Stir or knead in 3/4 cup of the oats, 1/3 cup of the brown sugar and 1 teaspoon of the vanilla until well blended.

2 With floured fingers, press mixture evenly in bottom of ungreased 13x9-inch pan to form crust. Bake 13 to 18 minutes or until light golden brown.

3 Meanwhile, in same bowl, break up remaining roll of cookie dough. Stir or knead in remaining 1 cup oats, 1/3 cup brown sugar and 1 teaspoon vanilla until well blended; set aside. In 2-quart heavy saucepan, heat caramels, butter and condensed milk over medium-low heat, stirring frequently, until caramels are melted and mixture is smooth.

4 Spread caramel mixture evenly over crust. Crumble remaining dough mixture evenly over caramel. Bake 20 to 25 minutes longer or until light golden brown. Cool 1 hour. Run knife around sides of pan to loosen bars. Refrigerate until firm, about 1 hour.

5 With small spoon, drizzle caramel topping over bars. For bars, cut into 8 rows by 6 rows. Cover and refrigerate any remaining bars.

NUTRITION INFORMATION PER SERVING: Calories 190 • Total Fat 7g • Saturated Fat 3g • Cholesterol 15mg • Sodium 115mg • Total Carbohydrate 29g • Dietary Fiber 0g • Protein 2g. DIETARY EXCHANGES: 1/2 Starch • 1-1/2 Other Carbohydrate • 1-1/2 Fat • 2 Carb Choices.

kitchen tip

The word "dulce" [DOOL-say] is Spanish for and generally refers to an intensely sweet confection made with sugar and cream. "Leche" [LAY-chay] is the Spanish word for "milk."

fabulous cashew scotchies with brown butter icing

PREP TIME: 25 Minutes ✳ **READY IN:** 1 Hour 25 Minutes ✳ **SERVINGS:** 24

BARS
1-1/4 cups all-purpose flour
1/2 teaspoon baking powder
1/4 teaspoon salt
1/2 cup butter or margarine
1-1/4 cups packed brown sugar
1 cup chopped cashews
1 teaspoon vanilla
2 eggs

ICING
2/3 cup butter (do not use margarine)
3 cups powdered sugar
1/2 teaspoon vanilla
2 to 3 tablespoons milk

1 Heat oven to 350°F. Grease 13x9-inch pan. In medium bowl, combine flour, baking powder and salt; mix well.

2 Melt 1/2 cup butter in large saucepan over low heat. Remove from heat. Add flour mixture, brown sugar, cashews, 1 teaspoon vanilla and eggs; mix well. Spread batter in greased pan.

3 Bake at 350°F for 25 to 30 minutes or until golden brown and bars begin to pull away from sides of pan. Cool 30 minutes or until completely cooled.

4 Melt 2/3 cup butter in medium saucepan over medium heat. Cook 13 to 15 minutes or until butter is light golden brown, stirring constantly. Remove from heat. Stir in powdered sugar, 1/2 teaspoon vanilla and enough milk for desired spreading consistency. Immediately spread icing over cooled bars. Cut into bars.

HIGH ALTITUDE (3500-6500 FT): When melting and cooking butter for icing, cook over medium-low heat.

NUTRITION INFORMATION PER SERVING: Calories 250 • Total Fat 12g • Saturated Fat 6g • Cholesterol 40mg • Sodium 140mg • Total Carbohydrate 33g • Dietary Fiber 0g • Protein 2g. DIETARY EXCHANGES: 1 Starch • 2-1/2 Fat • 2 Carb Choices.

confetti rocky road bars

PREP TIME: 20 Minutes ✳ **READY IN:** 2 Hours 20 Minutes ✳ **SERVINGS:** 36

1 roll (16.5 oz.) Pillsbury® refrigerated sugar cookies

3 cups miniature marshmallows

1-1/2 cups miniature creme-filled chocolate sandwich cookies, halved or coarsely broken

1 cup semisweet chocolate chips (6 oz.)

3/4 cup salted peanuts

1/3 cup miniature candy-coated chocolate pieces

1 Heat oven to 350°F. In ungreased 13x9-inch pan, break up cookie dough. With floured fingers, press dough evenly in pan. Bake 13 to 16 minutes or until light golden brown.

2 Immediately sprinkle marshmallows evenly over crust. Sprinkle with half of the cookies. Sprinkle with all of the chocolate chips, peanuts and candy-coated chocolate pieces. Sprinkle with remaining cookies; press lightly into marshmallows.

3 Bake 4 to 5 minutes longer or until marshmallows begin to puff. Cool completely on cooling rack, about 2 hours. For bars, cut into 6 rows by 6 rows.

HIGH ALTITUDE (3500-6500 FT): Stir or knead 2 tablespoons all-purpose flour into cookie dough before pressing in pan. In Step 2, bake 15 to 18 minutes.

NUTRITION INFORMATION PER SERVING: Calories 150 • Total Fat 7g • Saturated Fat 2g • Cholesterol 0mg • Sodium 80mg • Total Carbohydrate 20g • Dietary Fiber 1g • Protein 2g. DIETARY EXCHANGES: 1-1/2 Other Carbohydrate • 1-1/2 Fat • 1 Carb Choice.

cook's notes

To serve the bars quicker, place them in the refrigerator for about 15 minutes or until the chocolate chips are firm.

cook's notes

Use green food color to make green frosting, and use crushed green candies for the topping. To keep the tarts longer, wrap tightly, label and freeze up to 6 months.

peppermint candy tarts

READY IN: 1 Hour 30 Minutes ✳ SERVINGS: 32

TART SHELLS

1/2	cup granulated sugar
1/2	cup butter or margarine, softened
1/2	teaspoon peppermint extract
1	egg
1-1/2	cups all-purpose flour
1/4	teaspoon baking soda
1/4	teaspoon salt

FILLING AND GARNISH

2	cups powdered sugar
3	tablespoons butter or margarine, softened
2 or 3	drops red food color
2 to 3	tablespoons milk
1/2	cup crushed hard peppermint candies (about 18 candies)

1 Heat oven to 350°F. Grease bottoms only of 32 mini muffin cups with shortening or cooking spray. In large bowl, beat granulated sugar and 1/2 cup butter with electric mixer on medium speed until fluffy. Beat in peppermint extract and egg until blended. On low speed, beat in flour, baking soda and salt. Shape dough into 1-1/2-inch balls. Press each ball in bottom and up side of muffin cup.

2 Bake 9 to 12 minutes until set and edges are light golden brown. Cool 1 minute; remove from muffin cups to cooling racks. Cool completely, about 15 minutes.

3 In small bowl, beat filling ingredients except crushed candies with electric mixture on medium speed until smooth and creamy. Stir in 1/4 cup of the candies. Spoon or pipe 1 rounded measuring teaspoon filling into center of each tart shell. Sprinkle with remaining crushed candies.

NUTRITION INFORMATION PER SERVING: Calories 130 • Total Fat 4g • Saturated Fat 2.5g • Cholesterol 15mg • Sodium 60mg • Total Carbohydrate 21g • Dietary Fiber 0g • Protein 0g. DIETARY EXCHANGES: 1-1/2 Other Carbohydrate • 1 Fat • 1-1/2 Carb Choices.

crunchy cherry chippers

READY IN: 55 Minutes ✳ **SERVINGS:** 20

1 roll (16.5 oz.) Pillsbury® refrigerated oatmeal chocolate chip cookies

1/4 cup chopped maraschino cherries, well drained

1 tablespoon all-purpose flour

2 cups Wheaties® cereal, coarsely crushed

1 Heat oven to 350°F. Break up cookie dough into large bowl. Pat cherries dry with paper towels. Add cherries and flour to dough; mix well.

2 Drop dough by heaping teaspoonfuls into cereal crumbs; coat well, pressing cereal into dough. Shape into balls; place 2 inches apart on ungreased cookie sheets.

3 Bake at 350°F for 12 to 15 minutes or until golden brown. Immediately remove from cookie sheets to cooling racks.

NUTRITION INFORMATION PER SERVING: Calories 145 • Total Fat 6g • Saturated Fat 1g • Cholesterol 0mg • Sodium 125mg • Total Carbohydrate 20g • Dietary Fiber 1g • Protein 3g. DIETARY EXCHANGES: 1 Starch • 1-1/2 Fat • 1 Carb Choice.

cook's notes

To create this crunchy cherry treat, we updated the recipe for Quick Cherry Winks, a classic from the second Pillsbury Bake-Off® Contest in 1950.

quick cherry winks

READY IN: 1 Hour 15 Minutes ✳ **SERVINGS:** 4 Dozen

1 roll (16.5 oz.) Pillsbury® refrigerated sugar cookies

1 cup chopped pecans

1 cup chopped dates

1/3 cup chopped maraschino cherries, well drained

1-1/2 cups coarsely crushed cornflakes cereal

12 maraschino cherries, quartered

1 Heat oven to 375°F. Break up cookie dough into large bowl. Add pecans, dates and 1/3 cup chopped maraschino cherries; mix well. If necessary for easier handling, cover with plastic wrap; refrigerate 15 minutes.

2 Drop dough by level measuring tablespoonfuls into cereal; thoroughly coat. Shape into balls; place 2 inches apart on ungreased cookie sheets. Lightly press maraschino cherry quarter into top of each ball.

3 Bake at 375°F for 11 to 14 minutes or until edges are light golden brown. Cool 1 minute; remove from cookie sheets to cooling racks.

NUTRITION INFORMATION PER SERVING: Calories 80 • Total Fat 3g • Saturated Fat 1g • Cholesterol 2mg • Sodium 45mg • Total Carbohydrate 12g • Dietary Fiber 0g • Protein 1g. DIETARY EXCHANGES: 1 Other Carbohydrate • 1/2 Fat • 1 Carb Choice.

RUTH DEROUSSEAU
Rice Lake, Wisconsin
Bake-Off® Contest 2, 1950
Prize Winner

chocolate-filled russian tea cakes

PREP TIME: 2 Hours ✳ READY IN: 2 Hours 30 Minutes ✳ SERVINGS: 4 Dozen

COOKIES
    1 cup butter or margarine, softened
1/2 cup powdered sugar
    1 teaspoon vanilla
    2 cups all-purpose flour
1/4 teaspoon salt

3/4 cup finely chopped walnuts
  48 milk chocolate stars (from 14-oz. bag)

SUGAR COATING
    1 cup powdered sugar
    1 tablespoon red sugar
    1 tablespoon green sugar

1 Heat oven to 400°F. In large bowl, beat butter, 1/2 cup powdered sugar and the vanilla with electric mixture on medium speed until well mixed. On low speed, beat in flour, salt and walnuts.

2 For each cookie, shape scant measuring tablespoonfuls dough around chocolate star to make 1-inch ball; place 2 inches apart on ungreased cookie sheets.

3 Bake 12 to 15 minutes or until set and bottoms begin to turn golden brown. Meanwhile, in small bowl, mix sugar coating ingredients.

4 Immediately remove cookies from cookie sheets; roll in sugar coating. Cool completely on cooling racks, about 30 minutes. Roll in sugar coating again.

HIGH ALTITUDE (3500-6500 FT): Heat oven to 375°F.

NUTRITION INFORMATION PER SERVING: Calories 100 • Total Fat 6g • Saturated Fat 3g • Cholesterol 10mg • Sodium 45mg • Total Carbohydrate 11 g • Dietary Fiber 0g • Protein 1g. DIETARY EXCHANGES: 1 Other Carbohydrate • 1 Fat • 1 Carb Choice.

chocolate candy cookie bars

PREP TIME: 15 Minutes ✳ READY IN: 1 Hour 10 Minutes ✳ SERVINGS: 36

3/4 cup packed brown sugar
1/2 cup granulated sugar
1/2 cup butter or margarine, softened
1/2 cup shortening
1-1/2 teaspoons vanilla
    1 egg

1-3/4 cups all-purpose flour
    1 teaspoon baking soda
1/2 teaspoon salt
    1 cup candy-coated chocolate candies or semisweet chocolate chips
1/2 cup chopped nuts, if desired

1 Heat oven to 375°F. In large bowl, beat brown sugar, granulated sugar, butter and shortening with electric mixer on medium speed until light and fluffy, scraping bowl occasionally. Beat in vanilla and egg until well blended.

2 On low speed, beat in flour, baking soda and salt until dough forms. With spoon, stir in chocolate candies and nuts. Spread dough in ungreased 13x9-inch pan.

3 Bake 15 to 25 minutes or until light golden brown. Cool completely, about 30 minutes. Cut into 6 rows by 6 rows.

HIGH ALTITUDE (3500-6500 FT): Decrease granulated sugar to 1/4 cup, butter to 1/4 cup and baking soda to 3/4 teaspoon. Bake 18 to 23 minutes.

NUTRITION INFORMATION PER SERVING: Calories 130 • Total Fat 7g • Saturated Fat 3g • Cholesterol 15mg • Sodium 90mg • Total Carbohydrate 16g • Dietary Fiber 0g • Protein 1g. DIETARY EXCHANGES: 1/2 Starch • 1/2 Other Carbohydrate • 1-1/2 Fat • 1 Carb Choice.

chocolate-filled russian tea cakes

peanut butter-chocolate chip cookie bars

PREP TIME: 15 Minutes ✳ **READY IN:** 1 Hour 5 Minutes ✳ **SERVINGS:** 24

- 1 roll (16.5 oz.) Pillsbury® refrigerated chocolate chip cookies
- 1 cup creamy peanut butter
- 1/2 cup vanilla whipped ready-to-spread frosting (from 12-oz. container)

- 1 teaspoon oil
- 1/4 cup semisweet chocolate chips
- 1/4 cup miniature candy-coated milk chocolate baking bits

1 Heat oven to 350°F. In ungreased 13x9-inch pan, break up cookie dough. Press dough evenly in bottom of pan to form crust. Bake 14 to 18 minutes or until golden brown. Cool 5 minutes.

2 Meanwhile, in medium bowl, mix peanut butter, frosting and oil until well blended. Spread peanut butter mixture over warm crust. Place chocolate chips in small resealable food storage plastic bag; seal bag. Microwave on High 1 to 2 minutes or until melted. Snip very small hole in one corner of bag; squeeze bag to drizzle chocolate over peanut butter mixture. Sprinkle baking bits evenly over top. Let stand until chocolate is set, at least 30 minutes. For bars, cut into 6 rows by 4 rows.

NUTRITION INFORMATION PER SERVING: Calories 190 • Total Fat 11 g • Saturated Fat 3g • Cholesterol 0mg • Sodium 115mg • Total Carbohydrate 19g • Dietary Fiber 0g • Protein 4g. DIETARY EXCHANGES: 1/2 Starch • 1 Other Carbohydrate • 2 Fat • 1 Carb Choice.

Kitchen tip

Candied ginger is gingerroot that has been cooked in sugar syrup, dried and then coated in sugar. Look for candied ginger in the produce department of the supermarket...near the dried fruit.

---

walnut-topped ginger drops

READY IN: 1 Hour ✳ **SERVINGS:** 3-1/2 Dozen

- 1/2 cup packed brown sugar
- 1/2 cup butter or margarine, softened
- 1 teaspoon vanilla
- 1 egg
- 2 cups all-purpose flour
- 1/4 cup half-and-half

- 3 tablespoons finely chopped candied ginger
- 1/2 teaspoon baking soda
- 1/2 teaspoon salt
- 1/2 teaspoon ground cardamom
- 42 walnut halves
- 3 tablespoons white vanilla baking chips

1 Heat oven to 375°F. In large bowl, beat brown sugar and butter with electric mixer on medium speed until light and fluffy. Beat in vanilla and egg until well blended. On low speed, beat in remaining ingredients except walnuts and baking chips until well blended.

2 On ungreased cookie sheets, drop dough by rounded teaspoonfuls 2 inches apart. Press 1 walnut half onto each cookie.

3 Bake 6 to 9 minutes or until edges are set and light golden brown. Immediately remove from cookie sheets to cooling racks. Cool completely, about 5 minutes.

4 Meanwhile, place baking chips in small resealable freezer plastic bag; seal bag. Microwave on High 30 to 45 seconds or until softened. Squeeze bag until mixture is smooth. (If necessary, microwave 30 seconds longer or just until all chips are melted.) Cut small tip from one bottom corner of bag. Squeeze bag to drizzle melted chips over cookies.

HIGH ALTITUDE (3500-6500 FT): Increase flour to 2 cups plus 2 tablespoons.

NUTRITION INFORMATION PER SERVING: Calories 80 • Total Fat 4g • Saturated Fat 2g • Cholesterol 10mg • Sodium 65mg • Total Carbohydrate 8g • Dietary Fiber 0g • Protein 1g. DIETARY EXCHANGES: 1/2 Starch • 1 Fat • 1/2 Carb Choice.

peppermint-chocolate brownies

PREP TIME: 30 Minutes ✳ **READY IN:** 2 Hours 45 Minutes ✳ **SERVINGS:** 48

4 oz. unsweetened baking chocolate

1 cup butter or margarine

2 packages (8 oz. each) cream cheese, softened

2-1/2 cups sugar

5 eggs

1/2 teaspoon peppermint extract

1-1/2 cups all-purpose flour

1/2 teaspoon salt

2 cups crème de menthe baking chips (from two 10-oz. bags)

1 Heat oven to 350°F. Grease bottom and sides of 13x9-inch pan with shortening or cooking spray (do not use dark pan). In 3-quart saucepan, heat baking chocolate and butter over low heat, stirring frequently, until melted and smooth. Cool 5 minutes.

2 Meanwhile, in medium bowl, beat cream cheese, 1/2 cup of the sugar and 1 of the eggs with electric mixer on medium speed until smooth. Set aside.

3 Into chocolate mixture, stir remaining 2 cups sugar, remaining 4 eggs and the peppermint extract. Stir in flour and salt until well mixed. Spread half of chocolate batter in pan. Drop cream cheese filling by teaspoonfuls over batter. Carefully spoon and spread remaining batter over filling.

4 Bake 40 to 45 minutes or until toothpick inserted in center comes out clean. Sprinkle evenly with baking chips. Cool completely, about 1 hour 30 minutes. For brownies, cut into 8 rows by 6 rows. Store in refrigerator.

HIGH ALTITUDE (3500-6500 FT): In Step 1, heat baking chocolate and butter over medium-low heat.

NUTRITION INFORMATION PER SERVING: Calories 180 • Total Fat 11 g • Saturated Fat 7g • Cholesterol 45mg • Sodium 90mg • Total Carbohydrate 19g • Dietary Fiber 0g • Protein 2g. DIETARY EXCHANGES: 1-1/2 Other Carbohydrate • 2 Fat • 1 Carb Choice.

cook's notes

Small, round chocolate-covered creamy mints from a box can be used instead of the crème de menthe baking chips.

Divine Desserts

Decadent finales abound in this chapter, which offers after-dinner delights that will dazzle dinner guests. It's easy to satisfy your sweet tooth with these yummy sensations.

p. 296

p. 294

p. 282

p. 282

p. 286

snowball cupcakes p. 306

mini cherry cheesecakes

PREP TIME: 20 Minutes ✳ **READY IN:** 2 Hours 15 Minutes ✳ **SERVINGS:** 24

24 vanilla wafer cookies	2 eggs
2 packages (8 oz. each) cream cheese, softened	1 teaspoon almond or vanilla extract
3/4 cup sugar	1 can (21 oz.) cherry pie filling
	1/2 cup toasted, sliced almonds

1 Heat oven to 375°F. Line 24 regular-size muffin cups with paper liners. Place 1 vanilla wafer cookie in bottom of each cup.

2 In large bowl, beat cream cheese, sugar, eggs and almond extract with electric mixer on medium-high speed 1 to 2 minutes or until mixture is light and fluffy. Spoon evenly into muffin cups (about 2/3 full).

3 Bake 20 to 25 minutes or until toothpick inserted in center comes out clean. Remove from muffin cups to cooling rack. Cool completely, about 30 minutes. Refrigerate at least 1 hour or up to 24 hours before serving.

4 Just before serving, top each cheesecake with generous tablespoon pie filling; sprinkle with almonds.

HIGH ALTITUDE (3500-6500 FT): Bake 22 to 25 minutes.

NUTRITION INFORMATION PER SERVING: Calories 150 • Total Fat 9g • Saturated Fat 4.5g • Cholesterol 40mg • Sodium 75mg • Total Carbohydrate 16g • Dietary Fiber 0g • Protein 3g. DIETARY EXCHANGES: 1 Other Carbohydrate • 2 Fat • 1 Carb Choice.

noel napoleons

PREP TIME: 20 Minutes ✳ **READY IN:** 1 Hour ✳ **SERVINGS:** 12

1   sheet frozen puff pastry
     (from 17-1/4-oz. pkg.)

1   box (4-serving size) cheesecake instant
     pudding and pie filling mix

1-1/2   cups milk

2   tablespoons almond flavored liqueur or
     1 teaspoon almond extract

1   can (21 oz.) raspberry pie filling

1-1/2   cups frozen cranberry raspberry juice
     concentrate, thawed

1   tablespoon powdered sugar

1/4   cup toasted sliced almonds

cook's notes

The pastries, filling and sauce

can be made a day ahead of

time and then assembled in

minutes just before serving.

1 Heat oven to 400°F. Let puff pastry stand at room temperature 20 minutes to thaw. Unfold pastry; cut into 3 strips along fold lines. Cut each strip crosswise into 4 equal pieces; place on ungreased cookie sheet. Bake 12 to 15 minutes or until golden brown. Remove from cookie sheet to cooling racks.

2 In medium bowl, with wire whisk, beat pudding mix and milk 2 minutes. Stir in liqueur. Cover and refrigerate.

3 In medium bowl, mix raspberry pie filling and juice concentrate until well blended. Cover and refrigerate.

4 Just before serving, cut each pastry horizontally in half to make 2 layers. Place bottom half of each pastry on dessert plate. Spoon 2 tablespoons pudding evenly over pastry; cover with top half of pastry. Sprinkle each with powdered sugar and 1 teaspoon toasted almonds. Spoon 3 tablespoons raspberry sauce onto plate around each pastry.

NUTRITION INFORMATION PER SERVING: Calories 290 • Total Fat 8g • Saturated Fat 3g • Cholesterol 25mg • Sodium 180mg • Total Carbohydrate 49g • Dietary Fiber 1g • Protein 3g. DIETARY EXCHANGES: 1 Starch • 2-1/2 Other Carbohydrate • 1-1/2 Fat • 3 Carb Choices.

chocolate-eggnog cheesecake squares

PREP TIME: 20 Minutes ✸ **READY IN:** 4 Hours ✸ **SERVINGS:** 48

CRUST

- 2 cups chocolate cookie crumbs (from 15-oz. box)
- 1/2 cup butter or margarine, melted

FILLING

- 2 packages (8 oz. each) cream cheese, softened
- 1/2 cup sugar
- 1 tablespoon all-purpose flour
- 1/2 cup dairy eggnog
- 2 eggs
- 1/2 cup miniature semisweet chocolate chips
- 1/4 teaspoon ground nutmeg

1 Heat oven to 300°F. Line 13x9-inch pan with 18x18-inch square of heavy-duty foil so foil extends over long sides of pan. Spray foil with cooking spray. In small bowl, mix cookie crumbs and butter. Press in bottom of pan.

2 In large bowl, beat cream cheese and sugar with electric mixer on medium speed 1 to 2 minutes or until smooth. Beat in flour, eggnog and eggs on medium speed until smooth, scraping sides of bowl if necessary. With rubber spatula, fold in chocolate chips. Pour filling evenly over crust.

3 Bake 35 to 40 minutes or until edges are set. Center will be soft but will set when cool. Cool 1 hour. Refrigerate at least 2 hours. Sprinkle evenly with nutmeg. For squares, cut into 8 rows by 6 rows. Remove from foil. Store squares in refrigerator.

HIGH ALTITUDE (3500-6500 FT): Heat oven to 325°F.

NUTRITION INFORMATION PER SERVING: Calories 100 • Total Fat 7g • Saturated Fat 4g • Cholesterol 25mg • Sodium 75mg • Total Carbohydrate 7g • Dietary Fiber 0g • Protein 2g. DIETARY EXCHANGES: 1/2 Other Carbohydrate • 1-1/2 Fat • 1/2 Carb Choice.

peanut butter cups

PREP TIME: 20 Minutes ✸ **READY IN:** 55 Minutes ✸ **SERVINGS:** 24

- 1-3/4 cups all-purpose flour
- 1-1/4 cups packed brown sugar
- 3 teaspoons baking powder
- 1 teaspoon salt
- 1 cup milk
- 1/3 cup shortening
- 1/3 cup peanut butter
- 1 teaspoon vanilla
- 2 eggs
- 24 miniature chocolate-covered peanut butter cup candies, unwrapped

1 Heat oven to 350°F. Place paper baking cups in each of 24 regular-size muffin cups. In large bowl, beat all ingredients except peanut butter cups with electric mixer on low speed until moistened, scraping bowl occasionally. Beat on medium speed 2 minutes, scraping bowl occasionally.

2 Divide batter evenly among muffin cups, filling each 2/3 full. Press 1 peanut butter cup into batter in each cup until top edge of candy is even with batter.

3 Bake 18 to 28 minutes or until tops spring back when touched near center. Cool 5 minutes; remove from muffin cups. Serve warm or cool.

HIGH ALTITUDE (3500-6500 FT): Decrease baking powder to 2 teaspoons. Bake 23 to 28 minutes.

NUTRITION INFORMATION PER SERVING: Calories 170 • Total Fat 7g • Saturated Fat 2g • Cholesterol 20mg • Sodium 210mg • Total Carbohydrate 23g • Dietary Fiber 0g • Protein 3g. DIETARY EXCHANGES: 1/2 Starch • 1 Other Carbohydrate • 1-1/2 Fat • 1-1/2 Carb Choices.

chocolate-eggnog cheesecake squares

chocolate cranberry bread pudding

PREP TIME: 30 Minutes ✳ **READY IN:** 1 Hour 30 Minutes ✳ **SERVINGS:** 12

BREAD PUDDING

8	oz. day-old French bread, cut into 1/2-inch cubes (5 to 6 cups)
1	cup sweetened dried cranberries
4	eggs
1-1/4	cups packed brown sugar
1/2	cup unsweetened baking cocoa
3	cups half-and-half

SAUCE

1/2	cup granulated sugar
2	tablespoons butter
1	cup white vanilla baking chips
1	cup whipping cream
2	tablespoons bourbon or 1 teaspoon vanilla extract

1 Heat oven to 350°F. Spray 12x8-inch (2-quart) glass baking dish with cooking spray. Place bread and cranberries in baking dish; toss to mix.

2 In large bowl, with wire whisk, beat eggs, brown sugar, cocoa and half-and-half until well blended. Pour over bread mixture. Stir mixture gently with large spoon to coat bread with liquid. Let stand 10 minutes. Stir mixture. Bake uncovered 45 to 50 minutes or until knife inserted in center comes out clean.

3 In 1-quart saucepan, mix granulated sugar, butter, baking chips and whipping cream. Cook over medium heat 3 to 4 minutes, stirring frequently, until slightly thickened and smooth. Remove from heat; stir in bourbon (sauce will be thin). Serve sauce over warm bread pudding.

NUTRITION INFORMATION PER SERVING: Calories 510 • Total Fat 23g • Saturated Fat 14g • Cholesterol 120mg • Sodium 230mg • Total Carbohydrate 66g • Dietary Fiber 2g • Protein 8g. DIETARY EXCHANGES: 1 Starch • 3-1/2 Other Carbohydrate • 1/2 Medium-Fat Meat • 4 Fat • 4-1/2 Carb Choices.

black-bottom peanut butter pie

PREP TIME: 25 Minutes ✱ READY IN: 3 Hours 20 Minutes ✱ SERVINGS: 8

CRUST

1 Pillsbury® refrigerated pie crust, softened as directed on box

FUDGE LAYER

1-1/4 cups dark or semisweet chocolate chips

1/2 cup whipping cream

2 tablespoons butter or margarine, melted

FILLING

1 1/4 cups milk

1 container (6 oz.) French vanilla fat-free yogurt

1 box (4-serving size) white chocolate instant pudding and pie filling mix

3 tablespoons butter or margarine

1 bag (10 oz.) peanut butter chips (1-2/3 cups)

TOPPING

4 peanut butter crunchy granola bars (2 pouches from 8.9-oz. box), crushed (3/4 cup)

CLAUDIA SHEPARDSON
South Yarmouth,
Massachusetts
Bake-Off® Contest 42, 2006

1 Heat oven to 450°F. Make pie crust as directed on box for one-crust baked shell, using 9-inch glass pie plate. Cool on cooling rack 15 minutes.

2 Meanwhile, in 1-quart heavy saucepan, mix fudge layer ingredients. Cook over low heat, stirring constantly, until chips are melted. Remove from heat; stir until smooth. Reserve 1/4 cup fudge mixture in small microwavable bowl for drizzle; set remaining mixture aside to cool.

3 In large bowl, beat milk, yogurt and pudding mix with electric mixer on high speed about 3 minutes or until smooth and thickened. Set aside.

4 In another small microwavable bowl, microwave 3 tablespoons butter and the peanut butter chips uncovered on High 45 seconds. Stir; if necessary, continue to microwave in 10-second increments, stirring after each, until chips are melted and mixture is smooth. On low speed, gradually beat peanut butter mixture into pudding mixture until combined; beat on high speed until filling is smooth and fluffy, scraping side of bowl occasionally.

5 Spread cooled fudge layer mixture evenly into crust. Carefully spoon and spread filling over fudge layer. Sprinkle crushed granola bars evenly over top. Refrigerate until set, 3 to 4 hours.

6 To serve, microwave reserved fudge mixture uncovered on High 15 to 20 seconds or until drizzling consistency. Drizzle over top of pie. Cover and refrigerate any remaining pie.

NUTRITION INFORMATION PER SERVING: Calories 690 • Total Fat 40g • Saturated Fat 18g • Cholesterol 45mg • Sodium 520mg • Total Carbohydrate 72g • Dietary Fiber 4g • Protein 11g. DIETARY EXCHANGES: 1 Starch • 4 Other Carbohydrate • 1 High-Fat Meat • 6 Fat • 5 Carb Choices.

cook's notes

We don't recommend using chocolate chips to make this pie as they will not produce the same smooth filling as squares of baking chocolate.

chocolate-nut truffle pie

PREP TIME: 30 Minutes ✳ READY IN: 4 Hours 30 Minutes ✳ SERVINGS: 12

1 box Pillsbury® refrigerated pie crusts, softened as directed on box	12 oz. semisweet baking chocolate, coarsely chopped
1/4 cup finely chopped pecans	2-1/2 cups whipping (heavy) cream
	12 pecan halves

1 Heat oven to 450°F. Make pie crust as directed on box for one-crust baked shell using 9-inch glass pie plate. Before baking, sprinkle chopped pecans over bottom of crust; lightly press into crust. Bake 9 to 11 minutes or until lightly browned. Cool completely, about 15 minutes.

2 Meanwhile, in large bowl, place chocolate. In 2-quart saucepan, heat 2 cups of the whipping cream over medium heat just until it begins to boil. Pour over chocolate. With electric mixer on low speed, beat 1 minute or until chocolate mixture is smooth. Pour into cooled baked shell. Refrigerate at least 4 hours or until serving time.

3 Just before serving, in small bowl, beat remaining 1/2 cup whipping cream with electric mixer on high speed until stiff peaks form. Spoon or pipe whipped cream around outer edge of pie. Top each serving with pecan half.

NUTRITION INFORMATION PER SERVING: Calories 400 • Total Fat 31 g • Saturated Fat 17g • Cholesterol 55mg • Sodium 105mg • Total Carbohydrate 28g • Dietary Fiber 2g • Protein 3g. DIETARY EXCHANGES: 1 Starch • 1 Other Carbohydrate • 6 Fat • 2 Carb Choices.

minty ice cream squares

PREP TIME: 30 Minutes ✳ **READY IN:** 3 Hours 10 Minutes ✳ **SERVINGS:** 16

1/2 cup butter or margarine

1/4 cup unsweetened baking cocoa

2 cups coarsely crushed chocolate or regular graham crackers (about 20 cracker squares)

1/2 cup powdered sugar

1 carton (1/2 gallon) green mint chocolate chip ice cream, slightly softened

1 cup semisweet chocolate chips

2/3 cup whipping cream

16 thin rectangular crème de menthe chocolate candies, unwrapped

1 In 2-quart saucepan, heat butter and cocoa over medium heat, stirring frequently, until butter is melted and mixture is well blended. Remove from heat. Stir in graham cracker crumbs and powdered sugar. In bottom of ungreased 13x9-inch pan, press mixture to form crust.

2 Place heaping spoonfuls of ice cream on crust. With back of spoon, lightly press and smooth ice cream. Freeze 30 minutes.

3 Meanwhile, in 1-quart saucepan, heat chocolate chips and whipping cream over low heat 2 to 3 minutes, stirring constantly, until melted. Cool 15 minutes.

4 Drizzle chocolate mixture over ice cream. Arrange candies on top so each serving has 1 candy. Freeze until firm, about 2 hours. Let mixture stand at room temperature 10 minutes before cutting into squares.

NUTRITION INFORMATION PER SERVING: Calories 370 • Total Fat 22g • Saturated Fat 13g • Cholesterol 60mg • Sodium 150mg • Total Carbohydrate 38g • Dietary Fiber 2g • Protein 4g. DIETARY EXCHANGES: 1 Starch • 1-1/2 Other Carbohydrate • 4-1/2 Fat • 2-1/2 Carb Choices.

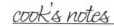

cook's notes

Purchased graham cracker crumbs are too fine to use for the crust in this recipe.

apple-cranberry crisp
with eggnog sauce

apple-cranberry crisp with eggnog sauce

PREP TIME: 25 Minutes ✳ READY IN: 1 Hour 5 Minutes ✳ SERVINGS: 10

SAUCE
- 2 containers (3.5 to 4 oz. each) refrigerated vanilla pudding
- 1 cup eggnog

FRUIT MIXTURE
- 5 cups sliced peeled apples (5 medium)
- 2 cups fresh or frozen cranberries
- 3/4 cup granulated sugar
- 2 tablespoons all-purpose flour

TOPPING
- 2/3 cup all-purpose flour
- 1 cup quick-cooking oats
- 3/4 cup packed brown sugar
- 1/2 teaspoon ground cinnamon
- 1/2 cup butter or margarine, cut into pieces

1 Place pudding in medium bowl. Gradually stir eggnog into pudding until blended. Cover and refrigerate.

2 Heat oven to 375°F. In large bowl, mix all fruit mixture ingredients. Spread evenly in ungreased 12x8-inch (2-quart) glass baking dish.

3 In another medium bowl, mix 2/3 cup flour, the oats, brown sugar and cinnamon. With pastry blender or fork, cut in butter until mixture resembles fine crumbs. Spoon over fruit mixture.

4 Bake 35 to 40 minutes or until deep golden brown and bubbly. Serve warm with chilled sauce. Store sauce in refrigerator.

NUTRITION INFORMATION PER SERVING: Calories 370 • Total Fat 13g • Saturated Fat 7g • Cholesterol 40mg • Sodium 110mg • Total Carbohydrate 62g • Dietary Fiber 3g • Protein 4g. DIETARY EXCHANGES: 1 Starch • 3 Other Carbohydrate • 2-1/2 Fat • 4 Carb Choices.

tres leches cake

PREP TIME: 30 Minutes ✳ READY IN: 4 Hours ✳ SERVINGS: 15

CAKE
- 1 box (1 lb. 2.25 oz.) yellow cake mix with pudding
- 1 cup water
- 1/3 cup vegetable oil
- 3 eggs

SAUCE
- 1 cup whipping cream
- 1/3 cup rum or 1 teaspoon rum extract plus 1/3 cup water

- 1 can (14 oz.) sweetened condensed milk (not evaporated)
- 1 can (12 oz.) evaporated milk

TOPPING
- 1 cup whipping cream
- 1/3 cup coconut chips, toasted
- 1/3 cup chopped macadamia nuts

1 Heat oven to 350°F. Grease 13x9-inch (3-quart) glass baking dish. In large bowl, beat cake mix, water, oil and eggs with electric mixer on low speed about 30 seconds or until blended. Beat on medium speed 2 minutes, scraping bowl occasionally. Pour batter into baking dish. Bake 25 to 35 minutes or until toothpick inserted in center comes out clean.

2 Meanwhile, in large bowl, mix sauce ingredients. Using long-tined fork, pierce hot cake in baking dish every 1 to 2 inches. Slowly pour sauce mixture over cake. Refrigerate cake at least 3 hours to chill. (Cake will absorb most of sauce mixture.)

3 Before serving, in small bowl, beat 1 cup whipping cream until stiff peaks form. Spread over cold cake. Sprinkle with coconut and macadamia nuts. Cover and refrigerate any remaining cake.

NUTRITION INFORMATION PER SERVING: Calories 440 • Total Fat 25g • Saturated Fat 11g • Cholesterol 90mg • Sodium 310mg • Total Carbohydrate 45g • Dietary Fiber 0g • Protein 6g. DIETARY EXCHANGES: 2 Starch • 1 Other Carbohydrate • 4-1/2 Fat • 3 Carb Choices.

cook's notes

Prepare the crisp and sauce a day ahead and store separately in the refrigerator. To warm the crisp, place it in a 325°F oven for about 15 minutes.

JANICE WEINRICK
La Mesa, California
Bake-Off® Contest 34, 1990
Prize Winner

mocha bread pudding with caramel topping

PREP TIME: 10 Minutes ✳ **READY IN:** 1 Hour 25 Minutes ✳ **SERVINGS:** 16

BREAD PUDDING

10	oz. day-old Italian or French bread, torn into pieces (about 8 cups)
1	cup chopped dates
1	cup chopped nuts
1/2	cup flaked coconut
1	teaspoon ground cinnamon
1/2	cup butter or margarine, melted

1/2	cup sugar
1/2	cup coffee-flavored liqueur or cold brewed coffee
3	eggs
2	cups half-and-half
1	cup milk

TOPPING

1	cup caramel ice cream topping, heated

1 Heat oven to 325°F. Spray 13x9-inch (3-quart) glass baking dish with cooking spray. In pan, gently mix bread pieces, dates, nuts, coconut and cinnamon.

2 In large bowl, mix butter, sugar and liqueur. Beat in eggs with spoon until well blended. Stir in half-and-half and milk. Pour over bread mixture in pan; toss to mix well. Let stand 10 to 15 minutes or until most of liquid has been absorbed.

3 Bake 1 hour or until set. Serve warm bread pudding with warm caramel topping. Store in refrigerator.

NUTRITION INFORMATION PER SERVING: Calories 320 • Total Fat 14g • Saturated Fat 5g • Cholesterol 55mg • Sodium 240mg • Total Carbohydrate 44g • Dietary Fiber 2g • Protein 5g. DIETARY EXCHANGES: 1 Starch • 2 Other Carbohydrate • 2-1/2 Fat • 3 Carb Choices.

chocolate silk raspberry tart

PREP TIME: 35 Minutes ✳ READY IN: 5 Hours ✳ SERVINGS: 12

20 creme-filled golden sandwich cookies, crushed (2 cups)
1/4 cup butter or margarine, melted
1-1/2 cups semisweet chocolate chips
2 cups whipping (heavy) cream

1 teaspoon vanilla
1 package (8 oz.) cream cheese, softened
1 cup fresh raspberries
2 tablespoons seedless raspberry jam

cook's notes

Any flavored sandwich cookies can be used in the crust of this rich dessert.

1 Heat oven to 375°F. In medium bowl, mix cookie crumbs and butter. In 9- or 10-inch springform pan, press mixture in bottom and 1 inch up side. Bake 7 to 9 minutes or until set. Cool completely, about 30 minutes.

2 Meanwhile, in 1-quart saucepan, heat chocolate chips and 1/2 cup of the whipping cream over low heat, stirring frequently, until chocolate is melted. Stir in vanilla. Cool to room temperature, about 15 minutes.

3 In large bowl with electric mixer, beat cream cheese on medium speed until smooth. Beat in chocolate mixture until creamy. Set aside.

4 In another large bowl with electric mixer, beat remaining 1-1/2 cups whipping cream on high speed until stiff peaks form. Fold half of whipped cream into cream cheese mixture until blended. Fold in remaining whipped cream. Spoon into cooled baked crust. Refrigerate until set, about 4 hours.

5 To serve, arrange raspberries around edge of tart. In small microwavable bowl, microwave jam on High 1 to 2 minutes, stirring every 30 seconds, until melted; lightly brush over raspberries. Remove side of pan. Cut tart into wedges. Store in refrigerator.

NUTRITION INFORMATION PER SERVING: Calories 430 • Total Fat 33g • Saturated Fat 18g • Cholesterol 75mg • Sodium 160mg • Total Carbohydrate 29g • Dietary Fiber 2g • Protein 4g. DIETARY EXCHANGES: 1 Starch • 1 Other Carbohydrate • 6-1/2 Fat • 2 Carb Choices.

peppermint-fudge pie

PREP TIME: 25 Minutes ❋ **READY IN:** 2 Hours 10 Minutes ❋ **SERVINGS:** 8

1 box Pillsbury® refrigerated pie crusts, softened as directed on box

2 cups milk

1 box (4-serving size) chocolate pudding and pie filling mix (not instant)

1/2 cup semisweet chocolate chips

1 package (8 oz.) cream cheese, softened

1/2 cup powdered sugar

1 teaspoon peppermint extract

2 drops red or green food color

2 cups frozen (thawed) whipped topping
    Shaved chocolate, if desired

1 Heat oven to 450°F. Make the pie crust as directed on the box for one-crust baked shell using a 9-inch glass pie plate. Bake 9 to 11 minutes or until light golden brown. Cool completely, about 30 minutes.

2 Meanwhile, in 2-quart saucepan, heat milk and pudding mix to a full boil over medium heat, stirring constantly. Remove from heat. Stir in chocolate chips until melted. Place plastic wrap directly over surface of pudding. Refrigerate 45 minutes or just until cooled.

3 In small bowl, beat cream cheese, powdered sugar, peppermint extract and food color with electric mixer on medium speed until smooth. On low speed, gradually beat in 1 cup of the whipped topping until combined. Spread in cooled baked shell.

4 Stir cooled pudding mixture; spread over cream cheese layer. Carefully spread remaining 1 cup whipped topping over pudding layer. Garnish with chocolate shavings. Refrigerate 1 hour or until chilled before serving. Store in refrigerator.

NUTRITION INFORMATION PER SERVING: Calories 420 • Total Fat 24g • Saturated Fat 14g • Cholesterol 40mg • Sodium 310mg • Total Carbohydrate 46g • Dietary Fiber 1g • Protein 5g. DIETARY EXCHANGES: 1 Starch • 2 Other Carbohydrate • 5 Fat • 3 Carb Choices.

pistachio-lime ice cream squares

PREP TIME: 35 Minutes ✴ **READY IN:** 7 Hours 35 Minutes ✴ **SERVINGS:** 16

LIME SWIRL
1/2 cup sugar

2 teaspoons grated lime peel

1/4 cup lime juice

2 eggs, beaten

1 egg yolk, beaten

3 to 4 drops green food color, if desired

CRUST AND FILLING
3/4 cup butter or margarine

1-1/2 cups all-purpose flour

1/3 cup sugar

1/2 cup chopped shelled pistachios

1/2 gallon (8 cups) vanilla ice cream, softened

1 In small non-aluminum saucepan, mix 1/2 cup sugar, lime peel, lime juice, eggs and egg yolk. Cook and stir over medium heat until mixture boils and thickens. Stir in food color. Cover; refrigerate about 1 hour or until chilled.

2 Melt margarine in large skillet over medium-high heat. Stir in flour, 1/3 cup sugar and pistachios. Cook and stir 5 to 7 minutes or until mixture is golden brown and crumbly. Reserve 1/2 cup crumbs for topping. With fork, press remaining mixture firmly in bottom of ungreased 13x9-inch pan. Place in freezer for at least 5 minutes to cool.

3 Spoon and spread half of ice cream over crust. Spread with half of lime mixture. Top with remaining ice cream; spread evenly. Top with remaining lime mixture. With knife, swirl lime mixture gently through ice cream, being careful to not disturb crust. Sprinkle with reserved crumbs. Cover; freeze 6 hours or until firm. Let stand at room temperature for about 10 minutes before serving. Cut into squares.

NUTRITION INFORMATION PER SERVING: Calories 335 • Total Fat 19g • Saturated Fat 10g • Cholesterol 90mg • Sodium 140mg • Total Carbohydrate 36g • Dietary Fiber 0g • Protein 5g. DIETARY EXCHANGES: 1-1/2 Starch • 1 Other Carbohydrate • 3-1/2 Fat • 2-1/2 Carb Choices.

kitchen tip

To remove the zest from a lime, peel thin strips with a small sharp knife, being careful not to include the white membrane, and mince finely. You can also take the whole fruit and rub it over a hand grater to remove the zest.

PAMELA KENNEY BASEY
Denver, Colorado
Bake-Off® Contest 40, 2002

kitchen tip

If flaked coconut has been frozen or becomes dried out, you can make it fresh again by placing the amount you need in a bowl and sprinkling with a few drops of water. Cover and microwave until warm.

mocha macaroon torte

PREP TIME: 20 Minutes ✳ READY IN: 3 Hours 35 Minutes ✳ SERVINGS: 12

CRUST AND FILLING
- 1 roll (16.5 oz.) Pillsbury® refrigerated double chocolate chip & chunk cookies
- 1 package (8 oz.) cream cheese, softened
- 1 egg
- 1/2 cup flaked coconut
- 1/4 cup sugar
- 2 tablespoons brewed coffee
- 1 teaspoon vanilla
- 1/3 cup semisweet chocolate chips

TOPPING
- 1/4 cup sugar
- 1/4 cup chopped pecans
- 1 cup semisweet chocolate chips
  French vanilla ice cream or vanilla frozen yogurt
  Chocolate-covered coffee beans

1 Heat oven to 350°F. Cut cookie dough in half crosswise; cut each section in half lengthwise. Press dough in bottom of ungreased 10- or 9-inch springform pan. Bake 12 to 18 minutes or until light golden brown. Cool 10 minutes.

2 While crust is cooling, in medium bowl, beat cream cheese with electric mixer on medium speed until light and fluffy. Add egg; beat until smooth. On low speed, beat in coconut, 1/4 cup sugar, the coffee and vanilla. With spoon, stir in 1/3 cup chocolate chips.

3 Spoon and carefully spread mixture over crust. Sprinkle with topping ingredients. Bake 30 to 45 minutes longer or until filling is set and edges are golden brown. Cool 10 minutes.

4 Run knife around side of pan to loosen; carefully remove side. Cool 1 hour. Refrigerate until chilled, 1 to 2 hours. Serve with ice cream garnished with coffee beans. Cover and refrigerate any remaining torte.

HIGH ALTITUDE (3500-6500 FT): Bake crust 16 to 20 minutes. After sprinkling with topping, bake 35 to 50 minutes.

NUTRITION INFORMATION PER SERVING: Calories 450 • Total Fat 26g • Saturated Fat 12g • Cholesterol 45mg • Sodium 200mg • Total Carbohydrate 48g • Dietary Fiber 1g • Protein 5g. DIETARY EXCHANGES: 1-1/2 Starch • 1-1/2 Other Carbohydrate • 5 Fat • 3 Carb Choices.

cook's notes

If you like, use 1/2 teaspoon almond extract in place of the amaretto.

raspberry-amaretto tarts

READY IN: 20 Minutes ✳ SERVINGS: 6

- 1 container (8 oz.) whipped cream cheese spread
- 1/4 cup powdered sugar
- 1 to 2 tablespoons amaretto
- 6 single-serve baked sweet tart shells (from 8.5-oz. pkg.) or graham cracker crusts (from 4-oz. pkg.)
- 36 fresh raspberries (about 3/4 cup)

1 In medium bowl, beat cream cheese spread, powdered sugar and amaretto until smooth. Divide cream cheese mixture evenly into tart shells. Top each with 6 raspberries.

NUTRITION INFORMATION PER SERVING: Calories 280 • Total Fat 18g • Saturated Fat 9g • Cholesterol 40mg • Sodium 240mg • Total Carbohydrate 25g • Dietary Fiber 1g • Protein 4g. DIETARY EXCHANGES: 1 Starch • 1 Other Carbohydrate • 3-1/2 Fat • 1-1/2 Carb Choices.

mocha macaroon torte

rich orange flan

PREP TIME: 30 Minutes ✳ **READY IN:** 3 Hours 15 Minutes ✳ **SERVINGS:** 12

3/4 cup sugar	1 teaspoon vanilla
3 tablespoons boiling water	1 can (14 oz.) sweetened condensed milk
6 eggs	1 can (12 oz.) evaporated milk
1/4 cup orange juice	Spun sugar, if desired
2 tablespoons finely grated orange peel	

1 Heat oven to 325°F. Spread sugar evenly over bottom of heavy skillet. Cook over medium heat, stirring constantly, until sugar melts and turns light caramel color. Add 3 tablespoons boiling water, stirring until sugar is dissolved. Pour into ungreased quiche dish or 10-inch glass deep-dish pie pan or 8-inch (2-quart) square baking dish. Tilt to evenly cover bottom; set aside.

2 In medium bowl, beat remaining ingredients with electric mixer on medium speed 1 to 2 minutes or until thoroughly blended. Pour over caramelized sugar. Place baking dish in large pan (broiler pan). Pour 1 inch hot water into broiler pan.

3 Bake 40 to 45 minutes or until mixture is almost set and knife inserted in center comes out clean. Cool 1 hour; refrigerate 1 hour. Run knife around outside edge to loosen; turn upside down onto 12-inch round serving plate with raised sides to hold liquid. Garnish with spun sugar.

HIGH ALTITUDE (3500-6500 FT): In Step 1, cook over medium-high heat, stirring constantly, until sugar melts and turns light caramel color. (Do not add water.) Pour into dish and continue as directed.

NUTRITION INFORMATION PER SERVING: Calories 240 • Total Fat 8g • Saturated Fat 4g • Cholesterol 125mg • Sodium 105mg • Total Carbohydrate 34g • Dietary Fiber 0g • Protein 8g, DIETARY EXCHANGES: 2-1/2 Other Carbohydrate • 1 Medium-Fat Meat • 1/2 Fat • 2 Carb Choices.

cranberry-topped cake

PREP TIME: 30 Minutes ✳ READY IN: 1 Hour 50 Minutes ✳ SERVINGS: 9

TOPPING

- 2/3 cup canned jellied cranberry sauce (from 16-oz. can)
- 1/3 cup chopped walnuts or pecans
- 3 tablespoons sugar
- 1 teaspoon grated lemon peel
- 1/4 teaspoon cinnamon, if desired

CAKE

- 2 cups all-purpose flour
- 2 teaspoons baking powder
- 1/2 to 1 teaspoon salt
- 1 cup sugar
- 1/3 cup shortening (or butter or margarine, softened)
- 1 teaspoon lemon extract or grated lemon peel
- 2 eggs
- 3/4 cup milk

1 Heat oven to 350°F. Generously grease and lightly flour 9-inch square pan. In medium bowl, combine all topping ingredients; mix well. Set aside.

2 In small bowl, combine flour, baking powder and salt; mix well. In large bowl, beat 1 cup sugar and shortening with electric mixer at medium speed until well blended. Add lemon extract and eggs; beat well. Alternately add flour mixture and milk to shortening mixture, beating until well combined. Pour into greased and floured pan.

3 Drop topping by teaspoonfuls evenly onto batter. Spread topping over batter. Bake at 350°F for 42 to 47 minutes or until toothpick inserted in center comes out clean. Cool at least 30 minutes. Serve warm or cool.

HIGH ALTITUDE (3500-6500 FT): Reduce baking powder to 1-1/2 teaspoons. Bake at 350°F for 47 to 52 minutes.

NUTRITION INFORMATION PER SERVING: Calories 365 • Total Fat 12g • Saturated Fat 3g • Cholesterol 50mg • Sodium 270mg • Total Carbohydrate 58g • Dietary Fiber 1g • Protein 6g. DIETARY EXCHANGES: 2 Starch • 2 Other Carbohydrate • 2 Fat • 4 Carb Choices.

MRS. JOSEPH SERAFINO
Muskegon, Michigan
Bake-Off® Contest 1, 1949

grasshopper cupcakes

PREP TIME: 35 Minutes ❋ READY IN: 2 Hours ❋ SERVINGS: 24

1	box (18.25 oz.) devil's food cake mix with pudding in the mix	1	container (12 oz.) fluffy white whipped ready-to-spread frosting
1-1/3	cups water	1/4	teaspoon peppermint extract
1/2	cup vegetable oil	4	drops green food color
3	eggs	24	thin rectangular crème de menthe chocolate candies, unwrapped, each cut in half crosswise

1 Heat oven to 350°F. Make cake mix into cupcakes as directed on box using water, oil and eggs. Cool completely, about 30 minutes.

2 In small bowl, reserve 1/2 cup frosting for garnish. Into remaining frosting, stir peppermint extract and food color until well blended. Frost cupcakes with green frosting.

3 Spoon 1 teaspoon reserved white frosting onto center of each frosted cupcake. Decorate each with 2 candy pieces, standing on edge.

HIGH ALTITUDE (3500-6500 FT): Heat oven to 375°F. Make cupcakes following High Altitude Directions on box. Pour batter into 30 muffin cups.

NUTRITION INFORMATION PER SERVING: Calories 220 • Total Fat 11g • Saturated Fat 3g • Cholesterol 30mg • Sodium 190mg • Total Carbohydrate 29g • Dietary Fiber 0g • Protein 2g. DIETARY EXCHANGES: 1/2 Starch • 1-1/2 Other Carbohydrate • 2 Fat • 2 Carb Choices.

merry cherry-chip pie

PREP TIME: 15 Minutes ✳ **READY IN:** 3 Hours 55 Minutes ✳ **SERVINGS:** 8

1 box Pillsbury® refrigerated pie crusts, softened as directed on box

1/2 cup sliced almonds

2 cans (21 oz. each) cherry pie filling

1/2 cup semisweet chocolate chips

1 teaspoon water

2 teaspoons sugar

1 Heat oven to 425°F. Make pie crusts as directed on box for two-crust pie using 9-inch glass pie pan. Reserve 1 tablespoon almonds; sprinkle remaining almonds in bottom of crust-lined pan.

2 In medium bowl, mix pie filling and chocolate chips. Spoon over almonds in pan. Top with second crust; seal edge and flute. Cut slits in several places in top crust. Brush water over top; sprinkle with reserved almonds and sugar.

3 Cover edge of crust with strips of foil; bake 30 to 40 minutes or until crust is golden brown. Cool at least 3 hours before serving.

HIGH ALTITUDE (3500-6500 FT): Use 9-inch deep-dish glass pie pan. Bake 35 to 45 minutes.

NUTRITION INFORMATION PER SERVING: Calories 470 • Total Fat 18g • Saturated Fat 7g • Cholesterol 5mg • Sodium 260mg • Total Carbohydrate 73g • Dietary Fiber 3g • Protein 4g. DIETARY EXCHANGES: 2-1/2 Starch • 2-1/2 Other Carbohydrate • 3 Fat • 5 Carb Choices.

cook's notes

Raspberry pie filling makes an equally delicious and festive-looking pie. Or, use one can of cherry pie filling and one of raspberry!

tiramisu ice cream squares

tiramisu ice cream squares

PREP TIME: 30 Minutes ✹ READY IN: 5 Hours 30 Minutes ✹ SERVINGS: 18

- 1 quart (4 cups) coffee ice cream
- 22 cream-filled chocolate sandwich cookies, crushed (2 cups)
- 1/4 cup butter, melted
- 1 quart (4 cups) cherry ice cream
- 1 container (8 oz.) mascarpone cheese
- 1/4 cup light rum or 1 teaspoon rum extract
- 2 cups frozen whipped topping, thawed

1 Place coffee ice cream in refrigerator for 15 to 20 minutes to soften slightly. In ungreased 13x9-inch pan, place cookie crumbs and butter. With fork, stir to mix and press evenly in bottom of pan.

2 Remove coffee ice cream from container into large bowl and stir with wooden spoon until softened. Spoon and carefully spread over cookie crumbs in pan. Freeze until firm, about 1 hour.

3 Place cherry ice cream in refrigerator for 15 to 20 minutes to soften slightly. Remove ice cream from container into large bowl and stir with wooden spoon until softened. Spoon and spread over coffee ice cream. Use back of spoon to smooth surface. Freeze until firm, about 1 hour.

4 In medium bowl, beat mascarpone cheese with electric mixer on medium speed 1 to 2 minutes or until light and fluffy. Beat in rum on low speed until well blended. With rubber spatula, fold in whipped topping. Spread evenly over ice cream. Cover and freeze at least 3 hours or up to 1 week.

NUTRITION INFORMATION PER SERVING: Calories 290 • Total Fat 17g • Saturated Fat 10g • Cholesterol 40mg • Sodium 160mg • Total Carbohydrate 29g • Dietary Fiber 1g • Protein 4g. DIETARY EXCHANGES: 1-1/2 Other Carbohydrate • 1/2 Low-Fat Milk • 3 Fat • 2 Carb Choices.

cook's notes

Substitute regular cream cheese for the mascarpone if you like—just soften it before you use it.

cherry cheesecake dessert

PREP TIME: 15 Minutes ✹ READY IN: 1 Hour 15 Minutes ✹ SERVINGS: 12

FILLING
- 1 package (8 oz.) cream cheese, softened
- 1/4 cup sugar
- 1 tablespoon all-purpose flour
- 1/2 teaspoon vanilla
- 1 egg

CRUST
- 1 package (16.5 oz.) Pillsbury® refrigerated sugar cookies

TOPPING
- 2 cans (21 oz. each) cherry pie filling
- 1/2 teaspoon almond extract

1 Heat oven to 375°F. In small bowl, combine all filling ingredients; beat until well blended. With floured fingers, press dough evenly in bottom of ungreased 13x9-inch pan to form crust. Spoon and spread filling over crust.

2 Bake at 375°F for 17 to 20 minutes or until edges begin to brown. Cool 40 minutes or until completely cooled.

3 Meanwhile, in medium bowl, combine topping ingredients; mix well. Spread over top. Cut into squares. Store in refrigerator.

NUTRITION INFORMATION PER SERVING: Calories 380 • Total Fat 14g • Saturated Fat 6g • Cholesterol 45mg • Sodium 240mg • Total Carbohydrate 60g • Dietary Fiber 1g • Protein 4g. DIETARY EXCHANGES: 1 Starch • 3 Fruit • 4 Other Carbohydrate • 2-1/2 Fat • 4 Carb Choices.

cook's notes

This easy dessert is perfect for any occasion. To ensure a satiny smooth filling, make sure to start with softened cream cheese and beat the cream cheese-egg mixture with an electric mixer.

rocky road cookie pizza

PREP TIME: 20 Minutes ✳ **READY IN:** 2 Hours 5 Minutes ✳ **SERVINGS:** 16

1 roll (16.5 oz) Pillsbury® refrigerated chocolate chip cookies

1 cup miniature marshmallows

1/2 cup salted peanuts

1/2 cup semisweet chocolate chips

1/3 cup caramel topping

1 Heat oven to 350°F. Grease 12-inch pizza pan with shortening or cooking spray. In pan, break up cookie dough. With floured fingers, press dough evenly in bottom of pan to form crust. Bake 12 to 17 minutes or until light golden brown.

2 Sprinkle marshmallows, peanuts and chocolate chips evenly over crust. Drizzle with caramel topping.

3 Bake 8 to 10 minutes longer or until topping is melted. Cool completely, about 1 hour 15 minutes. Cut into wedges.

NUTRITION INFORMATION PER SERVING: Calories 210 • Total Fat 9g • Saturated Fat 3g • Cholesterol 5mg • Sodium 150mg • Total Carbohydrate 29g • Dietary Fiber 0g • Protein 2g. DIETARY EXCHANGES: 1 Starch • 1 Other Carbohydrate • 1-1/2 Fat • 2 Carb Choices.

fancy-filled miniature shells with hazelnut filling

PREP TIME: 1 Hour 30 Minutes ✳ SERVINGS: 24

SHELLS
1/3 cup sugar
1/2 cup butter, softened
1 teaspoon vanilla
1 egg white
1-1/4 cups all-purpose flour

FILLING
2/3 cup hazelnuts (filberts)

1/2 cup firmly packed brown sugar
1/4 teaspoon salt
1/4 cup dark corn syrup
1 tablespoon butter, melted
1 teaspoon vanilla
1 egg
1 egg yolk

1 Heat oven to 350°F. Grease 24 miniature muffin cups or 1-1/2-inch tartlet tins. In small bowl, combine sugar and 1/2 cup butter; beat at medium speed until light and fluffy. Add 1 teaspoon vanilla and egg white; blend well.

2 Lightly spoon flour into measuring cup; level off. Add flour, mix at low speed just until well blended. Place about 2 teaspoons dough into each greased muffin cup. With floured fingers, press dough in bottom and up sides to form shells.

3 Place hazelnuts on ungreased cookie sheet. Bake at 350°F for 5 to 8 minutes or until lightly browned and skins have loosened. Turn hazelnuts onto clean cloth towel; rub hazelnuts between towel to remove skins. Cool 10 minutes. Reserve 12 whole nuts for garnish. Chop remaining nuts.

4 Spoon 1 teaspoon chopped nuts into each unbaked shell. In small bowl, combine all remaining filling ingredients except whole nuts; blend well. Spoon 1 tablespoon filling over chopped nuts in each shell. Cut whole nuts in half; place nut half in center of each filled shell.

5 Bake at 350°F for 18 to 22 minutes or until filling is set and golden brown. Cool in pan 5 minutes. Remove from muffin cups.

NUTRITION INFORMATION PER SERVING: Calories 140 • Total Fat 7g • Saturated Fat 3g • Cholesterol 30mg • Sodium 80mg • Total Carbohydrate 16g • Dietary Fiber 1g • Protein 2g. DIETARY EXCHANGES: 1/2 Starch • 1/2 Fruit • 1 Other Carbohydrate • 1-1/2 Fat.

kitchen tip

To soften brown sugar, place a slice of bread or an apple wedge with the brown sugar in a covered container for a few days. If you are in a hurry, microwave on High for 20-30 seconds. Repeat if necessary, but watch carefully, because the sugar will begin to melt.

raspberry-chocolate mousse

PREP TIME: 30 Minutes ✳ READY IN: 1 Hour 30 Minutes ✳ SERVINGS: 4

1-1/2 cups frozen unsweetened red raspberries, thawed

3/4 cup semisweet chocolate chips

2 tablespoons sugar

1 cup whipping cream

1 Place strainer over medium bowl; pour raspberries into strainer. Press berries with back of spoon through strainer to remove seeds; discard seeds. Reserve 2 tablespoons raspberry puree for topping.

2 In small saucepan, combine chocolate chips, 1 tablespoon of the sugar and 2 tablespoons of the whipping cream. Cook over low heat for 3 to 4 minutes or until chocolate is melted, stirring constantly. Stir in remaining raspberry puree. Cool 10 minutes or until completely cooled.

3 Meanwhile, in small bowl, beat remaining whipping cream until soft peaks form. Add remaining 1 tablespoon sugar; beat until stiff peaks form. Reserve 1/2 cup whipped cream for topping.

4 Gently fold remaining whipped cream into chocolate mixture. Spoon into dessert dishes or parfait glasses. Refrigerate at least 1 hour.

5 Fold reserved 2 tablespoons raspberry puree into reserved 1/2 cup whipped cream. Refrigerate until serving time. Just before serving, pipe raspberry whipped cream onto mousse. Garnish as desired.

NUTRITION INFORMATION PER SERVING: Calories 430 • Total Fat 32g • Saturated Fat 19g • Cholesterol 80mg • Sodium 25mg • Total Carbohydrate 33g • Dietary Fiber 4g • Protein 3g. DIETARY EXCHANGES: 1 Starch • 1 Fruit • 2 Other Carbohydrate • 2-1/2 Fat.

eggnog cheesecake with cherry sauce

PREP TIME: 25 Minutes ✳ READY IN: 6 Hours ✳ SERVINGS: 16

CRUST

- 1 cup vanilla wafer cookie crumbs (about 24 wafers)
- 3 tablespoons butter, melted

FILLING

- 3 package (8 oz.) cream cheese, softened
- 1 cup sugar
- 3 eggs
- 3/4 cup dairy eggnog (do not use canned)
- 1/2 teaspoon rum extract
- 1/4 teaspoon nutmeg

SAUCE

- 1 can (21 oz.) cherry pie filling
- 1/4 cup frozen cranberry juice concentrate, thawed
- 1/4 teaspoon rum extract

1 Heat oven to 350°F. In small bowl, combine crust ingredients; mix well. Press in bottom of ungreased 9-inch springform pan. Bake at 350°F for 8 to 10 minutes or until set.

2 Meanwhile, beat cream cheese in large bowl at medium speed until light and fluffy. Gradually beat in sugar until smooth. At low speed, add eggs 1 at a time, beating just until combined after each addition. Add eggnog, rum extract and nutmeg; beat until smooth.

3 Remove crust from oven. Reduce oven temperature to 325°F. Pour cream cheese mixture over partially baked crust. Return to oven; bake at 325°F for 55 to 65 minutes or until set. Cool in pan on wire rack for 30 minutes. Run knife around sides of pan to loosen. Cool 2 hours or until completely cooled. Refrigerate at least 2 hours.

4 Just before serving, in medium bowl, combine all sauce ingredients; mix well. To serve, carefully remove sides of pan. Cut cheesecake into wedges; place on individual dessert plates. Spoon sauce over each serving. Store in refrigerator.

NUTRITION INFORMATION PER SERVING: Calories 350 • Total Fat 21g • Saturated Fat 12g • Cholesterol 100mg • Sodium 200mg • Total Carbohydrate 35g • Dietary Fiber 0g • Protein 5g. DIETARY EXCHANGES: 1-1/2 Starch • 1 Fruit • 2-1/2 Other Carbohydrate • 4 Fat.

cook's notes

Open the oven door as little as possible while baking the cheesecake, especially during the first 30 minutes. Drafts can cause a cheesecake to crack.

snowball cupcakes

PREP TIME: 40 Minutes ✳ READY IN: 1 Hour 30 Minutes ✳ SERVINGS: 24

CUPCAKES

- 1 box (18.25 oz.) devil's food cake mix with pudding in the mix
- 1/2 cup water
- 1/3 cup vegetable oil
- 1/2 cup sour cream
- 2 eggs
- 1 package (3 oz.) cream cheese, cut into 24 cubes

FROSTING

- 1/2 cup sugar
- 2 tablespoons water
- 2 egg whites
- 1 jar (7 oz.) marshmallow creme
- 1 teaspoon vanilla
- 2 cups coconut

1 Heat oven to 350°F. Line 24 regular-size muffin cups with paper baking cups. In large bowl, beat cake mix, water, oil, sour cream and eggs with electric mixer on low speed 30 seconds, scraping bowl occasionally. Beat on medium speed 1 minute.

2 Spoon batter into muffin cups. Place 1 cube cream cheese in center of each cupcake; press down into batter almost to center (top of cream cheese will still show).

3 Bake 18 to 24 minutes or until toothpick inserted near center of cupcake comes out clean (test between cream cheese and edge). Remove cupcakes from pan to cooling racks. Cool completely, about 30 minutes.

4 In 2-quart stainless steel or other non-coated saucepan, mix sugar, water and egg whites. Cook over low heat, beating continuously with electric hand mixer at high speed until soft peaks form, about 4 minutes. Add marshmallow creme; beat until stiff peaks form. Remove saucepan from heat. Beat in vanilla.

5 Spread frosting evenly over cupcakes; sprinkle each with generous tablespoon coconut. Store cupcakes in refrigerator.

NUTRITION INFORMATION PER SERVING: Calories 220 • Total Fat 9g • Saturated Fat 4.5g • Cholesterol 25mg • Sodium 220mg • Total Carbohydrate 32g • Dietary Fiber 0g • Protein 2g. DIETARY EXCHANGES: 1 Starch • 1 Other Carbohydrate • 1-1/2 Fat • 2 Carb Choices.

chocolate espresso mousse

READY IN: 15 Minutes ✳ SERVINGS: 6

- 2 tablespoons light chocolate soymilk
- 1 tablespoon instant espresso powder or instant coffee granules or crystals
- 1 oz. semisweet or bittersweet baking chocolate

- 1 cup light chocolate soymilk
- 1 box (4-serving size) chocolate instant pudding and pie filling mix
- 2 cups frozen (thawed) fat-free whipped topping

1 In 1-quart saucepan, stir together 2 tablespoons soymilk, the espresso powder and chocolate. Cook over medium heat, stirring constantly, until chocolate is completely melted and mixture is well blended. Cool slightly.

2 In medium bowl, beat 1 cup soymilk and the pudding mix with electric mixer on medium speed or wire whisk 1 to 2 minutes, or until mixture is well blended and thickened.

3 Stir melted chocolate mixture into pudding mixture. Fold in whipped topping. Spoon into individual dessert dishes; serve immediately, or refrigerate until serving time. Cover and refrigerate any remaining mousse.

NUTRITION INFORMATION PER SERVING: Calories 140 • Total Fat 2.5g • Saturated Fat 1.5g • Cholesterol 0mg • Sodium 280mg • Total Carbohydrate 28g • Dietary Fiber 1g • Protein 2g. DIETARY EXCHANGES: 1 Starch • 1 Other Carbohydrate • 2 Carb Choices.

snowball cupcakes

rich and easy tiramisu dessert

PREP TIME: 25 Minutes ✹ READY IN: 5 Hours 15 Minutes ✹ SERVINGS: 15

CAKE

1/4	cup butter or margarine
1/4	cup milk
2	eggs
3/4	cup granulated sugar
3/4	cup all-purpose flour
1	teaspoon baking powder
1/4	teaspoon salt
1/4	teaspoon vanilla
3/4	cup hot strong brewed coffee
1	tablespoon granulated sugar

TOPPING

1	package (8 oz.) cream cheese, softened
1	container (8 oz.) mascarpone cheese (or cream cheese, softened)
1/3	cup powdered sugar
2	tablespoons Marsala wine, dark rum or cold strong brewed coffee
1	pint (2 cups) whipping cream
	Grated semisweet baking chocolate (about 1/2 oz.)

1 Heat oven to 375°F. Spray 13x9-inch pan with cooking spray. In small saucepan or 2-cup microwavable measuring cup, heat butter and milk until steaming hot (about 1 minute on High in microwave).

2 Meanwhile, in large bowl, beat eggs with electric mixer on high speed until light. Gradually beat in 3/4 cup granulated sugar; beat 2 minutes longer. Add flour, baking powder, salt, vanilla and hot milk mixture; beat on low speed until smooth. Pour batter into pan.

3 Bake 14 to 16 minutes or until cake springs back when touched lightly in center. In 1-cup measuring cup, mix coffee and 1 tablespoon granulated sugar. Drizzle over warm cake. Cool completely, about 30 minutes.

4 In large bowl, beat cream cheese and mascarpone cheese with electric mixer on medium speed until smooth and creamy. Beat in powdered sugar and wine.

5 In large bowl, beat whipping cream with electric mixer until stiff peaks form. Fold into cream cheese mixture until combined. Spread evenly on cake. Sprinkle grated chocolate over top of cake. Cover; refrigerate at least 4 hours or overnight. To serve, cut into squares. Store in refrigerator.

HIGH ALTITUDE (3500-6500 FT): Increase flour to 1 cup.

NUTRITION INFORMATION PER SERVING: Calories 330 • Total Fat 25g • Saturated Fat 15g • Cholesterol 105mg • Sodium 200mg • Total Carbohydrate 21g • Dietary Fiber 0g • Protein 5g. DIETARY EXCHANGES: 1/2 Starch • 1 Other Carbohydrate • 1/2 High-Fat Meat • 4 Fat • 1-1/2 Carb Choices.

pear and cranberry pie

PREP TIME: 20 Minutes ✳ READY IN: 1 Hour 35 Minutes ✳ SERVINGS: 8

CRUST AND FILLING

- 1 box Pillsbury® refrigerated pie crusts, softened as directed on box
- 2 medium ripe pears, peeled, cut into 1/4-inch slices
- 1 cup fresh cranberries
- 1/2 cup sugar
- 1/4 teaspoon nutmeg
- 1/2 cup sour cream
- 3 eggs

SAUCE

- 1 teaspoon cornstarch
- 1 cup dairy eggnog
- 1 tablespoon light rum or 1/2 teaspoon rum extract

1 Heat oven to 425°F. Make pie crust as directed on box for one-crust baked shell as directed on box using 9-inch glass pie plate. Prick crust generously with fork.

2 Bake 9 to 11 minutes or until golden brown. Reduce oven temperature to 350°F. Cool 5 minutes. Layer pear slices and cranberries in baked crust.

3 In medium bowl, with wire whisk, beat sugar, nutmeg, sour cream and eggs until smooth and well blended. Pour evenly over fruit.

4 Bake 15 minutes. Cover edge of crust with strips of foil to prevent excessive browning. Bake 40 to 45 minutes longer or until custard is just set and pears are fork-tender. Cool completely, about 1 hour.

5 In small saucepan, mix cornstarch with 1 tablespoon of the eggnog until mixture is smooth. With wire whisk, beat in remaining eggnog; cook over medium heat 6 to 8 minutes, stirring constantly, until mixture just begins to boil. Remove from heat; stir in rum. Serve warm sauce over pie. Store pie and sauce in refrigerator.

NUTRITION INFORMATION PER SERVING: Calories 290 • Total Fat 13g • Saturated Fat 6g • Cholesterol 110mg • Sodium 180mg • Total Carbohydrate 38g • Dietary Fiber 2g • Protein 5g. DIETARY EXCHANGES: 1 Starch • 1/2 Fruit • 1 Other Carbohydrate • 2-1/2 Fat • 2-1/2 Carb Choices.

cook's notes

This pie is best served the day it is baked. Our photo team actually chose it as their favorite dessert!

holiday ice cream pie

PREP TIME: 10 Minutes ✳ **READY IN:** 1 Hour 10 Minutes ✳ **SERVINGS:** 8

1 cup whole berry cranberry sauce
1 quart (4 cups) vanilla ice cream, softened
1 chocolate flavor crumb crust (6 oz.)

1 cup frozen whipped topping, thawed
1/2 cup fudge ice cream topping

1 In large bowl, stir cranberry sauce until softened. Add ice cream; fold until sauce is swirled throughout. Spoon mixture into crumb crust. Cover; freeze at least 1 hour or until firm.

2 To serve, cut into wedges. Place on dessert plates. Garnish each serving with whipped topping and ice cream topping.

NUTRITION INFORMATION PER SERVING: Calories 410 • Total Fat 17g • Saturated Fat 8g • Cholesterol 30mg • Sodium 240mg • Total Carbohydrate 59g • Dietary Fiber 1g • Protein 5g. DIETARY EXCHANGES: 2 Starch • 2 Fruit • 4 Other Carbohydrate • 3 Fat.

cook's notes

Use a small cookie or canapé cutter to cut leaf shapes out of the crust scraps. Bake them on ungreased cookie sheet 6 to 8 minutes or until golden brown.

cranberry-chocolate tart

PREP TIME: 50 Minutes ✳ **READY IN:** 2 Hours 25 Minutes ✳ **SERVINGS:** 10

PASTRY
1/3 cup shortening
1-1/4 cups all-purpose flour
1 teaspoon vinegar
2 to 4 tablespoons cold water
1/2 cup semisweet chocolate chips
1/4 cup half-and-half

TOPPING
2 cups fresh or frozen cranberries

1 cup sugar
1/2 cup water

FILLING
3/4 cup milk
1 box (4-serving size) vanilla instant pudding and pie filling mix
1 cup sour cream
1 tablespoon grated orange peel or 2 tablespoons orange-flavored liqueur

1 Heat oven to 450°F. In medium bowl, using pastry blender, cut shortening into flour until mixture looks like coarse crumbs. Sprinkle flour mixture with vinegar; add water, 1 tablespoon at a time, while tossing and mixing lightly with fork. Add water until dough is just moist enough to hold together.

2 Shape dough into ball. With floured fingers, press dough evenly over bottom and up side of 10-inch tart pan with removable bottom or 9-inch glass pie plate. Flute edge, if desired. Prick bottom and sides of pastry generously with fork. Bake 8 to 12 minutes or until lightly browned. In 1-quart saucepan, melt chocolate chips and half-and-half, stirring until smooth. Spread in shell. Cool slightly; refrigerate until chocolate is firm, about 15 minutes.

3 Meanwhile, in 1-quart saucepan, heat topping ingredients to boiling, stirring until sugar is dissolved. Boil gently 3 to 4 minutes or until most of cranberries pop. Cool at least 30 minutes.

4 In small bowl, beat milk and pudding with electric mixer on low speed about 1 minute or until blended; stir in sour cream and orange peel. Let stand 5 minutes. Pour over chocolate layer in shell, spreading to cover evenly. Spoon cooled cranberries over filling, covering completely. Refrigerate at least 1 hour until serving time. Let stand at room temperature 10 minutes before serving. Cover and refrigerate any remaining tart.

HIGH ALTITUDE (3500-6500 FT): Increase cold water in pastry to 4 to 6 tablespoons. Bake 12 to 16 minutes.

NUTRITION INFORMATION PER SERVING: Calories 350 • Total Fat 15g • Saturated Fat 7g • Cholesterol 20mg • Sodium 160mg • Total Carbohydrate 51g • Dietary Fiber 2g • Protein 3g. DIETARY EXCHANGES: 1/2 Starch • 3 Other Carbohydrate • 3 Fat • 3-1/2 Carb Choices.

white chocolate-cranberry-pecan tart

PREP TIME: 25 Minutes ✶ READY IN: 3 Hours 15 Minutes ✶ SERVINGS: 12

CRUST
- 1 box Pillsbury® refrigerated pie crusts, softened as directed on box

FILLING
- 1 cup fresh or frozen cranberries
- 1 cup pecan halves
- 1 cup white vanilla chips
- 3 eggs
- 3/4 cup packed brown sugar
- 3/4 cup light corn syrup
- 2 tablespoons all-purpose flour
- 1 teaspoon grated orange peel

1 Place cookie sheet in oven on middle oven rack; heat oven to 400°F. Spray sheet of foil (large enough to cover pie) with cooking spray. Place pie crust in 10-inch tart pan with removable bottom as directed on box for one-crust filled pie.

2 Layer cranberries, pecans and vanilla chips in crust-lined pan. In large bowl, beat eggs with wire whisk. Beat in brown sugar, corn syrup, flour and orange peel until well blended. Pour over cranberry mixture.

3 Place tart on cookie sheet in oven; bake 35 to 45 minutes or until crust is golden brown and filling is set in center. After 25 minutes of baking, cover pie with foil, sprayed side down, to prevent excessive browning. Cool completely, about 2 hours. If desired, serve pie with whipped cream. Store in refrigerator.

HIGH ALTITUDE (3500-6500 FT): Bake at 400°F 35 to 40 minutes.

NUTRITION INFORMATION PER SERVING: Calories 400 • Total Fat 18g • Saturated Fat 7g • Cholesterol 60mg • Sodium 140mg • Total Carbohydrate 54g • Dietary Fiber 1g • Protein 4g. DIETARY EXCHANGES: 1/2 Starch • 1/2 Fruit • 2-1/2 Other Carbohydrate • 4 Fat • 3-1/2 Carb Choices.

cook's notes

Placing the tart pan on a cookie sheet helps to brown the bottom crust. The cookie sheet also makes it easy to remove the tart pan from the oven and prevents leaks onto the oven floor.

general recipe index

alphabetical recipe index